A potted history
of
ILFORD

To Muriel & Morton
to commemorate your recent visit
to Ilford.
With my best wishes for your
Good Health. Fortune and Happiness.

Norman

30th June '93

Aerial photograph of central Ilford and beyond – the spread of bricks, concrete and tarmac.

This photograph taken by Aerofilms in 1981 at an altitude of approximately 2000 feet illustrates how most of the forest land and (later) farmland which covered Ilford for centuries has disappeared. In its place, to meet the needs of an increasing and more affluent population, are roads and railway lines, houses, shops, schools, offices and commercial buildings, etc. Beneath the ground lie hundreds of miles of pipes carrying water supplies, drainage and sewerage, and gas mains as well as cables and wires for electricity supplies and telephones.

What cannot be seen, of course, is the ever-present transmission of air-borne signals or impulses converted from electromagnetic waves and transformed into sounds, words, figures, symbols and pictures for communication, information and entertainment purposes, which most of us take for granted and which are part of our present everyday life.

A potted history
of
ILFORD

Norman Gunby

Published privately by the author

1991

© 1991 Norman Gunby

All rights reserved

ISBN 0 9515832 0 4 (hardback)
ISBN 0 9515822 1 2 (paperback)

Typeset in Times New Roman
Printed in Great Britain by
Circle Services (Southend) Ltd, Southend-on-Sea, Essex SS1 1BJ

Contents

with over 170 Illustrations, Maps and Photographs

Acknowledgements

I am greatly indebted to and thank the following – to whom all appropriate credit is due – for their permission to use certain information, and in some cases photographs etc., contained in this publication: Barnardo's (for information regarding Doctor Barnardo & Mrs. Barnardo), A & C Black (Publishers) Ltd. (Publishers of WHO'S WHO and WHO WAS WHO), British Rail Engineering Depot, Ilford (Mr. E. Birchler), Harrison Gibson (Mr. E.R. Guy, Asst. General Manager), Hodder & Stoughton (Publishers of Arthur Mee's "Essex" and Cardinal Heenan's autobiography), Ilford Guardian, Ilford Limited, Ilford Recorder, Imperial War Museum, London, Kelvin Hughes Ltd. (Mr. D.J. Parselle), Local Studies Library Stratford Reference Library Newham, London Borough of Redbridge (Mr. G.U. Price, Chief Executive), National Maritime Museum Greenwich, Oxford University Press (Publishers of the Diary of John Evelyn), Passmore Edwards Museum Stratford, P.D.S.A. (for information regarding its founder, Mrs. Maria Dickin, etc.), R.A.F. Museum Hendon, The Plessey Company PLC, Redbridge Central Reference Library and Local History Room (Mr. Ian Dowling and Mrs. Rosemary Meakins), The Daily Telegraph (Obituary Department), Unwin Hyman Ltd. (Publishers of the Diary of Samuel Pepys).

I also pay tribute to my friends the late Basil Amps (a former Editor of Ilford Recorder), George Gowing, Peter Foley and Brian Page – all of whom share or have shared with me an interest in Ilford's history – and to Miss Madge Carter (a fellow Vice-President of Barking & District Historical Society) for her valuable work in typing out many of my pages of handwriting. Lastly, but by no means least, I pay tribute to my wife for her forbearance during the long time it has taken me to bring this book to publication.

Because this publication is basically a condensed history of Ilford, to anyone interested in furthering their knowledge of local happenings I commend the reading of George Tasker's "Ilford Past and Present" (published in 1901) and George Caunt's interesting "Ilford's Yesterdays" (first published in 1963, and re-published by Mrs. Rose Caunt in 1980) as well as the Barking and Ilford extract from the official Victoria History of the County of Essex published jointly by Barking and Dagenham Libraries and Redbridge Libraries in 1987.

Acknowledgements

Additionally the five recent booklets entitled "Ilford Old and New" (Vols. 1-5) which are a pictorial record of roads and buildings in Ilford showing how they were and how they are now are a valuable contribution to Ilford's archives. They have been published by husband-and-wife team Brian and Joyce Piggott in conjunction with Brian Page.

Few books, if any, written specifically to tell the first 100 years' history of a business firm can excel "Silver by the Ton" by R.J. Hercock and G.A. Jones which deals with the firm of Ilford Limited (1879-1979) which firm was founded by Mr. Alfred Hugh Harman who came to Ilford in 1879 expressly to manufacture photographic plates in a district close to London and with a dust-free atmosphere. Another well-known manufacturing firm in Ilford for many years was Howards & Sons Ltd. whose chemical and pharmaceutical products were sold world-wide and their book published in 1947 to celebrate their 150 years from 1797 documents their history for those years. For local cricket enthusiasts I commend the excellent book on the first 100 years of Ilford Cricket Club (1879-1979) written by the Club's former President and local resident John Polson.

A century has also been scored in Ilford by the Salvation Army for they established themselves here in the year 1886 and the book by Cyril Barnes entitled "A Century at Ilford (1886-1986)" is also of historic interest.

Another commendable book which has recently come to my notice is the 125 page story of the 4th/17th Ilford Scout Group 1911-1986, researched and written by Roy Barnes with a foreword by Group Scout Leader Roy Sharland.

Interested in local history? If so, why not join the Ilford & District Historical Society (President: Mr. H.H. Lockwood; Chairman: Mr. Peter Wright, c/o Central Reference Library) or the Seven Kings & Goodmayes Historical Society, or the Barking & District Historical Society.

NOTE: Any profit resulting from the sale of this publication which is dedicated to my two grandchildren James and Fiona will be divided equally between Barnardo's, the P.D.S.A., and the Local Tree Fund.

NORMAN GUNBY
31 Falmouth Gardens
Redbridge,
ILFORD,
Essex IG4 5JU

Prologue: Our Town

At first 'twas mostly Sea or Ice and then dense Woodland, and much later (when the Trees were felled) productive Agricultural Farmland.

Now, with many Flats and Houses, it's mainly Residential with a little Industry and Commerce including Plessey, Kelvin Hughes, Wiggins Teape, Filofax, Sun Alliance and the Prudential.

Some fine Shops, Stores, and Supermarkets too, notably Harrison Gibson, Boots, Marks & Spencer, Bodgers, Sainsbury, Tesco, Gateway (at Barkingside), Do-It-All and B & Q.

And in building at the present time a large new costly Shopping Complex named "The Exchange" increasing still further the choice of Ilford's shoppers in variety and range. *[Opened 4 September '91]*

Also here are many Schools in keeping with the needs of Ilford's younger population, Schools in which numerous people of repute have, over the years, received their basic education:

Whilst Parks, Recreation Centres, Golf Courses, Baths, Theatre, Cinema, Hainault Forest and now Fairlop Waters, provide extensive Leisure Activities for all adults, and sons and daughters.

* * *

READ, if you will, herein of Ilford's history; it will then no longer be to you unknown, much less a mystery.

Facts and figures too (though a few, no doubt, you already knew) some of years long gone and some quite new.

Also of men and women with an Ilford association who by their work, occupation, endeavour, diligence, and dedication have made an outstanding contribution to our Society, some even to the World, as well as to our Nation, bringing justified renown not only to themselves, but to Our Town in which many of you either go to School, or work, or have grown up or reside and which deserves your care, and merits your unqualified Civic Pride.

* * *

Lastly, 'tis hoped you'll find this book a handy Local Reference for past events or happenings, and for certain information of appropriate relevance.

Preface

This Potted History of Ilford is based on a short talk which I gave a few years ago to the Barkingside branch of a retired businessmen's Club, a talk I was asked to give by a then neighbour of mine, the late Major John Beazley, MBE, JP, TD, only because the Club was short of a Speaker for their forthcoming monthly luncheon meeting and because he knew that I was "into local history". I have since given it to a few other local Clubs following their requests and expanded it somewhat for this book.

Apart from "Ilford Past and Present" by George E. Tasker MBE, published as long ago as 1901, and "Ilford's Yesterdays" by George Caunt OBE, first published in 1963, there is nothing similar, so far as I am aware, which deals specifically and exclusively with the history of Ilford.* The purpose of this condensed history, which in the main relates events in chronological order, is to give local residents and, in particular, schoolchildren an account of local happenings which can be read in a comparatively short time. Excluding my several years of Army service from 1940 when for most of the time I was in other parts of the country or overseas, I have lived nearly all of my fairly long life in Ilford and have, therefore, witnessed many events and changes during that time. Some of these are related in my Recollections to be found in this book, recollections which, in fact, it was suggested by a Club member I should record.

I hope you will find some enjoyment in reading what I have written and will, as a result, acquire some further knowledge of the town (which in 1964/65 was merged with the adjoining Borough of Wanstead and Woodford to become the London Borough of Redbridge) in which, presumably, most of the readers of this book reside.

NORMAN GUNBY

*Since the above was initially written a book entitled "Bygone Ilford" by Brian Evans has been published. Mainly pictorial it makes a further and welcome addition to the archives of Ilford's past.

The Armorial Bearings of the Borough of Ilford 1926-1965

The Official Description or Blazon:
Ermine an oak tree eradicated and fructed proper surrounded by seven crowns Or, in base waves proper.
Crest: Issuant from a chaplet of oak a demi buck supporting between the legs a seax proper pomel and hilt Or.
Supporting: Dexter, a forester holding in the exterior hand a bow proper. Sinister, a female figure habited as an Abbess and holding in the exterior hand a book proper.

(eradicated = rooted out. fructed = having fruit – acorns. Or = the tincture gold or yellow. chaplet = a garland of leaves. pomel = the knob terminating the hilt of a sword, etc. Dexter = situated on the right-hand side (from the bearer's point of view). Sinister = the opposite of Dexter.)

NOTES DESCRIPTIVE OF THE BOROUGH OF ILFORD ARMS
By the HONBLE. PHILLIP P. CARY, YORK HERALD, College of Arms

Three main considerations govern the construction of Armorial Bearings.

The design should be simple: it should be easily distinguished at a distance; and the various components should have meaning, that is they should refer either to some historical or geographical feature, or, as in the case of many old coats of Arms, be a pun on the name or part of the name.

It has been our endeavour to bear these considerations in mind, and it is our hope that a design has been evolved at once pleasing to the eye, emblematic of Ilford, and worthy of the best traditions of heraldry.

The Shield

Upon a background of Royal ermine are arranged seven crowns representing the seven Kings of the Saxon heptarchy and in their midst an oak tree in memory of the Fairlop Oak in Hainault Forest, perhaps one of Essex's most celebrated trees. Under this oak, from 1725 until the tree was blown down in 1820, an annual fair was held on the first Friday in July.

In the base of the shield is conventional water representing the "ford" which forms part of the name of the Borough.

The Crest

In the upper part of the design is the Crest depicted, as is the rule in the case of a Borough, upon an Esquire's closed helmet.

The Crest itself is composed of a demi buck symbolic of the Forest of Hainault, which is so closely bound up with the History of Ilford, supporting a seax or scimitar, a weapon also found connected with Essex.

The Mantling

The ornamental foliage surrounding the helm is the mantling or lambrequin, a cloth usually worn to protect the wearer of the helm from the heat of the sun. The rough usage to which it was necessarily exposed led to the now conventional arrangement of its tattered edges.

The mantling in the case of Ilford, and indeed in most cases, give the livery colours. *The livery colours of Ilford are blue and white, or blue and silver.*

The Supporters

On the dexter side is a representation of a forester in further allusion to the Forest of Hainault. He is armed with his bow, quiver and hunting knife and carries a hunting horn.

On the sinister side is a representation of a lady in the dress of an Abbess. This is an allusion to Adeliza, the sister of Payne Fitzjohn, who was appointed Abbess of Barking Abbey by King Stephen.

Adeliza is connected with Ilford through the fact that she was the founder of Ilford Chapel and Hospital in about 1145. She died in about 1173 and was succeeded as Abbess by Mary, sister of Thomas A'Beckett.

The Motto

The motto "In Unity Progress" alludes to the rise of Ilford from a village to the status of a Borough and its determination to rise still higher – by Unity. The Fairlop Fair actually continued for many years after 1820, and it was not until the disafforesting act of 1852 that the power of holding it was taken away. Some 4 or 5 years later the ground was enclosed and became part of what then was called Crown Farm. Even until the end of the century the

Blockmakers of Wapping were visiting Barkingside annually with their decorated horse-drawn mounted boats to dine at the Maypole or one of the neighbouring inns and a fair of sorts continued to be held on unenclosed land.

* * *

Permission to reproduce the above notes, written by the late Honble. Phillip P. Cary, York Herald in 1926, has been kindly given by the present York Herald and Registrar of the College of Arms, Conrad Swan Esquire.

* * *

It will be observed that following the amalgamation with the Borough of Wanstead and Woodford in 1965 most of the Borough of Ilford's Arms has been incorporated in the Arms of the newly created London Borough of Redbridge. The main differences are :
1) The supporters (a forester and a benedictine Abbess who now has a crook) have changed places.
2) The 7 crowns have been replaced by 4 leopards' faces and 3 martlets (martins).
3) The buck in the crest now supports a cross instead of a seax.

As to the Fairlop Oak tree (The Fairlop Oak) which occupies the centre of the shield, its age when it was blown down in 1820 is not recorded but it must have been several hundred years old and its girth of 36 feet is very little less than Britain's largest Oaks mentioned in the Guiness Book of Records.

History : A written narrative constituting a continuous methodical record in order of time, of important or public events, especially those connected with a particular country, place, or people etc. Definition : Oxford English Dictionary

Introduction

When you walk in one of Ilford's Parks, or in Hainault Forest, or in what is now called Fairlop Waters, you are walking on local history, for there is history in the very ground beneath your feet. It is the association of the ground on which we walk, and any buildings erected on it, with past happenings which makes history – and history is all around us.

Imagine, if you can, the locality during the Ice Age, and the pre-historic animals which, through various Ages, roamed these parts, the Iron Age settlers at Uphall in their enclosed, roughly fortified settlement, the Romans who were here for a few hundred years and who made the road from London to Colchester which passed through here – a road which from that time meant that people living hereabouts were never an isolated community.

Envisage what life was like after the Romans had departed and the country was left open to invasion by the Saxons and others, and later by the Normans under William the Conqueror who, doubtless, would have passed through part of Ilford with his army to take up quarters in the Winter of 1066/1067 at Barking Abbey.

See in your mind's eye the building here of a hospital and chapel for lepers around 1145 AD and when King Edward II was here in 1321, of the Black Death in 1348 and the "Peasants Revolt" in 1381, the years of religious persecution under Queen Mary I and, to a lesser extent, under Queen Elzabeth I who would have passed this way on one of her Royal Progresses as did Shakespeare's companion Will Kemp who danced his way from London to Norwich in 9 days in 1599, and the soldiers engaged in skirmishings in 1648 during the Civil War in the time of King Charles I and Cromwell.

In the 1650's John Evelyn, that cultured and much travelled gentleman and diarist, would have passed through Ilford on his way to see his woods at Warley from his home at Sayes Court, Deptford. Samuel Pepys records in his diary two visits to Ilford in the 1660's. Picture the Stage Coaches which ran regular services in the 1700's and 1800's, stopping here on their way to and from London, and the cattle, sheep and turkeys being driven along the Great Essex Road (as it was then called) on their way to market in London often from faraway places. And the many farms which replaced much of the forest here, and the transportation of their produce to London.

Conceive the effect the coming of the Railway in 1839 had on Ilford and the great activity in the subsequent building of the many houses, schools, shops, and other buildings which changed a village into an expanding town in the late

1800's. Think, if you can, of the effect the First World War had on the people of Ilford when 1159 Ilford men were killed and many more were wounded, and the death and destruction caused by enemy planes, flying bombs and rockets during the Second World War and the consequent hardship, grief, pain and suffering.

Read in these pages of some of the men and women who have played such an important part in Ilford's development or who have contributed to the welfare of others; such people as Doctor Barnardo and the equally dedicated Mrs. Barnardo, of Mrs. Maria Dickin, the founder of the P.D.S.A., Archaeologist Sir Antonio Brady, Alfred Hugh Harman the early manufacturer of photographic plates and founder of Ilford Limited. Also of Arthur Hughes whose inventions have saved many lives, Television pioneer John Logie Baird, the dynamic A.G. (Sir Allen) Clark, co-founder of the great Plessey Company. Notice the exceptional tradesmen J. Harrison Gibson, A.W. Green, John Bodger and George Fairhead who founded businesses here in Ilford many years ago. Discover benefactors Miss Eleanor Thompson and the Ingleby's (Mrs. Sarah, and her son Holcombe), Ben Bailey who played such a prominent part in Ilford's early development and in the acquisition of land for Valentines Park, of photographer Watson Hornby, historian Frederick Brand, and Archibald Cameron Corbett (Lord Rowallan) who like W.P. (Sir Peter) Griggs and his nephew A.P. Griggs built many of the houses here. Peruse of authors Mrs. Walford, George Tasker and George Caunt, of Ilford's M.P.'s and of some of its councillors including Edmund Beal, George Gott, Revd. Sir Herbert Dunnico, and Alderman Dane, of Ilford's Grand Old Man Joe Pates, and of Edward Tuck a teacher here for 57 years. Observe men born here and who went to school here who have gone on to have distinguished careers, men such as Cardinal Heenan, Admiral Sir Raymond Lygo, Air Vice-Marshall Sir Bernard Chacksfield, and Raymond Baxter, also of ex-Ilford County High Schoolboy Sir Allen Sheppard currently Group Chief Executive of Grand Metropolitan Plc., of Ilford-born John Bairstow, founder of Queens Moat Houses Plc., and more.

You will as a result, I think, be better informed about Ilford and its people and have a greater understanding of what has gone before and what has been achieved.

Cheers!

Précis

According to scientists – Einstein among them – the Universe of which our Planet Earth is but an infinitesimal part, inexplicably began with a gigantic explosion thousands of millions of years ago and has been expanding ever since, with distant galaxies moving away from us at great speed. Encyclopaedias and other relevant publications tell us that our Planet is between 4,500 million and 4,600 million years old, being formed by consolidation of interstellar dust.

Such length of time is beyond human comprehension but if equated to a 24-hour day the last 2000 years – which covers most of present day history – would be equivalent to it being within the last second before midnight! During the existence of Earth, Ilford like much of the rest of Britain has been alternately submerged under the sea, covered by sandstone, by swamps, and by ice, been inhabited by pre-historic animals and by early man, was part of the mainland of Europe, and covered by a primeval forest which was here even when the Romans came approximately 2000 years ago and, to a slightly lesser extent, when the Normans came in 1066 AD. According to an ancient map, so dense was the forest when the Romans came that it was said that a squirrel freed in the Thames valley could travel to The Wash (between Lincolnshire and Norfolk) from tree to tree without once touching the ground.

Since then, over the years, most of the forest has been cut down and in comparatively recent years and for a relatively short time became farmland producing vegetables, milk and cereals for the London market.

An ever-increasing human population in the London area and improved standard of living accommodation for the majority of people has resulted in much of the land in Ilford being built on for housing, and to a lesser extent businesses, commerce and industry, and to serve the inhabitants in other ways – shops, schools, public utility buildings, and leisure activities etc.

Excluding the many social and other events which have taken place over the years this, very briefly, is the history of Ilford. To narrate in detail all that has happened over the years would fill a large volume. This Potted History of Ilford attempts to relate some of the more important local happenings up to the present time.

Potted History

In the Beginning: Early History

To anyone who may wonder or ask what history Ilford has, I would answer that there is history in every stone, in every particle of earth, and in every grain of sand.

And speaking of sand I would remind you that although our Planet is estimated to be between 4,500 million and 4,600 million years old it is less than 10,000 years since Britain was joined by land to the mainland of Europe and that certain rivers such as the Thames and the Rhine then flowed into a large inland lake, dammed by ice to the north, where the North Sea is today. Through the Ages climatic conditions have varied enormously, ranging from extreme heat to extreme cold and extraordinary changes have taken place. Long ago the land masses of the World were different in size, shape and location to what and to where they are now. For example, South America was joined to Africa, and India was separated from Asia by a sea, and Australia was joined to Antarctica, and for millions of years much of Britain including Essex was covered by forests, or by ice, or was under water. The evidence for the latter is mainly in the deposits of sand and of gravel (which is a mixture of coarse sand and waterworn stones) which have been extracted from various parts of the Ilford district for building purposes over the past 150 years or more. A Geological map of the district, in fact, shows that the subsoil is largely of gravel with areas of London Clay to the north, and, until much of it was extracted, deposits of brick-earth in central and south Ilford. It is known that the course of the Thames has undergone changes throughout its history and at one time, before it was deflected, it flowed through the Vale of St. Albans and probably out where the River Blackwater (between the Crouch and the Colne) is today. As to the Ice one has only to go to the Natural History Museum in South Kensington to see that many thousands of years ago – during the period known as the Pleistocene Glaciation – the vast Lowestoft Ice Sheet as it is called extended as far south as the northern part of Ilford. With the gradual return of temperate conditions the ice melted and the water level rose. Water and pack-ice flowing southward eroded the coastlines of England and France and formed the Straits of Dover.

In the Natural History Museum one will see that the Ilford Terrace as it is called, along with the Alluvium Terrace, the Upper and Lower Flood Plains, and the Swanscombe Terrace, is evidence of former levels of the Thames which with their deposits of silt and stones etc. laid down over former years are of especial interest to geologists.

There is not space to say more about this Prehistoric Era except that because Britain was then joined to the mainland of Europe and climatic conditions were different, such animals as the mammoth, rhinoceros, tiger, bear and elk, to name but a few, lived hereabouts. The bones and teeth (the hardest part of the body) of such animals were first discovered in an Ilford brickfield off Ilford Lane – then called Barking Lane – in 1786. Year by year many more were unearthed and in 1857 the first great mammoth tusk over 9 feet in length came to light. In 1863 the first perfect skull of a mammoth with a tusk 8 ft. 8 in. long was discovered in the Uphall brick-earth pits which became known as the Ilford Elephant Ground. Large quantities of fossil shells were also found.

In recent years there have been finds of this kind when the excavations for the present Harrison Gibson building were in progress in 1959 and more recently for subways etc. in connection with the re-developed Town Centre and during the construction of the M11 through Redbridge. Some of these finds have since been on display in the Local History Room of the Central Library. There must undoubtedly be many more lying buried beneath the streets, houses and shops etc. of Ilford still.

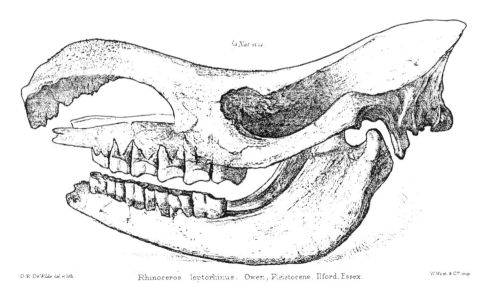

G R De'Wilde del et lith   Rhinoceros leptorhinus. Owen, Pleistocene, Ilford, Essex.   W.West & Cº imp

Rhinoceros leptorhinus. Drawing from Sir Antonio Brady's Catalogue of Prehistoric Animal Remains unearthed at Ilford from approximately 1834 to 1874. Note: These remains are estimated to be at least 100,000 years old.

How it all began

History books tell us that life on Earth appeared some two thousand million years ago. According to a recent report it was due to our planet having a moon which together with the Sun causes gravitational forces which create tides and it is these tides which enabled early forms of life from the sea to inhabit the land. Be that as it may the Homo Erectus stage occurred probably less than half a million years ago and the Homo Sapiens (modern Man) stage about 40,000 years ago. The earliest inhabitants of Britain are thought to be the Palaeolithic or early Stone Age people (before 5000 BC) and the Neolithic or later Stone Age people (from 5000 to about 1500 BC) followed by the Bronze Age people. It is known that from about 5000 BC Celtic immigrants from the Rhineland began to settle here and that around 200 BC the South-east of England was occupied by the Belgae, from Northern France. Between 200 and 100 BC there was a Settlement of these people, or of people before them, by the Roding at Uphall. Various artefacts used by these early settlers have been discovered over the years including some very recently unearthed from the cleared Laporte site (now being re-developed) by archaeologists from Stratford's Passmore Edwards Museum.

Occupation by the Romans, Saxons, and the Normans

I now come to historic times starting with the invasion of Britain in 55 BC by the Romans under Julius Caesar with his 12,000 legionaries and their superior weaponry and battle tactics and their strict discipline. After a short stay in Kent they withdrew and invaded again the following year when part of south-east England was temporarily occupied.

Ninety seven years later – in 43 AD – the Romans came again, this time numbering about 24,000 under their general Aulus Plautius, followed soon afterwards by the Emperor Claudius himself. Then began an occupation which was to last until the year 406 AD, some 363 years – a span of time which from now would take us back to the third year of the reign of Charles I.

Before the coming of the Romans when a large part of the country was forest-land there were no roads in Britain in the accepted sense nor were there towns. However Colchester was one of the principal settlements. Here the Romans established their first colony which they named Camulodunom. The road they built from London (Londinium) to Colchester passed through where Ilford is today so this locality would have witnessed the sight of Roman legions during the many years of their occupation and some Romans probably lived hereabouts for a Roman coffin containing a skeleton was discovered at Valentines in 1729 and Uphall Mount in south Ilford and Carswell near Woodford Bridge Road, as well as Wanstead, are known to have had Roman associations. Along the road from London to Colchester were Roman

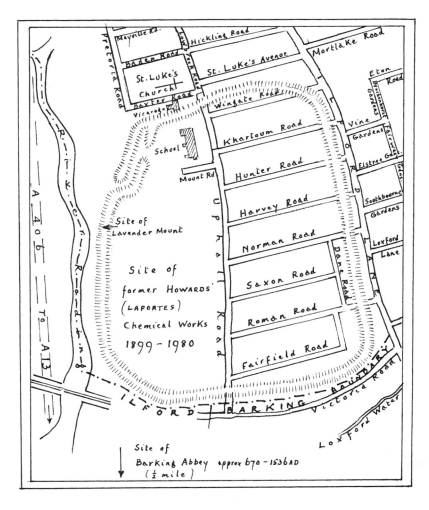

The estimated extent of the Iron Age Camp at Uphall c. 200–100 BC. (Reproduced courtesy of Passmore Edwards Museum.)

stations. One, named Durolitum, was between Romford and Brentwood; another Canonium, was near Kelvedon, and a third named Ad Ansam was probably at Stratford.

At the end of the 4th century and at the beginning of the 5th the huge and extended Roman Empire was falling to the Goths, the Huns, and the Vandals and in consequence the Roman forces were withdrawn from Britain leaving it virtually defenceless. Although the Britons were told to arrange for their own defences an appeal was made to Rome some years later for the Romans to return but to no avail. In the centuries that immediately followed came invasions by the Saxons from Saxony, the Angles (from whom England takes its name) from Schleswig-Holstein, the Jutes from Jutland, the Vikings from Scandinavia, and later the Danes, many of whom settled here and gave their names to settlements from which many of our towns and villages have grown. Under the Angles and Saxons there were seven small Kingdoms each with its own ruler though one of these was usually supreme. The Kingdom of the East Saxons (which eventually became known as Essex) was established about the year 527 and remained a separate Kingdom for nearly 300 years. London was selected as its capital and Colchester, though the second place of importance, was thus deprived of the position it had held for nearly five centuries.

Between the years 666 and 670 AD the Saxons began the building of an

(*left*) Roman legionary (bronze model). A bronze statue of a Roman legionary of the 2nd century AD. Soldiers serving in chillier provinces such as Britain were issued with leather breeches and heavy red cloaks, and often stuffed their open-toed boots with fur.

(*right*) William, Duke of Normandy ("The Conqueror") as depicted on the Bayeaux tapestry.

Abbey at Barking. It was founded by Erkenwald, Bishop of London, at the request of his sister Ethelburga who became its first abbess. It is believed to have been the first nunnery established for women in the Kingdom and was undoubtedly one of the most important. Erkenwald was the grandson of the King of the East Angles and was the first bishop to preach in St. Pauls. Whilst on a visit to his sister at Barking, Erkenwald died there about 685. He was later canonized (made a Saint).

We owe our knowledge of historical happenings of the time to a scholar, the Venerable Bede, who lived from 673 to 735 AD and recorded many of the place-names in his Historia Ecclesiastical written in a Northumbrian monastery. Many of these names in their original or slightly altered form are in use to this day. Barking, of Saxon origin, for example means the settlement of Berica's people. It was at Barking Abbey that William the Conqueror and his Norman army took up Winter quarters in January 1067 – little more than ten weeks after the Battle of Hastings and almost immediately following William's Coronation in the then Westminster Abbey on Christmas Day 1066. Because there was no direct road from Barking to London then (and, in fact, not until about 1810) there would have been a great coming and going of Norman troops through Ilford to and from Barking during that time. And it was to William at Barking that the nobles came to swear fealty to him.

When in the year 1085 William ordered the so-called Domesday Book to be completed (it was actually in two volumes and was a most detailed Inventory of land, stock, buildings, equipment and people primarily for the imposition of Taxes) Ilford, within the Hundred of Becontree, was part of Barking. Barking (including Ilford) is recorded as being worth 80 pounds. In contrast Woodford was worth 100 shillings and Wanstead 40 shillings. The name Ilefort is recorded in one volume but refers to the separate parish of Little Ilford which was then owned by a minor Norman "Lord" named Goscelinas Loremarius (Joselyn Lorimer). The entry (translated) reads "2 free men held Ilford before 1066 as a manor for 3 hides less 30 acres. Then 2 ploughs in lordship, now 1. Then 2 1/2 men's ploughs, now 1. Then 7 villagers, now 4. Then 4 small-holders, now 6. Then 1 slave, now none. Woodland 20 pigs, meadows 20 acres." (A hide was normally 100 acres but the size of the acre varied). Ironically William was not to profit from this meticulous survey for while campaigning against the King of France he received an injury from which, on 9 September 1087, he died. He was buried in Caen.

In later documents the name of Ilford is spelled as Yleford (1171) and Hileford (1234) and in a document dating from the time of Edward I (1271-1307) setting out the boundaries of the old forest of Essex, as Hyleford – the ford through the Hyle (the name then of the River Roding or, at least the lower stretches of it).

In those days and for a period of over 250 years after the Norman Conquest men could be detailed by the county Sheriff to travel long distances on foot from their homes to construct Castles in various parts of England and Wales.

They would, undoubtedly, have been away for a very long time, and some no doubt, were never to return.

Just as Wanstead and Woodford were held by their monastic overlords the Abbeys of Westminster and Waltham respectively so, until the dissolution of the monasteries by Henry VIII in the late 1530's and early 1540's, Ilford was held by the Abbey of Barking and it was in the 12th Century (approx. 1145 AD) that a Hospital on Ilford Hill was founded by Adeliza, the then Abbess of Barking to house 13 lepers. (In 1572 during the reign of Queen Elizabeth I the purpose of the Hospital was changed to maintaining six poor aged men under the care of a master and a chaplain.)

Another monarch who it is said visited Ilford a long time ago was the then King David of Scotland who came to see his sister at the Ilford hospital and on his arrival found her washing the feet of the lepers.

The palace at Havering-atte-Bower (near Romford) was one of the residences of English Kings and Queens for several hundred years and in the year 1321 Edward II while staying there spent two days, 25th and 26th November, in Ilford. In those days the centre of government was wherever the King happened to be and no less than seven documents issued on those two days gives the place of issue as Ilford. Where precisely in Ilford were they written I wonder, and what was life like here in those days?

From documents in the Public Records Office and in the British Museum we know that even in the 14th century lands were being enclosed and trees and bushes in parts of the forest were being grubbed up to make the land arable. Manor houses had been built, many of them surrounded by moats for keeping out cattle and intruders. The moats also served as fishponds to provide fish for the table. Fields were ploughed with oxen and crops of corn, barley, rye, peas, beans and herbs were grown. Sheep (their wool and the cloth woven from it brought much wealth to England) and cows grazed in the fields, pigs foraged for acorns and beechmast in the forest, geese and fowls were kept and dovecots stocked for fresh meat in winter. Cheeses were made from ewes milk, and watermills and windmills were to be seen over a wide area. A scene of some prosperity was emerging.

King Edward II

The Hospital Chapel, Ilford Hill – Ilford's most historical building. (Photo: Author.)

The Hospital Chapel entrance: the letter 'A' over the doorway stands for Adeliza, the Abbess of Barking Abbey who founded the Chapel and its Hospital in about the year 1145.
(Photo: Author.)

The Black Death and subsequent Peasants Revolt

But in the year 1348 disaster struck, for in that year the Black Death reached England from Europe – brought in by merchant ships from Black Sea ports via Italy and transmitted to man by fleas from black rats. The epidemic wiped out at least one quarter of the European population, and of England, and one tenth of the population of London, from 1348 to 1350. No doubt Ilford, small though it was then, had its share of fatalities. All this was to have an effect on the labour available on the land and resulted eventually in the Peasants Revolt of 1381. This was a time of widespread rebellion and local men joined the marches advancing on Mile End Common and Aldgate eventually with dire consequences including the slaying of Wat Tyler the Kentish leader, and later, the massacre of many of the followers of Jack Straw, the Essex leader, at Billericay.

(Under the fuedal system, which William the Conqueror introduced into Britain from Europe, the monarch owned all land, much of which he allowed his lords to hold in return for their allegiance and, when required, military and other services and obligations. The lords in turn could sub-let their holdings. At the bottom of the system were the serfs who were "attached to the soil" and could not leave it without their master's permission. Partly due to the growth of commerce and trade and partly due to the Peasants Revolt serfdom gradually began to disappear and ended completely in this country two hundred years or so later. In France it continued until the beginning of the French Revolution (1789), in Western Europe until the early 1800's, and in Russia until 1861.)

Religious Persecution in the 16th Century

Certainly the lot of many people in olden times was not a happy one. Following the break with Rome by Henry VIII his daughter Mary I who remained a Roman Catholic reversed the religious changes made by her father and by her half-brother, the young Edward VI, and some 300 Protestants in England (73 from Essex) were put to death during her short reign of just over five years (1553-1558). Sad to relate, on one day – Saturday 27th June 1556 – at nearby Stratford eleven men and two women were burnt at the stake. (A memorial outside the Church there marks the spot where these and others were put to death in 1555 and 1556). And during the 44-year reign of Elizabeth I some 200 Catholics were put to death – mainly by hanging – for their religion. Some no doubt would have been Catholic priests who had clandestinely infiltrated into Britain from the Continent. (These figures have been taken from "A History of England" by Sir Keith Feiling. However according to fellow local historian Peter Foley in a letter to Essex Countryside magazine (July 1990 issue) the number of Catholic martyrs during Elizabeth's reign, based on records in Rome and in Douai, France, was well in excess of 200). Many more during both reigns were imprisoned. Good old days indeed! Thank goodness there is more tolerance today.

Royal Palaces in Essex

I have already mentioned the Palace at Havering but there was another Palace in Essex which is not so well known. It was New Hall at Boreham – one of the finest houses in Essex and considered second only to Audley End – and was built by Henry VII and Henry VIII. Both Mary Tudor and Elizabeth lived there for a time. The many distinguished personages who were associated with this Palace over the years, including Oliver Cromwell, would no doubt have passed through Ilford on their way from there to London.

The Threat of Occupation by Spain

During the reign of Elizabeth I – in that eventful year of 1588 – England was threatened by invasion and occupation by Spain. There was great activity in the area at the time with troops marching through Ilford on their way to camps at Stratford, Romford, Billericay and Tilbury. The road from London to Tilbury was at that time through Ilford village and Barking. As many a schoolboy and schoolgirl knows, due to a combination of various factors, the Spanish Armada comprising 124 ships laden with many thousands of troops, and horses, guns and equipment, failed in its objective of landing and taking London during those fateful days in July and August 1588, and being at the mercy of storms and high seas around the coasts of Scotland and Ireland so many ships were sunk or shipwrecked that barely one half of the fleet eventually got back to Spain.

At the Cranbrook Hall which existed at the time, four Spanish noblemen who had survived shipwreck were held pending their ultimate release – three being in exchange for ransom and the fourth being exchanged for a Huguenot prisoner in Spanish hands.

Queen Elizabeth I's Royal Progress

When Elizabeth made one of her many "Royal Progresses" and stayed at Ingatestone Hall with her vast attendant retinue, all of whom had to be accommodated and fed by her host Lord Petre, it is almost certain that she would have passed through Ilford on her way there from London. It is said that until Elizabeth's time carriages were not used in England and that she was one of the first persons in this country to ride in one, though in fact it would have been little more than an enclosed cart and almost certainly had no springs and no glass windows. Compared with travel today – especially with the roads as they were then – it must have been very slow and uncomfortable. But, no doubt, to her servants it was a great adventure.

Will Kemp's "Nine Day Wonder"   ———————>

Elizabeth died in 1603, aged 69, but she would no doubt have heard of Will Kemp, who in 1599 danced his way from London through Ilford (where he stopped for refreshment) to Norwich which he reached in nine days. The feat was said to have been done as a publicity stunt and to win a wager. Will Kemp was regarded as the greatest comic actor of his time – "a fellow of infinite jest" – and a contemporary and associate of William Shakespeare.

"Forward I went with my hey-de-gaies to Ilford, where I again rested, and was by the people of the town and country thereabout very well welcomed, being offered carouses in the great spoon, one whole draught being able at that time to have drawn my little wit dry; but being afraid of the old proverb (He had need of a long spoon that eats with the devil) I soberly gave my boon companions the slip".

Note : The great spoon referred to held more than a quart and was kept at one of the inns in Ilford for special drinking occasions.

A Wedding at the Hospital Chapel

It is on record that in the year 1608 in the Hospital Chapel in Ilford the marriage took place between Sir Ferdinande Fairfax and Mrs. Mary Sheffield, daughter of Lord Sheffield. In 1644 Sir Ferdinande was in command at the battle of Marston Moor when the Royalists, under Prince Rupert, were severly defeated. He died in 1648. His son Sir Thomas Fairfax captured Colchester in 1648 towards the end of the Civil War.

Civil War

It was during the Cvil War in June 1648 that Ilford witnessed the sight of Royalist troops fighting a rearguard action against the Parliamentarians during the Royalist' retreat to Colchester.

Commonwealth Period

The year 1650 is important in Ilford's history because in that year the decision (brought about by the inhabitants of Ilford) was made to split the ecclesiastic-

; was one, Great Ilford (as it
:o it, was the second and
's later before Ilford had its
:fore Barkingside had theirs
ld either to go all the way to
)el (which many did) or stay
was very much a part of the
e fined for not attending. At
omprised about 50 houses.
ultured and much travelled
June 1649 he purchased the
for six years until September
; that time when he visited
:ain, and Ford of Europe are
he was living at Sayes Court
is life it is almost certain that
of those occasions. There are
h etc. when he would almost
:o Sayes Court, crossing the

Author's Note:

Although Will Kemp published an account of his "nine daies wonder," according to the book entitled "Ingatestone and the Essex Great Road" by E. E. Wilde, the journey took four weeks. It was the actual dancing that took nine days with days taken off for resting. Throughout the journey Will Kemp was accompanied by his companion Tom Slye who played a fife with one hand and beat a tabor (small drum) with the other.

Ilford

Samuel Pepys was in Ilford.
Privy Seal and on that day,
'se" and rode to Bow where
at the "King's Head" he ate a breakfast of eggs. There he was joined by a Mr. Deane (later to become Sir Anthony Deane, the King's Master Shipbuilder). Together they rode into the Forest – then called Waltham Forest – to see some trees being felled for the building of naval ships. They had dinner in Ilford – most probably at "The Angel" – where while waiting for dinner Pepys was instructed by Mr. Deane on the measurement of timber. They later set off for Barking, from where the forest timber was shipped to the shipyards at Woolwich. Pepys was at Ilford again in 1665 (June 13) when he came out by coach to meet the Duke of York (who became King James II in 1685) on his way home from Harwich. It is all recorded in his famous Diary. At the time of Pepys' visit the forest extended from the River Lea at Bow and along the main road – the Great Essex Road as it was called then – to Whalebone Lane, then northwards as far as Harlow and Roydon. It was then some 60,000 acres in area, ten times the size of Epping Forest today. (On the other side of the River Lea was the Forest of Middlesex).

Extracts from Samuel Pepys' Diary. Year 1662: 18 August

Up very early, and up upon my house to see how work goes on, which doth
please me very well. So about 7 o'clock took horse and rode to Bowe; and
there stayed at the King's Head and eat a breakfast of eggs till Mr. Deane of
Woolwich came to me; and he and I rid into Waltham Forest and there we
saw many trees of the King's a-hewing and he showed me the whole mystery
of off-square, wherein the King is abused in the timber that he buys, which I
shall with much pleasure be able to correct. After we had been a good while
in the wood, we rode to Ilford; and there, while dinner was getting ready, he
and I practised measuring of the tables and other things till I did understand
measure of timber and board very well. So to dinner, and by and by, being
sent for, comes Mr. Cooper, our officer in the forest, and did give me an
account of things there, and how the country is backward to come in with
their carts. By and by comes one Mr. Marshall, of whom the King hath many
carriages for his timber, and they stayed and drank with me. And while I am
here Sir Wm. Batten passed by in his coach homeward from Colchester where

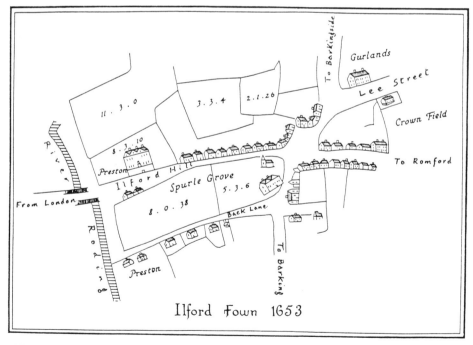

Ilford in 1653. Scale c. 15 in. to 1 mile. As it was a few years before Samuel Pepys' visits in 1662
and 1665.

he hath been seeing his son-in-law Lemon, that lies a-dying; but I would take no notice of him, but let him go. By and by I got a-horse-back again and rode to Barking, and there saw the place where they ship this timber for Woolwich; and so Deane and I home again. And parted at Bow, and I home just before a great shower of rain as God would have it. Whiled away the evening at my office, trying to repeat my rules of measuring learnt this day; and so to bed – with my mind very well pleased with this day's work.

Year 1665: 13 June

At noon with Sir G. Carteret to my Lord Mayor's to dinner ..... My Lord Mayor very respectful of me. And so I after dinner away, and found Sir J. Minnes ready with his coach and four horses at our office-gate for him and me to go out of town to meet the Duke of York, coming from Harwich tonight. And so as far as Ilford, and there light. By and by comes to us Sir Jo. Shaw and Mr. Neale that married the rich widow Gold upon the same errand. After eating a dish of Creame, we took coach again, hearing nothing of the Duke; and away home, a most pleasant evening and road.

From Forest to Farmland

Over the ensuing years the continued felling of trees for the building of ships and houses resulted in the clearing of much of this land. Fortunately some of the woodland survived and some was incorporated in the grounds of some of the larger houses. Part, too, survived to give us the Epping Forest and Hainault Forest of today. Most of the remainder became farmland which for well over 200 years produced corn, vegetables and milk for the London market. At one time there were over forty small farms in Ilford alone. Today all but one or two have gone.

The Great Essex Road

Being on the Great Essex Road which was the main route from London to Chelmsford and Colchester, Harwich, Ipswich and Norwich Ilford was never an isolated community. It could hardly have been otherwise for the road was the main reason for its existence. At one time sixty stage coaches ran through Ilford to and from London and various towns in Essex and beyond, and horses were changed at "The Angel" and at the "White Horse". In 1740 Ilford had its own daily Stage Coach to London starting from the "Red Lion" (now re-named "Mainstreet") and in 1786 this was increased to two daily coaches. There were also two from London to Barking via Ilford.

The Great Essex Road was also used extensively for the driving of cattle and sheep, and at certain times of the year turkeys, from considerable distances to London, the journey often taking several days. At night the turkeys would roost in the roadside hedgerows.

Robbery on the Highway

Of course, roads were not surfaced as they are today nor were they lit and this great highway was dust or mud according to the season. For the majority of travellers, who could not afford to travel on horseback or by coach, transport was on foot and all travellers ran the risk of being robbed by footpads or mounted highwaymen. One such person who frequented these parts in the 1720's and 1730's was the notorious Dick Turpin. Born at Hempstead in North Essex in September 1700 he was on leaving school apprenticed to a butcher in Whitechapel. He married a local girl named Lily Palmer who lived at Aldborough Hatch. Turpin took to sheep and deer stealing, became a member of a gang of burglars robbing country houses at night, and a member of a gang of smugglers before becoming a highwayman holding up coaches on the main roads, and seeking refuge in Hainault and Epping Forests. It was in Epping Forest that he shot and killed a gentleman's servant who had gone there in an attempt to capture him. Fleeing north with his friend Tom King, whom he accidentally shot and killed during another hold-up, Turpin was eventually hanged at York in April 1739 for horse-stealing.

The River Roding made navigable to Ilford Bridge

In the year 1737 an Act of Parliament provided for the improvement of the River Roding to permit barge navigation between Barking Quay and Ilford Bridge. This stretch of commercial waterway was used extensively until the early 1930's.

Ilford Hill and Back Lane

The section of the main road between Ilford Bridge and the Broadway known as Ilford Hill was much steeper years ago and much of the horse-drawn traffic preferred to use Roden Street, or Back Lane as it was then called. Here, for the shoeing of horses, and repairs, was a blacksmith's forge which existed until the 1930's in the ownership of a Mr. Kingsnorth, and where Sainsbury's Supermarket is now.

Valentines

Of the several fine old houses that were once in Ilford only "Valentines" now remains. This was built in the 1690's. Enlarged and improved from 1724 to 1769 it was lived in until 1906 when Mrs. Sarah Ingleby, the last resident, died there. The house was surrounded by fine grounds, woodland and gardens, and it was here that the Valentines Vine grew. Planted in April 1758 it was a Black Hamburgh and from it many cuttings were taken including the one in 1769 which became the great vine at Hampton Court still producing grapes in abundance to this day. On the garden wall of Valentines is a tablet marking the spot where the Valentines Vine grew. It was placed there by the Ilford Borough Council in 1951. Recently a cutting from the Hampton Court Vine was taken and planted at Valentines by local school children thus renewing the link between the two. Apart from Valentines Mansion, as it now called, Claybury Hall built about 1790, and Loxford Hall, built about 1830 (all three no longer privately owned) some of the oldest surviving houses in Ilford today are in Park Avenue (south side) dating from about 1850. Some small well-built and recently refurbished cottages in Tanners Lane also date from 1851.

Cranbrook Hall and Cranbrook Castle

Another fine house in Ilford was Cranbrook Hall which with its grounds and parkland occupied 190 acres. The last house which survived for over 200 years, was demolished in 1900 when the estate was bought for housebuilding. The Drive in Ilford follows the route of the old drive from Cranbrook Road to Cranbrook Hall which was sited where Endsleigh Gardens is now. There was also a house named "Highlands" built in 1768 by Sir Charles Raymond who also built a tower nearby which became known as Cranbrook Castle and which survived until 1923. Built with the intention of it being used as a mausoleum it was never used as such but in later days accommodated a farm worker and his family and during the 1914-1918 War was used as an Observation post.

In the year 1796 Ilford village contained 149 houses, so the number since 1653 had trebled, and by 1801 the population of Ilford was 1,724. There were a further 317 in Chadwell ward.

The Farlop Oak and Fairlop Fair

A map of Essex published in 1777 by John Chapman and Peter Andre shows how much larger Hainault Forest was then compared with its present size for then it extended almost to Woodford Bridge, to Claybury, to Barkingside and to Marks Gate (Whalebone Lane). In the forest was an immense and very old oak tree which became known as the "Fairlop Oak". It is recorded that this celebrated Oak measured thirty-six feet in girth at three feet from the ground

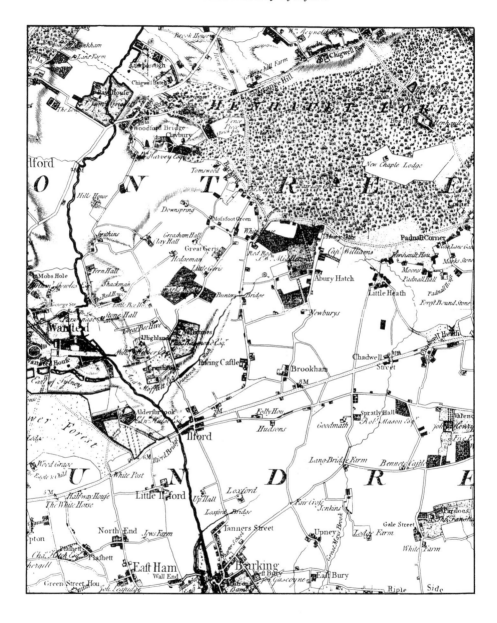

Extract from the Survey of Essex conducted by John Chapman and Peter Andre published on October 1st, 1777.

Queen Anne – seen above with her son William, Duke of Gloucester (National Portrait Gallery). During her short reign from 1702 to 1714, Queen Anne rode out to Ilford to see the famous Fairlop Oak. Already several hundred years old, it was probably then past its prime and was gone a little over a hundred years later. The last of the Stuarts, this unfortunate lady (born in 1665 and married in 1683) was the mother of seventeen children all of whom died in infancy except William who lived only until he was eleven. She was the second daughter of James II and sister of Mary II and lived in a palace on the site of the present Downing Street. She was married to Prince George of Denmark who died in 1708. Her reign saw the union of England and Wales with Scotland which previously had separate legislative procedures. When she died the succession to the British throne had to be traced back to the sister (Elizabeth) of Charles I who had married Frederick V, Elector Palatine of the Rhine and through her marriage became the grandmother of George I the first of the Hanoverians. In the Redbridge Magistrates Court, built on the site of Mossford Lodge at Barkingside, is a handsome painted Royal Coat of Arms bearing the date 1718 (reign of George I) which used to hang in the "Angel" public house in the High Road, where upstairs the judiciary courts known as Petty Sessions were regularly held for many years in the 1700's and 1800's.

Fairlop Oak with a Meeting of the Hainault Foresters.

The Fairlop Oak

One of the decorated boats
drawn by six horses on its way
to Fairlop Fair around 1840.

FAIRLOP "FRIGATE."

and its branches extended three hundred feet in circumference. The shadow cast by its branches and foliage covered at least an acre of ground. During her reign (1702-1714) Queen Anne, accompanied by her retinue, came to see it. It was around this tree that a Fair was held on the first Friday in July of each year. In later years it had grown into a three-day event, lasting until Sunday. What started as a private picnic or bean-feast given by a Mr. Daniel Day of Wapping in the early 1700's had by 1725 grown into a public event enjoyed by a great multitude of people many travelling from the Mile End area to Fairlop in a long procession of decorated horse-drawn carts and floats and vehicles of every description and in 1840 an estimated 200,000 people were there. By this time the Oak had been finally cut down after having been damaged by fire and storm and high winds. Its timber was purchased by a builder and from part of it was made the pulpit and reading desk for St. Pancras Church in Euston Road.

Another Royal Visitor

In 1795 the Prince of Wales (who in 1811 due to the insanity of George III became Prince Regent, and in 1820 became George IV) came through Ilford to review troops raised locally. This was at a time when France had by then become a Republic, Louis XVI had been beheaded, and Napoleon Bonaparte was emerging as a would-be conqueror of Europe with Britain soon to be left almost alone to oppose him.

Funeral Procession of Caroline of Brunswick

In 1821 (August 14th) Ilford witnessed a procession of a more sombre kind than the ones that were part of the annual Fairlop Fair celebrations from the east end of London. It was the very long funeral cortege of Caroline of Brunswick which had started from London that day. Accompanied by Royal Horse Guards and a large number of private carriages with mourners and sympathisers the long procession passed through Ilford in the evening on the way to Chelmsford and then to Harwich, where the body of Caroline of Brunswick (whose marriage to her cousin the Prince of Wales had been a disaster) was taken by boat to be buried in the family tomb in Germany.

(George IV had been strictly educated and he reacted by entering a life of debauchery. In 1795 (after marrying a Mrs. Fitzherbert in 1785) he married Princess Caroline in return for payment of his debts. In 1820 a Bill which George IV forced the Government to bring in deprived Her Majesty Caroline Amelia Elizabeth of the title of Queen.)

The Coming of the Railway

We now come to the event which was to make the greatest impact on the development of Ilford – the coming of the Railway. Only nine years after the opening of the Liverpool and Manchester Railway in 1830 when George Stephenson's Rocket was the proven locomotive of the day the Eastern Counties Railway, as it was called, opened the first section of the line from Devonshire Street Mile End to Romford on 20th June 1839 though three months earlier a special train of two carriages drawn by the latest locomotive named "The Ilford" had made the journey to Ilford in a trial run. By the following year the line had been extended to Shoreditch and, eastwards, to Brentwood. Fenchurch Street Station came into use in 1854 and Liverpool Street Staton in 1874. Just how primitive the rolling stock looked when the first steam passenger line opened in 1830 was illustrated in a set of postage stamps issued by the Post Office in 1980 but advancements rapidly followed. Much of the rolling stock serving Ilford was made at Stratford though some of the locomotives were made in France. When the Railway was eventually extended to Great Yarmouth it meant that fresh fish from the North Sea could be brought to London in a few hours. Until then Barking had been a busy and important port but with the opening of the Railway to the East Coast this was soon to end.

By 1872 twenty trains in each direction were in daily service on the London, Ilford, Romford, and Brentwood line.

Over the ensuing years the railway was to open up Ilford as a dormitory suburb. City men who had lived at Stepney Green and Bow were beginning to move out to the quieter areas of East Ham and Ilford. At first, however, the service was expensive and slow and when a lad of 16 was summonsed for travelling on a train with a child's ticket it was offered as a defence that when the lad commenced his journey he was only 12! Later the service improved and fares were reduced, particularly for those passengers travelling between 5 am. and 7.30 am. (most people started work early in those days) and in 1891 the journey from Ilford took only 19 minutes. (Nearly 100 years later it is not much faster). In 1903 the loop line serving Newbury Park, Hainault and Woodford was built though this was closed in 1908 until 1930.

Ilford no longer a village – the building of houses transforms the scene

Many builders saw the potential of housing development in Ilford and it began in earnest after the Clements Estate which extended from Ilford Lane to St. Mary's Church was sold in 1879. Other housing Estates quickly followed: Ilford Lodge in 1883, Birkbeck (Newbury Park) in 1893, Grange (north of Ilford Station) in 1894; Cranbrook, Loxford and Uphall in about 1897, and Downshall (Seven Kings) and Mayfield (Goodmayes) in 1898.

Train crossing Stratford marsh 1839.

Illustrated courtesy of Local Studies Library, Stratford.

The Starting Train circa 1865.

Illustrated courtesy of Local Studies Library, Stratford.

Two men stand out above all others in connection with this house building. They are Archibald Cameron Corbett who later became the first Lord Rowallan, and W.P. Griggs who in 1916 became Sir Peter Griggs and was the first Member of Parliament for Ilford in 1918 when it was made a separate parliamentary constituency. Corbett's houses, built by Corbett in association with a local contractor, Robert Stroud, sold for between £217 and £520 and over 3000 were built. It is recorded that the houses were built at cost price and that Corbett was looking to the annual ground rents for income. (He was also responsible for the building of Seven Kings and Goodmayes Stations – having first to give the Railway a guarantee of a certain annual income). Griggs' houses ranged from £260 to £495 and over 2000 were built. The twenty or so years between 1879 and 1900 saw the beginning of the Ilford that we know today.

Because large deposits of brick-earth had been found in many parts of Ilford many of the bricks used in the building of the houses then were manufactured locally. There were brickfields off Ilford Lane, another at Cricklefield, and one on the north side of the High Road, facing St. Mary's Church. The map of 1777 already mentioned shows a brick kiln at Fencepiece (then bounded by Hainault Forest). There were gravel and sand pits in the district and one such gravel pit I remember was where the open-air Swimming Pool is in Valentines Park. There were also Lime and Cement works and timber yards by Ilford Bridge up to which point following the deepening of the Roding ships and barges from the Thames could reach.

Ilford breaks away from Barking

In 1888 Ilford which for over twelve hundred years had been one of the four wards of the parish of Barking, became by Act of Parliament, a separate civil parish and in 1894 became an Urban District. It had earlier (in 1836) become a separate Ecclesiastical parish.

Ilford's People and Population

A study I have made of the Census of 1851 shows that in the fairly extensive parish of Great Ilford (as it was then termed) there were over 4500 inhabitants of all ages sharing 913 different names. Of this Smith was the most popular, there being 84 people living here then by that name. This was followed by such good old English names as Wright (74), Clark (57), Stringer (43), Skiggs (42), Green (39), Hunt (39), Brown (35), Young (35), Webb (32), Miller (31), and Wood (31). In 1861 the population had increased to 5405, by 1881 it was 7645, by 1891 it was 10,913 but by 1901 it had increased almost fourfold in ten years to 41,234. There was a further increase to 78,188 by 1911 and by 1931 to 131,061. In 1938 it was an estimated 166,900 and in 1951 with a population of 184,706 Ilford was the most populous town in Essex and the second largest non-county borough in England. At the last census taken (in 1961) before the merging of Ilford with Wanstead and Woodford for administrative and local Government purposes the population had decreased slightly to 178,024.

Public Services and Amenities

Of course a rapid rise in the population such as occurred in Ilford in the late 1800's and early 1900's brings many problems which have to be solved and difficulties which have to be overcome. As Ilford grew from the village that it was up until the late 1870's to an enlarging town so what today are referred to as back-up services and amenities had of necessity or desirability to be provided as part of what Politicians now like to term the Infrastructure. With the building of houses came people of all ages from other areas and so followed the need for shops, schools, churches, offices for local administrative staff, a hospital, fire station, police station, a highways depot and refuse plant, cemetery, swimming bath, facilities for recreation including parks, places of entertainment, and improved roads, bridges, lighting, local transport and, very importantly, adequate mains water, drainage and gas supplies and later, electricity.

As early as 1895 a public Swimming Bath was opened by the Council. Its site by the side of the River Roding was off Uphall Road (now the Riverdene Road Section) and chosen because there was a supply of water from a well there – later to prove inadequate. I remember going to it in the mid-1920's with my class from Christchurch Road School. It was just 60 feet long by 20 feet wide, and there were six slipper baths. In January 1931 the Baths in the High Road were opened. They have since been modernised.

Wanstead Park

Regarding Recreation, we in Ilford are fortunate indeed that in those early days were some men who had great foresight enabling them to visualise that Ilford would not long continue to be on the edge of London with the open country beyond and that, therefore, public Parks – mainly an innovation of the Victorian era – would be a most desirable asset to possess. Wanstead Park was opened to the public on 1st August 1882 but except for a small part of it was beyond the Ilford boundary. In the early 1800's Wanstead Park was part of the grounds of the magnificent Wanstead House, the home of Miss Tylney-Long. After only ten years of her marriage to the spendthrift the Hon. Pole-Wellesley (later to become the 4th Earl of Mornington) the house of this unfortunate lady, its contents and the grounds were disposed of under the Auctioneer's hammer.

Valentines Park

In the late 1890's Ilford's Council acquired 47½ acres of grounds from Mrs. Sarah Ingleby of "Valentines", and Central Park, as it was called at first, was opened to the public on September 16, 1899. Money (a small sum by today's standard) had to be raised by a Government loan for the purchase of the land and it was not without opposition from certain members of the Council led by the Chairman Alderman E.J. Beal. However, due to the tireless efforts of such Councillors as Ben Bailey, William Ashmole, W.P. Griggs and W.W. Gilson the loan was obtained to the benefit of us all. After Mrs. Ingleby's death in January 1906, 12 acres of the grounds including the gardens and the house, were presented to Ilford by her son Mr. Holcombe Ingleby in memory of his mother. A further addition was made by the purchase of some of the grounds when put up for sale to give us the Valentines Park of some 146 acres we have today. Part of the grounds was sold for the building of the "Ilford Garden Suburb" where Emerson, Tillotson and Holcombe Roads, Bethell Avenue and The Square are. Here were built some of Ilford's best houses. Two types sold for £750 and £720 Freehold or £570 and £555 Leasehold. Of course no one then saw what most people nowadays want – a garage or garage space.

Further Parks and Recreation Grounds

Other Parks were to follow and in one week Councillor Gott, who was a local farmer at Fencepiece Farm, Barkingside, opened three Parks – South Park (32 acres), the first part of Seven Kings Park (9½ acres) and Barkingside (14½ acres). The land for the original Seven Kings Park and Goodmayes Park was presented to the town by Mr. Corbett as was the Westwood Recreation Ground on the Downshall Estate which stretched from Aldborough Road to Barley Lane. Councillor W.P. Griggs who in 1901 presented to the town the Clock Tower and Dinking Fountain which stood in Ilford Broadway for many years also presented for use in Valentines Park a marble drinking fountain (from which I often quenched my thirst on a hot day when I was a boy) and a Clock and Bell Tower – the clock having come from over the stables at old Cranbrook Hall.

Many people today, without the knowledge of what has happened in former years, not unnaturally take for granted the many amenities and facilities which now exist for us to enjoy.

Whereas the Parks and Recreation Grounds in Ilford have come about through the foresight of our early Councillors or have in one or two cases been donated by benefactors, much other land to which we now have unrestricted access has been acquired only after a great struggle for its preservation.

Land Enclosure

By the 1850's enclosure of land by the Lords of the Manors and other owners had reached alarming proportions. For example, most of Hampstead Heath, including Parliament Hill Fields, Ken Wood and Golders Green Park – some 800 acres in extent – would have been built on had it not been for the action taken by certain members of the public residing in the surrounding districts, as a result of which much of it was eventually purchased by the old Metropolitan Board of Works, and some 80 acres given by the Eton College Trustees, for the public's permanent use.

Epping Forest Saved

And so it was with what remained of the old Forest of Waltham which included our present Epping and Hainault Forests. In the twenty years from 1851 to 1871 the illegal enclosure of part of Epping Forest was greater than in the previous 250 years. At that time with the rapid development of London, land increased considerably in value. It was a poor villager of Loughton, Thomas Willingale, who had earned a scanty living collecting wood and by grazing cattle, who flung himself into the battle for the preservation of the Forest and sought the support of the City of London Corporation. There was also a great deal of support from the public and after fifteen years of battles in Parliament and the Courts, costing a great deal of money in legal fees, Epping Forest was declared free for the people again and in celebration a dedication ceremony was held on 6 May 1882 attended by Queen Victoria.

The Destruction and Reduction of Hainault Forest

George Tasker in his detailed account of the destruction of Hainault Forest tells us that in the year 1793 the Commissioners of Woods and Forest estimated the entire area of Hainault Forest (as distinct from Epping Forest) to be 17,000 acres and that 2939 acres were the King's Woods or Royal Forest. Less than 60 years later, in 1851, as a result of enclosures and claims by land owners, and land grabbers, the forest had dwindled down to only about 4000 acres. In that year it was decided to disafforest much of the land and an Act of Parliament was passed enabling the Government to cut down the timber, remove the deer, and enclose the land. The work went on for many months and in order to get the land cleared as speedily as possible was carried out by night as well as by day, the timber being transported by wagons along Barley Lane or Aldborough Road to Barking.

Old farm building, Hainault Farm. The date (1855), the crown and the letters VR (Victoria Regina) and AP (Prince Albert) indicate that it was a Crown property. (Photo: Author.)

Hainault Farm cottages. (Photo: Author.)

St. Peter's Church, Aldborough Hatch. This church was built by the Government in 1863 for the use of the inhabitants of Aldborough Hatch after the disafforestation of much of Hainault Forest. Much of the stone used in construction of the church came from the old Westminster Bridge (built between 1738 and 1750) which had recently been demolished. (Photo: Author.)

Looking across part of Hainault Farm towards Fairlop Waters. In 1852, after a large part of the then extensive Hainault Forest, when approximately 100,000 trees (oak, hornbeam and the like) had been cut down, an area of 1870 acres was allocated to the Crown and converted into farmland. The long straight roads (New North Road, Forest Road, Hainault Road and Painter's Road) across the consequent treeless plain date from this time. (Photo: Author.)

Approximately 100,000 trees – oak, beech, hornbeam and others – were cut down, the land drained and made arable and long, straight roads formed without a field path and with scarcely a tree left to relieve the dreary uniformity resulting in what has been described as one of the most uninviting and wearisome tracts around London. An area of 1870 acres, alloted to the Crown, was converted into a farm (Hainault Farm) and farm buildings and cottages erected. For the use of the relatively few inhabitants the Government built, in 1863, the little church of St. Peter, Aldborough Hatch. Thus was formed what became known as Fairlop Plain which included the land on which all the houses and other buildings have been erected on the housing Estates at Hainault – mainly from the 1930's – and the land allocated to the various playing fields at Fairlop. Part of the Plain – some 360 acres – following the extraction of sand and gravel, and the burying of household rubbish by the local Council mainly in the 1970's and 1980's, has now become the recreational and leisure area called Fairlop Waters.

In 1903 our present Hainault Forest – approximately 1100 acres in area – (belonging at that time to the Lord of the Manor of Lambourne, Mr. A.R. Lockwood, afterwards Lord Lambourne) was acquired by the London County Council and local authorities including Ilford Urban District Council at a total cost of £21,830 and opened in July 1906. Though but a relatively small portion of the Hainault Forest shown on that map of 1777 already referred to it was nevertheless a welcome amenity for future generations in perpetuity.

The Town Hall and other public building and services

Before the Town Hall was opened in December 1901 meetings of the Council were held at first in a house in Brandon Grove on Ilford Hill (where the British Telecom building is now), then over a shop at No.3 Cranbrook Road (where the NatWest bank is), and later at Ilford Hall on which site Harrison Gibson's has stood for many years. Besides providing the Council with an appropriate conference chamber and offices for Council officials, the Town Hall provided the people of Ilford with a fine hall for public meetings, concerts, displays and other functions. In 1908 a Public Hall was opened in Seven Kings for the use of residents in that part of the town, together with Ilford's first public Library. Towards this Library and the Central Library erected in Oakfield Road in 1927 the sum of £10,600 was given by the Carnegie Trust – a considerable amount in those days. In 1871 the fire appliances in Ilford consisted only of a few lengths of leather hose. In 1884 a Fire Escape ladder was purchased which, with other appliances was housed at the "Red Lion" near the Broadway. The first Fire Station, built in 1893, was in Oakfield Road, and in 1905 the Central Fire Station was opened in Ley Street. Horse-drawn machines were then in use until 1914. The Ley Street Station was replaced in 1987 by the new Fire Station in the High Road – near the Baths.

Ilford's Schools

The few schools in Ilford until the year 1832 were private ones. The first of which there is any record was the Ilford House Academy on Ilford Hill. In 1832 the National Schools, which adjoined St. Mary's Church in the High Road, were built by subscriptions and by various benefactors and accommodated 500 children. The name of the Schools was eventually changed to "Church Schools". There were similar schools founded in 1842 in Barkingside. Through the benevolence of Mrs. Ingleby a school for 120 children was built in Beehive Lane and this building stood until about three years ago when it was demolished to make way for some privately built retirement homes. There was also an Infants School at Aldborough Hatch. Following the formation of the School Board in 1893 the first school built by the Board was the Horns School – opened in 1895 – for 264 children. However the Education acts of 1902 abolished School Boards throughout the country and transferred their powers and duties to local Authorities.

According to the Ilford Guardian dated 4th August 1933 a Mr. Charles J. Dawson (whose death was reported in that issue which also contained a detailed report of my sister's wedding) designed most of the schools in Ilford between 1896 and 1909. They were : Cleveland Road 1896, Christchurch Road 1900, Downshall 1902, Loxford Junior 1903, Loxford Boys & Girls 1904, Highlands 1905, Goodmayes 1906, South Park 1908 and Uphall 1909. His firm C.J. Dawson & Son and Allardyce, which had an office at the corner of Cranbrook Road and Balfour Road, were also responsible for the design of King George Hosptal.

St. Peter's Church, Aldborough Hatch, and the former Chapel there

Mention has already been made of the Hospital Chapel – Ilford's oldest building – but another ecclesiastical building of historical interest is St. Peter's, Aldborough Hatch, for it is built mainly with stones from the first Westminster Bridge which itself was built between 1738 and 1750 and demolished in 1861. The reason these stones were used is, apparently, that the contractor for the building of the new (existing) Westminster Bridge and, presumably, the demolition of the former one, also had the contract for the building of St. Peter's, Aldborough Hatch. It was on that first Westminster Bridge, which in 1750 was the only bridge across the Thames in London in addition to London Bridge, that the poet Wordsworth stood early one morning and after admiring the view of the City therefrom wrote those memorable lines: "Earth has not anything to show more fair: Dull would be he of soul who could pass by a sight so touching in its majesty: This City now doth, like a garment, wear the beauty of the morning, silent bare. Ships, towers, domes, theatres and temples lie Open unto the fields and to the sky. All bright and glittering in the smokeless air."

St. Peter's Aldborough Hatch is so named because Westminster Abbey, close to Westminster Bridge, is officially the Collegiate Church of St. Peter.

In the vicinity of Aldborough Hatch stood, until about the year 1808, Aldborough Hall which had attached to it a chapel, built to obviate the inconvenience of parishioners having to journey to Barking parish church and home again. Services were held in the Chapel until 1863 by which time St. Peter's had been built. This chapel is now sadly in a derelict state it having been further damaged during the gale of October 16th 1987. According to Mr. H.H. Lockwood, President of the Ilford & Dstrict Historical Society, there is evidence that this chapel was built before 1690. This would make it Ilford's second oldest building – pre-dating Valentines Mansion which was built in the 1690's. It is hoped that the local Council whose attention has been drawn to the condition of the chapel by Mr. Lockwood will do what it can to save the building. Incidentally John Donne (1571–1631) English Poet and Dean of St. Pauls cathedral lived at Aldborough Hatch for a time.

Ilford's many other churches

Although Ilford's many Church of England and Nonfonformist Churches have declined in number in recent years – largely through lack of support and

Butcher's Shop, Ilford Broadway 1865 (an early photograph).

a changing population – I feel that no history of a town, however short that history, should omit reference to a few more of them. In 1803 Ilford's first Baptist Church was founded. When Ilford was made a separate ecclesiastical parish and not merely a division of the Barking parish, in 1836 St. Mary's Church in the High Road which had already been built and consecrated in 1831 was our Parish Church. It had then, and for over a hundred years afterwards, a spire as well as a tower. In 1840 Holy Trinity Church, Barkingside, was built. In 1889 the building of St. Clement's Church in Park Avenue began, the foundation stone being laid by the Marchioness of Salisbury whose husband the Marquis of Salisbury was Prime Minister at the time. In 1902 St. Clement's replaced St. Mary's as the Parish Church of Great Ilford. Then followed the building of St. Albans (1900), St. John's Seven Kings (1902-1913), St. Paul's Goodmayes (1903), the Church Hall of St. Andrew's (built in just over four months in 1906), All Saints, Goodmayes (1914) St. Margaret's (1914) and St. Luke's (1915). Many nonconformist churches were also built during those years including, in 1906, the Wycliffe (Congregational) Church in Cranbrook Road. St. Andrew's (in The Drive) was built in 1923 and the present St. Laurence's, Barkingside in 1939. The Roman Catholic Church of St. Peter and St. Paul in the High Road was consecrated as early as 1899. The Synagogues in Coventry Road and Beehive Lane were founded in 1927 and 1936 respectively.

It may be of interest to mention that after the Gants Hill (Wesleyan) Methodist Church in Gants Hill Crescent was opened in 1928 the congregations were so large that it was sometimes necessary to display "Church Full" notices outside.

In recent years we have seen the disappearance of St. Clement's Church as a building – the site now occupied by flats – though the Cecil Hall across the road now serves as the church. Also long gone are several nonconformist churches in the High Road and in Cranbrook Road to make way for shops, the Methodist Church in the Drive (now occupied by "sheltered housing") and the Wycliffe Church which for several years was used as a Theatre and which has now been converted into an office building.

Doctor Barnardo's Village Homes for Girls, Barkingside

An important event in Ilford's history occurred in 1874 when Mossford Lodge in Cranbrook Road, Barkingside was offered by the owner, Mr. Sands, to Doctor Barnardo on a lease, free of rent, of 21 years.

Dr. Barnardo had already established a home in Stepney mainly for destitute boys and the offer of Mossford Lodge gave him and his dedicated wife Mrs. Syrie Barnardo the opportunity to start a home for orphaned and destitute girls. This eventually grew into the Village Homes of 48 separate cottages and five large households spread over 50 acres in all.

Ilford Limited

Another important event in Ilford's history occurred in 1879 when Mr. Alfred Hugh Harman came to Ilford and set up his business of making photographic dry plates in the basement of his house on the corner of Cranbrook Road and Park Avenue (where "The Cranbrook" P.H. stands). His business prospered and in 1880 it operated from premises in Roden Street, trading as the Britannia Works Company later to become Ilford Limited.

A book by Messrs. R.J. Hercock and G.A. Jones entitled "Silver by the Ton" tells the story of Ilford Limited from 1879 to 1979 and makes very interesting reading. A copy is available in the Central Reference Library.

Howards of Ilford

In 1897 30 acres of land alongside the Roding at Lavender Mount, Uphall were purchased by the old-established firm of chemical manufacturers Howards & Sons Ltd. of Stratford. At the factory built at Lavender Mount pharmaceutical products and photographic chemicals were manufactured for many years (Howards aspirin tablets were world famous). It was while digging the foundations at this site that several pieces of Roman pottery and many coins were unearthed.

Local Newspapers

The first newspaper to cater specifically for the town of Ilford was the Ilford Guardian which was published on 27th August 1898 from premises on Ilford

Ilford Broadway in 1880.

Hill. The proprietor was a Mr. J. Wilmott, a builder of High Road, Ilford who considered that with Ilford growing apace there was a need for such a paper. Previously the local news had been covered by the Essex and Middlesex Guardian. In the first issue of the Ilford Guardian was an article on the new printing method and an illustration of a Linotype machine purchased for the purpose. The article stated that the machine "does the work of the hand compositor by mechanical means increasing one man's output by at least 5 or 6 times". In its first issues the Ilford Guardian ran features on some of the outstanding Ilfordians of the day including Mr. Ben Bailey who was described as the shrewdest and cleverest businessman and Councillor in Ilford and Mr. William Ashmole who was born in Roden Street in 1850 and was the sole County Councillor for Ilford at the time, and Chairman of the Ilford Gas

Alfred Hugh Harman, 1841–1913, founder of ILFORD limited.

Light and Coke Company. Mr. Ashmole who in 1876 saved the life of a would-be suicide who had thrown himself into the Roding near the Red Bridge was quoted as saying it was evident to everybody at that time that Ilford was increasing more rapidly in population than probably any other town in England. The Ilford Guardian's premises near the old skating rink were demolished when the new Chapel Road was built behind the Hospital Chapel (from Ilford Lane to Ilford Hill). However before that (in November 1954) the name of the paper was changed to the Ilford Pictorial and since October 1978 has been the Ilford and Redbridge Post and Pictorial which is published by Greater London & Essex Newspapers Ltd. from premises at 2 Whalebone Lane South. Its editor is Mr. David Russell. The Ilford Recorder – part of South Essex Recorders Ltd. – was first published on the 17th September 1898 and began in premises at the rear of Dunn's in the Broadway. It later moved to Cranbrook Road (on the corner of Balfour Road) and in 1903 into the Recorder Buildings in the High Road almost opposite the Town Hall. The name can still be seen on the building. In 1961 it moved from there to its present purpose-built premises, Recorder House, at 539 High Road (the new Fire Staton is situated opposite). However, the printing of this weekly newspaper is now carried out at Peterborough. The editor for several years was Mr. Tom Duncan, but is now Mr. Mark Sweetingham. The issue of the several free weekly newspapers with their many advertisements is something that has come about in recent years.

Local Crime and Punishment in Former Days

In an ideal world there would, presumably, be no crime, no felonies nor misdemeanours of any kind and very little need for a Police force. The money thus saved could be put to far better use to improve the quality of life generally. But people being as they are with their varying degree of desires, emotions, vices and passions as well as virtues, there have been and always will be those whose behaviour and actions are sometimes not in the best interest of the public at large. I have already mentioned the burglaries, armed robberies and killing by the notorious Dick Turpin who met his end on the scaffold in 1739. Criminal records as far back as the year 1379 (during the reign of Richard II) tell us that one John Tanner was found guilty of stealing a horse locally and in consequence his land and properties were taken into the King's possession. In 1588 – the year of the Spanish Armada – Richard Nightingall was found guilty of stealing six lambs at Ilford. He was probably hanged. On 25 February 1608 John Clifton of Ilford was sentenced to be branded for stealing two silver rings and a shilling from a William Huggett. On 25 May 1785 William Grace was hanged at Chelmsford for stealing a horse at Aldborough Hatch. Travelling on foot or by coach could be dangerous and several footpads and mounted highwaymen were hanged for robberies (*Continued on p. 56.*)

This photograph taken in the late 1880's is of where Park Avenue is today. The house on the left is one of eighteen that were built in about 1850. Eight faced the main road and ten were on the right-hand side of the avenue. The location at that time and for many years afterwards was called South Park. To the right of the picture stood the house named "Elmhurst" which was the first home to be occupied by Mr. Alfred Hugh Harman when he came to live in Ilford in 1879. In the cellar and ground floor of this house he made his photographic dry plates assisted by two men and three boys and, at times, by his wife and the housekeeper. He also travelled daily from this house to London in his horse and trap to deliver his wares. Today the Cranbrook Public House occupies part of the site of the house as seen below.

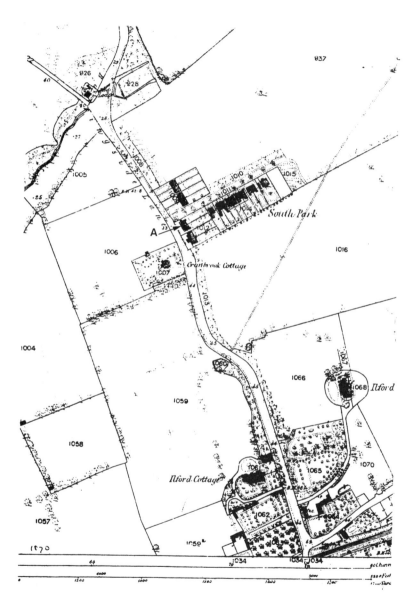

Map showing the Cranbrook Road area of Ilford in 1881. The railway station and Ilford Broadway are just off the bottom of the plate. Harman's house is marked 'A'.

A view of the Cranbrook Road looking towards Wellesley Road as it was in Harman's time. His second residence in Ilford was on the corner of Wellesley Road where McDonald's is now.

Cranbrook Hall c. 1890. Located where DeVere Gardens and Endsleigh Gardens are now, it was demolished in 1900 its 190 acres of grounds and parklands having been sold for house building.

The ILFORD trademark
Harman introduced in 1886.

Cranbrook Road from the Railway Station, showing corner of York Road, in 1890.

The Drive, showing the old Lodge at the Wash c. 1890. A telephone exchange now occupies the site of the Lodge but the house, now No. 6 The Drive (Sidney Villa), is still standing and occupied.

Another view of the same area in about 1900 showing how well-wooded it was then and showing also the access to the stream (the Cran brook) used to water and cool cart-horses. The author recalls the felling of these trees in the 1920's in his Recollections.

ILFORD CRICKET GROUND.

AN INTERESTING

CRICKET MATCH

will be played between the following

18 HONORARY MEMBERS

And the first

ELEVEN OF THE CRICKET CLUB,

On Saturday, August 20th, 1892.

HONORARY MEMBERS:

Wm. ASHMOLE, Esq.	G. DOUBELL, Esq.	CAPT. Mc. ALLUM,
H. A. BISHOP, ,,	H. FAREY, ,,	GORDON PRYNN, Esq.
F. W. BEAL, ,,	H. GILBEY, ,,	J. H. SMITH, ,,
J. W. BENTON, ,,	W. W. GILSON, Esq.	E B. SCRUTON, ,,
W. CARTER, ,,	C. E. HUME, ,,	J. THOMAS, ,,
J. DENNEY, ,,	J. W. JOPSON, ,,	C. WOOD. ,,

The 18 will appear in

SILK HATS AND RED BRACES.

The 11 Cricketers are to Bat and Field one hand only,
and to Bowl underhand.

WICKETS PITCHED AT 3 O'CLOCK.

W. G. FERRAR, ESQ., and J. W. F. MUMFORD, ESQ.,
Have kindly consented to umpire.

THE BAND OF THE ILFORD VOLUNTEERS,

(By permission of Capt. Meggy) has been engaged and will play selections during the
evening.

Arrangements have also been made for the attendance of
C. HART'S WELL KNOWN STEAM CIRCUS SWINGS &c.

ADMISSION 6d.   CHILDREN 3d.

Half-price after 6 o'clock.

S. W. Hayden, Printer, High Street, Ilford.

Poster for a cricket match held on Saturday August 20th 1892 on Ilford Cricket Ground.

Group photo. Players in the above match. Photo courtesy of Mr. John Polson.

A Foden Steam Wagon: the earliest mechanical vehicle used by ILFORD Limited.

High Road, Ilford near Willow Walk 1893. The large "Boots" store is now next door to what for many years was known as Willow Walk. Another small side turning was called Chapel Row and was where "Marks & Spencer" is now.

Cranbrook Castle: built in 1765 (reign of George III). It was demolished in 1923. The PLA pavilion off the Drive stands on the site.

Ilford Bridge c. 1900 (looking towards the Broadway).

Ilford Railway Station entrance: opened in 1894, it replaced the original entrance off the Broadway.

W.P. Griggs' advertisement in George Tasker's "Ilford Past and Present" published January 1901. Mr. Griggs, who was knighted in 1916 and became known as Sir Peter Griggs, built over 2000 houses in all ranging in price from £260 to £495.

ADVERTISEMENTS.

Cranbrook Park and
Central Park Estates.

Without question the choicest positions in Ilford and surrounding districts.

Substantially-built Residences are being erected on these unique Estates, near to two Public Parks. All Houses nearing completion are sold; intending purchasers should therefore book early.
Leases 99 years.   Drainage Perfect.   Gas or Electric Light.

· · · SINGLE-FRONTED RESIDENCES, · · ·
£260, £270, and £295.

Four Bedrooms, £375 and £395; Five Bedrooms, £450.
· · · DOUBLE-FRONTED RESIDENCES, · · ·

FOR FULL PARTICULARS APPLY TO

W. P. GRIGGS and CO.,
· · · Cranbrook Park, ILFORD.

Ilford Lane 1902. This section was in Ilford Lane near the Broadway and is now part of what has been named Chapel Road.

The opening tram car, Ilford Lane, May 27th, 1903. The track to Barkingside and to Chadwell Heath from the Broadway had already come into service from 14th March of that year. Motormen were paid 6¼d per hour. Two cash clerks were paid £1.00 per week and a junior clerk £30 per year.

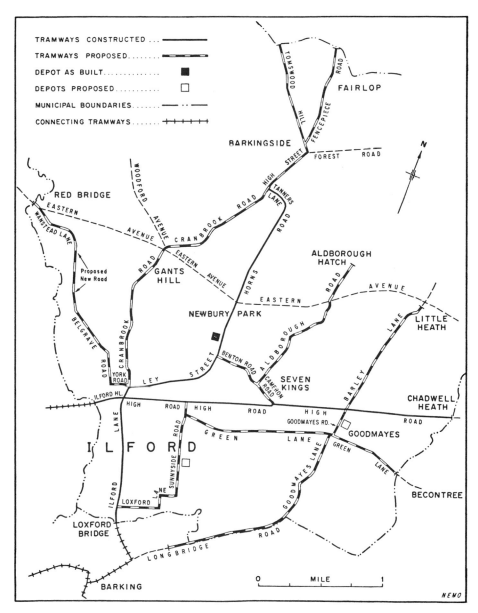

TRAMWAYS CONSTRUCTED ...
TRAMWAYS PROPOSED ....
DEPOT AS BUILT ....
DEPOTS PROPOSED ....
MUNICIPAL BOUNDARIES ......
CONNECTING TRAMWAYS ....

Map of tram routes constructed and those proposed

The full extent of the Ilford tramway system as originally proposed (Eastern Avenue not then constructed).

Entrance to Valentines Mansion at junction of Cranbrook Road and Beehive Lane in 1903.

Valentines Park (the canal): formerly part of the grounds of "Valentines".

High Street, Barkingside c. 1905.

High Street, Barkingside: The Chequers P.H. and tram terminus.

Ilford Broadway (1905) showing the Griggs' clock tower which was removed in 1923 to South Park. It was destroyed by enemy action in 1944.

At the end of an extensive tour abroad and of Britain, 76-year-old General William Booth, founder of the Salvation Army drove into Ilford, 9 September 1905. After being greeted by 5000 people who thronged the High Road, he addressed Ilfordians in the Town Hall for over half an hour. Five years later General Booth was in Ilford again leading a series of meetings in the newly built Hippodrome.

A photograph of Ilford Wharf taken from Ilford Bridge in 1906. In 1737 an Act of Parliament was passed for the improvement of the river Roding from Barking to Ilford Bridge and this stretch of the river was the scene of much activity until the early 1930's. (Photo: Redbridge Local History Library.)

Valentines Mansion c. 1910.

An Edwardian wedding group. Photograph taken by Watson Hornby at Christchurch Road School, Sept. 1909. Note the enormous hats worn by some of the ladies.

The Ilford Military Band assembled at The Wash prior to leading the Hospital Carnival Procession in 1911.

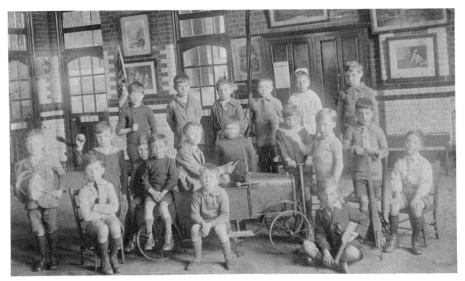

Boys of 5 to 6 years old at Christchurch Road Junior School, 1919 or 1920. (The author is on extreme left, back row, with flag.)

committed on the road between Ilford and Romford. With the Forest close at hand it is little wonder that the stealing of deer (regarded as the property of the King) was a common occurrence. No Social Security payments in those days such as we have now!

At one time when ale and other alcoholic liquor was cheap to buy and was regularly consumed and drunkenness was commonplace there was a lock-up or cage behind the "Angel" Public House (where the newly-built "Angel" now stands). In an upper room of the "Angel" Petty Sessions were held every alternate Saturday. In 1791 a slightly larger lock-up was erected at what was then the junction of Ilford Lane and Back Lane (Roden Street) near where Sainsbury's Supermarket now stands. Misdemeanants found guilty were sent to Barking prison until Ilford Gaol (or Jail – which spelling do you prefer?) was built. This was actually located in Manor Park near the "Three Rabbits" Public House in Romford Road. The building, which housed a treadmill – used as an instrument of prison discipline – was demolished in 1880.

It is probable that some local persons found guilty of theft, of smuggling, deer poaching, or some other crime including some relatively minor ones by today's standards would have been among those transported overseas. This transportation began in the late 1600's (first to the West Indies and America) and in the year 1788 the first shipment set sail for Australia (later Tasmania and New Zealand became additional destinations). It continued until 1864 when it was abolished by Parliament.

On display in the National Maritime Museum at Greenwich are graphic details of those convicts transported to Australia in the very first fleet of ships, two of which sailed from nearby Woolwich. Included in the manifest are John Hall found guilty of stealing a handkerchief, Edward Perkins who had stolen a chicken, and another man who had stolen a pair of shoes. There was also a lad of 16, and also servant girls found guilty of petty larceny. Harsh treatment indeed, especially when corruption by officials in high places and by Government contractors was prevalent, and when with Royal and Governmental cognizance men's liberty was imperilled by the possibility of their being kidnapped by press gangs to serve as soldiers and sailors in the 18th and early 19th centuries!

The Ilford Murder

Until recent years murders appear to have been relatively infrequent locally and when the murder of Mr. Percy Thompson occurred just after midnight on 3/4th October 1922 a great deal of prominence was given to it in the National newspapers no doubt because a woman (Mrs. Edith Thompson) was involved. Both she and her young lover, Frederick Bywaters, were hanged after a trial whose verdict so far as Mrs. Thompson was concerned has never ceased to be the subject of some controversy. It was the last double hanging.

Subsequently the Executioner committed suicide and the Prison Governor and the Chaplain retired.

Ilford's Electricity Works and its Trams

By the year 1901 Ilford had its own Electricity works, situated in Ley Street. Again this was the result of the imaginative foresight by certain Councillors who served the Community well and voluntarily. The Electricity produced gradually replaced the Gas Lighting supplied by the privately-owned Ilford Gas Company which had begun as early as 1839. In 1903 this Electricity was driving Ilford's own trams serving Ilford from Chadwell Heath and from Barkingside to Barking. This tramway system was one of the few to be run at a profit (to the benefit of Ratepayers) though fares were low. Incidentally Ilford had the first tram in the London area to have a covered top. I can still remember when the Trams from the Horns and Barkingside carried a letter posting-box at the front, the mail inside being collected at Ilford Broadway and taken to the Post Office in Clements Road. The trams ran until 1938

The type of horse-drawn hearse in regular use before the days of motor hearses. These hearses were often to be seen drawn by a team of four horses and followed by numerous black horse-drawn coaches. Photograph courtesy of Mr. J. Crewe of Gilderson's.

when they were replaced by the very quiet and fast trolley buses. These in turn were replaced by motor buses in the late 1950's. For anyone interested in Ilford's trams and trolley buses I commend the reading of a book on the subject written by an old school-mate of mine, Len Thomson, who died in 1986.

Water, Water – and Necessary Drainage!

Today an abundant supply of water at the turn of a tap is something which (as with Electricity and Gas) nearly all of us take for granted. Yet it is not so very long ago that water was obtained from wells or communal pumps, or even drawn direct from streams and rivers and used without prior purification. There was, in fact, a Town pump in the Broadway – erected in 1887 to commemorate the 50th year of Queen Victoria's reign – the water supply being pumped up from a well. With Ilford's development came the laying of pipes bringing water from the South Essex Water Company's and the Metropolitan Water Board's newly built reservoirs. Pumps and the drawing of water from wells, therefore, became a thing of the past.

The problem of drainage of surface water and of sewerage, to which again most people do not give a second's thought, also had to be solved by the installation of countless miles of pipes (30" in diameter) and the building of a pumping station and an outfall works. Just as important was the raising of the money for this work and Councillors Ben Bailey and Robert Stroud were very much involved with this in the late 1890's and early 1900's. Nothwithstanding, following three days of continuous rain, on 15th June 1903, there was extensive flooding in Ilford (especially in the vicinity of the Roding) and Seven Kings where parts were under two or three feet of water and the Railway track in places was like a shallow river.

Flooding is nowadays a rare occurrence locally not only because of better drainage but because a greater amount of water is now taken from rivers by Water Companies to meet the ever-increasing demand, especially for domestic purposes. As more houses and flats are built the need to conserve water and use it prudently, particularly in dry seasons, will be increasingly of the utmost importance.

Ilford's Hospitals

In 1898 the Isolation Hospital as it was first called (and for many years afterwards) – now Chadwell Heath Hospital – was opened at the junction of what was then Cat Lane and Brickhill Lane. The Ilford Emergency Hospital was built in 1912 and in 1930 this was replaced by the King George Hospital, extensions to which were opened by King George V accompanied by Queen

Mary on 18th July 1931. In the meantime the Ilford Maternity Home was built, and opened in 1926.

Claybury Hospital dating from about 1890 was built by the Middlesex Justices and the London County Council and was for many years known as Claybury Lunatic Asylum. It stands on a hill some 230 feet above ordnance datum and its distinctive tower is a feature that can be seen over a wide area. The large Hospital in Barley Lane dating from 1899 was originally built to care for West Ham pauper lunatics and was known for many years as the West Ham Lunatic Asylum. It is now designated Redbridge Community and Mental Health Nursing Unit Goodmayes Hospital and in its grounds is now being built a large new General Hospital to serve the district.

The Boer War

On October 10, 1899 the Boer War began and many local men volunteered to serve in South Africa to augment the Regulars of the British Army. There were great celebrations in Ilford, as elsewhere, following the news of the relief of Mafeking (May 17, 1900) and the occupation of Pretoria three weeks later, and at the end of the war on May 31st, 1902. Particularly after Pretoria the celebrations got very much out of hand and fires were started, people were hurt, fire hoses were slashed and damage done to property. As sometimes happens today the Police in their attempt to contain the excesses of some of the populace were severely criticised for their methods.

Ilford Town Hall

On 17th March 1900 the foundation stone of the Town Hall was laid by Councillor W.W. Gilson, Charman of Ilford U.D.C. at the time. Only twenty-one months later, in December 1901 the Town Hall, which had been built for £24,900 was opened by Councillor Ben Bailey.

St. Andrews Church Hall

On 30th June 1906 the foundation stone of St. Andrews Church Hall was laid and in four months and a day later, on November 1st, the building was opened. Compare that with the interminable time relatively minor works take to be completed today!

Ilford's Ploughing Matches

In the early part of the century much of the land around Ilford was farmed and in October 1909 a Ploughing match – the largest in the south of England and organised by the Ilford Farmers Association – was held at Forest Farm on Fairlop Plain with 69 ploughs competing. A second Ploughing match was held in 1911 when 76 Ploughs competed.

The 1910 General Elections

During 1910 there were two General Elections (January and December) and Lloyd George addressed a public meeting in Ilford Town Hall in support of Sir John Bethell the Liberal Candidate who was elected on the two occasions (and after whom Bethell Avenue is named). Ilford was then part of the Southern Parliamentary Division of Essex which also included Romford, Dagenham, Barking, and part of East Ham. Lloyd George at that time was Chancellor of the Exchequer who introduced Social Insurance in 1908-11. In the December election the Conservative candidate was Mr. W.P. Griggs who used the Ilford Skating Rink on Ilford Hill for his final meeting which drew an audience of 7000 people. At that time the Suffragettes ("Votes for Women" – and why not?) were very active in Ilford and elsewhere.

The First World War (1914-1918). The Menace of the German Airships: Hainault Farm Airfield

By the early part of August 1914 War had broken out which involved not only most of Europe but much of the rest of the World, a War that was to last well over four years during which time millions of lives would be lost and countless injuries and unprecedented destruction suffered and more than 10,000 men from Ilford were to answer the call to arms. How did this terrible event come about and what sparked it off? Very briefly it was this:

On 28 June 1914 in Sarajevo, Serbia (which is now part of Yugoslavia) a Serbian student shot dead the heir to the Austrian Empire, Archduke Francis Ferdinand, and a month later Austria-Hungary declared war against Serbia. On August 1st Germany declared war against Russia and two days later declared war on France which had a mutual treaty with Russia. In order to attack France Germany invaded Belgium which Britain had a moral obligation to defend and to whose aid Britain immediately went, resulting in warfare and land, sea and air battles which were to continue for the whole of the duration.

For several years previously Count Ferdinand von Zeppelin who had been retired from the German Army at the age of 52 in 1891 had been experimenting with and building dirigible airships for the main purpose of using them as a weapon of war. By 1914 a fleet of these airships was operating commercially all over Germany and after the outbreak of war it was decided by the German warlords to use them so that the war could be carried into Britain with the object of terrorizing the population and breaking its morale.

Although the first Zeppelin appeared over the British coast on December 20, 1914, the first raid on Britain was on January 19th, 1915 when bombs were dropped on Gt. Yarmouth and King's Lynn killing 20 people and injuring 40 besides causing damage to property and a ship. Further raids were made over the next eight months mainly on Tyneside, eastern England and London before serious attention was given to combatting these raids by aeroplanes in addition to the very few guns and searchlights in use at the time. The unpreparedness of the Liberal Government under Mr. H.H. Asquith gave vent to public anger especially after a further raid on London and the suburbs on 8 September 1915 when there were more fatalities and injuries.

In addition to the Royal Flying Corps stations at Hounslow, Northolt, Joyce Green (near Dartford) and Dover for the defence of London it was decided to have a further two to the east of London and consequently reconnaissance parties were sent out to find suitable fields. One was a 90 acre piece of Suttons Farm, Hornchurch growing root crops (turnips etc.). The other was a 60 acre piece of grassland at Hainault Farm, Ilford in the possession of a Mr. W. Poulter. These two fields were officially requisitioned and designated Landing Grounds Nos. II and III respectively. Further, a ring of Observers on the ground would be in direct communication with the War Office and a cordon of 13-pounder mobile and anti-aircraft guns and searchlights set up around the north-eastern fringe including Becontree Heath and Chigwell Row.

And so it was that between 4th and 12th October 1915 Landing Ground No. III at Hainault Farm came into use. Portable canvas hangars were erected for the two planes that were to operate initially from here, as well as two Royal Engineers sheds. The farmhouse on the opposite side of the road which was unoccupied and unfurnished at the time was used to billet the pilots who were required to provide their own bedding etc. A telephone was installed in the house and a 13-pounder gun was allocated to defend the airfield.

No sooner had the airfield become operational than, on October 13th, another Zeppelin raid on London took place. On this occasion at least 40 people (men, women and children) were killed and 85 injured at the several places where bombs were dropped but neither the few planes which went up from Hainault, Hornchurch and Joyce Green nor the A.A. guns met with any success.

It was to be over five months later during a raid on 31 March 1916 that a Zeppelin (the L15) – one of three – which had dropped bombs on Suffolk and Essex was damaged by A.A. guns over the Thames Estuary and by concerted attacks by 2nd Lieut. Alfred de Bathe Brandon (who had come to England from New Zealand at the outbreak of war to volunteer and who had learnt to fly privately) flying from Hainault Farm. Slowly losing height the Zeppelin eventually foundered in the sea at Knock Deep some 20 miles from Foulness Point (Essex) and 15 miles north of Margate. One of the 15-man crew was killed, the others captured.

Shortly afterwards six aeroplanes were maintained at both Hainault Farm and Suttons Farm which became part of No.39 Home Defence Squadron. However it was not until the beginning of September 1916 that a German airship was shot down over British soil. This was one of an armada of eighteen German airships (mostly Zeppelins) that had set out from Germany to bomb London and the shooting down was accomplished by 21 year old Lieut. William Leefe Robinson in the early hours of Sunday 3rd September 1916 using a newly invented explosive and incendiary bullet. The airship – a Schütte Lanz 11 – which had already dropped its bombs on London suburbs fell in flames from a great height and was witnessed by many people over a wide area of London and Essex including Ilford. (The spot where it met its end at Cuffley, Hertfordshire, six miles north of Enfield is marked by a memorial paid for by readers of the "Daily Express"). The destruction of this airship was rightly hailed as a major success when things were going so badly for us. Heavy losses were being sustained at sea and unprecedented casualties were being suffered during the prolonged Battle of the Somme.

Soon afterwards, on the night of 23/24th September 1916, two Super Zeppelins were brought down. One (the L32) which was shot down by 2nd Lieut. Fred Sowrey, also flying from Suttons Farm, fell at Great Burstead near Billericay when all on board were killed. The other (L33) force-landed at Little Wigborough south of Colchester, and exploded shortly afterwards possibly being fired by the crew, all of whom survived. It was in the bringing down of this Zeppelin that 2nd Lieut. Brandon, flying from Hainault Farm, also played a major role. Exactly one week later (Sunday, October 1st) a fourth Zeppelin (the L31) commanded by the experienced Commander Mathy, was shot down falling in flames from a great height at Potters Bar, Hertfordshire. The successful pilot on this occasion was 2nd Lieut. W. Tempest flying from Suttons Farm. Never again, after this raid, did Zeppelins raid London – though they continued on other parts of Britain – but later came the Gothas and Giant planes which did more damage and killed and injured more people than did the Zeppelins. On January 25, 1918 two pilots from Hainault Farm shared in the shooting down of a Gotha plane which fell at Wickford.

In 1917 Hainault Farm airfield was equipped with new planes, the Sopwith Camels, Hainault Farm being the first airfield to receive them. I can remember seeing them taking off and landing when my father (who had been wounded on the Somme) took me to the airfield towards the end of the war. By that time the Royal Flying Corps had (from 1st April 1918) become the Royal Air Force.

In November 1918 the late Air Marshall Sir Arthur "Bomber" Harris was based at Hainault Farm airfield where he was in command of a night fighter squadron.

By the end of 1919 the airfield had been closed and reverted to farmland.

A German airship of the type that dropped 13 high explosive bombs on the Ilford area on the night of 25th April 1916. Most were built to the design of Count Ferdinand von Zeppelin and so were called Zeppelins. This photograph – courtesy of the Imperial War Museum – gives some impression of their immense size, one being 530 feet long. Capable of flying at 15,000 feet or more, a height beyond the reach of the relatively few guns we had at the time – they could remain aloft for at least 24 hours.

In one raid carried out on 8 September 1915, a bomb weighing 660 lbs (300 kilograms) – the heaviest ever put on board a German airship – was dropped on the City of London, falling in Bartholomew Close adjoining St. Bartholomew's Hospital. This was in addition to numerous other high explosive bombs and incendiaries inevitably causing fatalities and injuries and damage to buildings, gas and water mains and a bus with 20 people on board, 9 of whom were killed including the driver who died after having both his legs blown off.

At left: (*Above*) A 2-seater version of the original BE2c bi-plane, as used in the First World War over the Western Front and in the defence of London. (The letters BE stand for Bleriot Experimental.)

The frail-looking, primitive, crude, clumsy but stable machines made of wood, wire and fabric and with engines of early design, which were prone to failure and caused the whole plane to vibrate, were used by such Royal Flying Corps pilots as Lieut. Robinson, 2/Lt. Brandon, 2/Lt. Sowrey and 2/Lt. Tempest in the later, successful attacks on German airships over England.

Armed with a single Lewis gun which was fixed to fire over the top wings and which would often jam and whose ammunition drum would sometimes slip out and hit the pilot's head, these planes (at first very few in number and with very few pilots either) could take up to five minutes to start and the best part of an hour to reach 10,000 feet. The pilot in his shallow open cockpit with primitive flying instruments, had no protection from the bitter cold at such a height other than perhaps a scarf, leather coat or British Warm (overcoat) and leather helmet and goggles in addition to his normal clothing. Primitive flares on the ground of the airfields which had no proper runways and which were often shrouded in ground mist made flying then – especially at night – a very hazardous occupation. (Photo: courtesy of RAF Museum, Hendon.)

(*Below*) The Sopwith Camel bi-plane as used in the First World War and flown from Hainault Farm airfield – a 60 acre field of grassland owned by a Mr. W. Poulter – which was the first to use these planes in the defence of London. This was one of several planes designed by Sir Thomas Octave Murdoch Sopwith who died aged 100 as recently as January 1989. He was also joint developer of the Hurricanes used in World War II. (Photo: courtesy of RAF Museum, Hendon.)

Belgian Refugees in Ilford

During the First World War Valentines Mansion was used to house Belgian refugees. For a time it was also used as an annexe to the Ilford Emergency Hospital.

An Unhappy New Year's Day

On the morning of New Year's day 1915 a serious Rail Crash occurred just outside Ilford Station when an Express train running late from Clacton ran into the side of a crowded local train crossing on to the main line to London. 10 people were killed and over 80 injured.

Kelvin Hughes

In 1916 the Kelvin Hughes factory in New North Road, Hainault, was started by Mr. Arthur Hughes to meet the demands of the Royal Flying Corps (later to become the Royal Air Force) for compasses and navigational aids.

The Silvertown Explosion

In 1917 (January 19) the Silvertown munition works explosion occurred killing 69 people and causing widespread damage. It was heard as far away as Salisbury, in Wiltshire. The Ilford Fire Brigade rendered assistance as it did when a German Gotha plane was brought down at Beckton in the last raid of the First World War.

Lest we forget: for our tomorrow they gave their today

After the 1914-1918 War a list of the names of those who had "paid the supreme sacrifice" was published in the Ilford War Memorial gazette. There were as many as 1159. Very many more were wounded.

On Armstice Day (November 11th) 1922 the Ilford War Memorial in the garden adjoining what was then the Ilford Emergency Hospital (now the King George Hospital) was unveiled. It now also serves as a memorial to those who lost their lives in the Second World War 1939-1945.

King George V at Ilford Town Hall

In the early 1920's the building of the Becontree Housing Estate began coinciding with the Limehouse Slum Clearance scheme, and on June 12th, 1923 the Estate was visited by King George V who stopped at Ilford Town Hall on his way to Becontree.

In the same year (1923) the Clock Tower (the gift of Mr. W.P. Griggs) was removed from Ilford Broadway to the entrance to South Park. Also that year the building known as Cranbrook Castle (which had been erected in 1765) was demolished.

The Plessey Company's commencement in Ilford: Harrison Gibson's first fire, etc.

1923 saw the start of the Plessey Company's factory in Vicarage Lane, and in 1924 the building of the parade of shops with offices above known as Cranbrook House (in Cranbrook Road), and the first Harrison Gibson's fire. Also in that year Valentines Mansion was first used by the Ilford Council for their public health offices.

More of Ilford's farms disappear

Although there had been a great deal of house building in Ilford before the First World War when much farmland or Estates were built on there were still several small farms in active production for some time afterwards in the Ilford area. I clearly remember Stringer's (Middlefield) Farm where Perth Road now continues through to Gants Hill (the farmhouse – now divided into two cottages – is still there) and Brown's Farm where the Clayhall Estate off Woodford Avenue is now. And most of Barkingside and Hainault was still farmland until the 1930's and some even later.

The P.D.S.A. Animal Treatment Centre at St. Swithin's Farm

In 1927 the People's Dispensary for Sick Animals (founded by Mrs. Maria Dickin in the East End in 1917) acquired the 30-acre St. Swithin's Farm in Woodford Bridge Road, Ilford.

House Building in the 1920's and 1930's

Much house building took place in Ilford between the two wars and those builders whom I remember as being foremost in such development included Suburban Developments, New Ideal Homesteads, Haines & Warwick, Holmes White, R. Stroud, P.E. Brand, A.P. Griggs, Hobbs Bros., J.W. Moore, W. Wakeling, Baskett & Brown, and J.W. Lohden.

Eastern Avenue opened

In 1925 Eastern Avenue was opened by H.R.H. Prince Henry, who later became the Duke of Gloucester (died 1974). It was later made a dual carriageway all the way to Southend and was, I believe, the first of such roads in Britain. This was in the days before Traffic Lights – introduced in the late 1920's and early 1930's – which is why so many "roundabouts" were built at road junctions. With the building of Eastern Avenue the High Road ceased to be the main road for through traffic which it had been for many centuries previously.

Ilford becomes a Borough

On October 21st 1926 the then Duke of York (who on December 12th 1936 became King George VI) accompanied by the Duchess of York – our present Queen Mother – came to Ilford and at the Town Hall presented the Royal Charter by which the Urban District of Ilford was raised to the status of a Municipal Borough.

Entertainment

In Victorian and Edwardian times and even well into the 1920's many people enjoyed musical evenings in their homes, the music being created by themselves around the then popular piano. The playing of a musical instrument was regarded very much as a desirable social accomplishment and singing, monologues accompanied by a pianist, and even recitations were enjoyed as were local brass bands which played in the parks and other public places including other parts of London to which they travelled. Card games, particularly Whist, were popular too with many a Whist Drive (with prizes) taking place in halls throughout the town. Several amateur dramatic and operatic societies also performed locally. It must be said that the meeting of one's relations and friends was very much more widespread then than it is today, especially on a Sunday when usually in their "family best" the whole family would go together and probably stay to tea.

Before the coming of the Cinema music halls attracted large audiences. Ilford had its own music hall or Variety Theatre, the Hippodrome, which stood in Ilford Lane by the Broadway. Many were the nationally-known Variety Artists who appeared there over the years, very often having appeared on stage the same evening at the Stratford Empire and the East Ham Palace. They included Marie Lloyd, George Robey, Gracie Fields, George Formby, Nellie Wallace, Robb Wilton, Clapham & Dwyer, Stainless Stephen, Nosmo King, Wee Georgie Wood, Max Miller, Nervo & Knox and the rest of the Crazy Gang, and Renee Houston. A seat in the gallery in the early days cost 4d (four old pennies – less than 2p today) and a programme for a further penny. A seat in the pit was 1/- (one shilling). I can remember seeing Vera Lynn singing there with Ambrose and his orchestra in 1938 before she was well known. The Hippodrome was still attracting large audiences until towards the end of the Second World War when it was extensively damaged by a V2 Rocket in January 1945.

It was in the 1920's and 1930's that the Cinema became the No.1 form of entertainment for many people, especially with courting couples. The first of Ilford's several Cinemas to be built was the Biograph on Ilford Hill. There was also the Cinema de luxe in the High Road (opposite where BhS is now), the Empire Kinema in Ilford Lane and the Astoria (now the Shannon Club) in Seven Kings. But Ilford's most popular cinema was the Super Cinema – opened in October 1922 – which stood opposite Ilford Railway Station (where C & A now stands). Sadly this Cinema, like the Hippodrome, was extensively damaged by a V2 Rocket in 1945. Such cinemas as the Premier Electric (now the Ilford Palais), and the Regal in the High Road, the Savoy at Gants Hill and the State at Barkingside were also well patronised.

Ilford Football Club

Football, like Cricket, has its origin in rural Britain going back several centuries but as a game played by a team to a laid-down set of rules dates from the year 1863 when the Football Association was formed since when the game has been known as Association Football. This is to distinguish it from Rugby Football which dates from 1823 when a boy at Rugby Public School picked up and ran with the ball for the first time. The Ilford Football Club which ceased as a separate club in 1979 when it sold its ground at Lynn Road Newbury Park – one of the best in Amateur football – and merged with Leytonstone to become Leytonstone Ilford (subsequently merged with Walthamstow Avenue and now playing on Dagenham F.C.'s ground as Redbridge Forest) dates from 20 October 1881 when the population of Ilford was less than 8000. For a large part of its 98 years' life Ilford Football Club was one of the most senior and well-known amateur football clubs in the London area, in Essex, and indeed in England. It was also known and respected in the Channel Islands and in Germany, France, Holland, Spain, Belgium, Denmark and Eire all of which the club visited on various playing tours starting in 1903 and, the war years excluded, continuing for well over 50 years. Many were the trophies which were won but most importantly the Ilford Football Club always had a reputation for fair play and sportsmanship, acting and playing in the true spirit of amateur football. It is worth mentioning that in those years nearly all of the team's players lived locally and each member had great pride in playing for his home town. A brief outline of the Club's history and its achievements are given elsewhere in this book.

(*Continued on p. 83.*)

The staff of the Ilford Laundry in the late 1910's or early 1920's.

The company's letter heading showing the Laundry's drying ground alongside.

T. S. S. *Ocean Monarch*. One of the many passenger and cargo ships furnished by the Ilford store of C. W. Burnes Ltd.

C. W. Burnes' Wellesley Road frontage 1953.

This bridge over the Roding near the Red House P.H. was demolished when Eastern Avenue was constructed in 1924/1925.

The forerunner of Marks & Spencer, located opposite The Angel P.H., 1922.

This photograph was taken in the early 1920's before The Drive, Ilford was extended to where Eastern Avenue is now.

Eastern Avenue under construction in 1924. This section is near Barley Lane, Goodmayes.

SUPER CINEMA, CRANBROOK ROAD, ILFORD

THE WASH, CRANBROOK ROAD, ILFORD

(*Above*) The Super Cinema c. 1924. (Photo: W. Hornby.) (*Below*) The Wash, Cranbrook Road c. 1924. (Photo: W. Hornby.)

Ilford War Memorial (adjoining King George Hospital) unveiled 11th November 1922. (Photo: Author.)

A London Co-operative Society staff outing in 1924 from their shop in the High Road on the corner of Oaklands Park Avenue – destroyed in World War II.

IN UNITY PROGRESS

ILFORD'S CHARTER DAY SONG
(21 October, 1926)

Words by
DOROTHY M. HOBBS

Music by
HERBERT H. GOODACRE

Lowe & Brydone Printers Ltd., London, N.W. 10.

Charter Day 21 October 1926. The then Duke and Duchess of York at Ilford War Memorial with Sir Frederic Wise M.P. (Charter Mayor), Mr. Adam Partington (Town Clark) and Mr. Drane (Mace Bearer). The Duke of York, who became King George VI on 12 December 1936, was 31 years old at the time of the visit; the Duchess of York – our present Queen Mother – was then only 26.

Gants Hill c. 1928 (no Underground station there then).

Head offices of ILFORD Limited in Roden Street: built in 1928, they were demolished to make way for Sainsbury's supermarket.

Freddie Drane scoring Ilford's first goal against Leyton in the Amateur Cup Final at Highbury: 20 April 1929. Ilford won 3–1 and the following year won the Amateur Cup again beating Bournemouth Gas Works 5–1 at Upton Park.

Ilford Football Team: season 1928–1929. Winners: F.A. Amateur Cup; London Senior Cup; Essex Senior Cup; Ilford Hospital Shield.
Top row – J. Young, F. Duffin, W. Golding, C.F. Duffin, E.N. Cowley, F. Murray. Middle row – C. Dawson (Trainer), A. Stokes, L. Cramer, P.S. Banks, H. Norman, A.K. Barrett, V.F. Welsh, A. Bott, A. Willats (Trainer). Front row – E.C. Porter (Hon. Sec.), V.C. Potter, G. Peploe, R.C. Dellow, Reg Wade (Captain), F.A. Drane, E. Gilderson, G.W. Drane (Hon. Fin. Sec.).

Sowing the last crop on land at Clay Hall Farm, which was acquired by Ilford Borough Council for use as a public park, October 1930. (Photo: Ilford Recorder.)

(*Above*) King George V and Queen Mary opening the extensions to King George Hospital, 18 July 1931. (Photo: Local History Collection, Central Library.) (*Below*) King George Hospital today. (Photo: Author.)

ILFORD............

2007 REASONS

for buying B**RAND** **HOUSES**
BUILT

1 PRICES FROM £699 to £1,150.

2 THEY'RE WORTH IT

3 ROUGHLY 10% DOWN

4 26/10d. to 30/- A WEEK (all-in).

5 NO ROAD CHARGES

6 ALL HOUSES FREEHOLD

7 7 MILES FROM LIVERPOOL STREET

And the other 2,000 reasons are the best of the lot — the 2,000 satisfied customers which Brand built houses have made during the past 30 years. The " GREAT GEARIES " and " HIGH VIEW " Estates are on gravel sub-soil 100 feet above sea level. The houses contain Drawing and Dining rooms, 3/4 Bedrooms and usual offices. Some have garages and central heating, They are convenient for schools and shops.

Our Estate Office is at the corner of Cranbrook Road and Eastern Avenue. The houses are always open for inspection and a salesman there to help you. Car available if necessary.

Write for booklet P. Address enquiries to:

BRAND & WHITE, LTD.,
Builders, EASTERN AVENUE,   ILFORD

Tel. : Valent'ne 4148.

Buy a **B**RAND *House*
BUILT

House advertisement reprinted from Pageant of Essex programme, July 1932.

Ilford's Schoolboys Triumph

Ilford's schoolboys have also distinguished themselves at Soccer. In May 1952 the gates at the Lynn Road ground were closed for the one and only occasion when an all-time record of 17,000 spectators crammed into the ground to see Ilford Boys defeat Swansea Boys 4-2 in the first leg of the English Shield Final. Ilford went on to win the trophy in the second leg and they also won the Cook Cup and the Robert Johnson trophy the same year – an achievement unequalled by a local schools representative side. Also in the 1928/29 season when Ilford Football Club won the Amateur cup for the first time, Ilford schoolboys reached the final of the Corinthian Shield when they lost to West Ham. In Ilford's team then was W.F. Asker of Goodmayes School who that season captained England boys against Scotland at Glasgow.

Ilford Cricket Club: Athletics, Swimming, Bowls and Golf

Ilford Cricket Club – founded in 1879 – has also performed well over the years, with such players as John Lever (who lives in Ilford) and Graham Gooch (born in Leytonstone) going on to play for England – as Graham Gooch is still doing. An excellent book on the first 100 years of the Club (involving a great deal of research) has been written by the former Club President – described by T.N. Pearce, a former Essex Captain, as "the indefatigable John Polson". Ilford has also been well represented at various times by the Ilford Athletic Club, the Ilford Swimming Club, local Bowls Clubs, and by members of the Ilford Golf Club. The latter Club with Mr. Holcombe Ingleby as its President was founded in 1907 playing on land which for a number of years (from 1887) had been a Company-owned Rifle Range. With ranges up to 900 yards, being handy to London, it was very much used until, as a result of the inherent danger of stray bullets to an increasing public requiring access to Wanstead Park, Ilford Council decided to purchase the land of which it is still the owner (though now as Redbridge Council). It is unfortunate for the Club, which has recently been granted a new lease of the land by the Council, that the Woodford to Barking Relief Road (now linking up with both the North Circular Road and the M11) has reduced the size of the Course and separated it from the Club House but it is still a popular playing area.

The Hospital Chapel

Around 1930 the buildings at each side of the Hospital Chapel on Ilford Hill – all of which had been extensively restored in 1889 – were replaced by those that are there today. The history of the Chapel with its associations now going back over 800 years is dealt with at some length by George Tasker in his "Ilford Past and Present" published in 1901 and reference to it is recommended to anyone wanting to research Ilford's oldest building, as is George Caunt's "Ilford's Yesterdays".

Pageant of Essex

In July 1932 a spectacular event took place over a period of nine days which attracted vast numbers of people to Valentines Park where it was held. This was the colourful Pageant of Essex in aid of King George Hospital, extensions to which had been opened by King George V accompanied by Queen Mary the previous July. The Pageant Master was Mr. Frank Lascelles, and Chairman of the Pageant Historical Committee was Ilford's celebrated Essex and local historian Mr. Fred Brand who played an important part in the Pageant's success which was widely acclaimed in the National press.

Set on the Melbourne field, with over 900 performers, there were seven episodes. The first dealt with the Roman invasion and early occupation of Britain and the resistance to it led by Boadicea (Boudicca), Queen of the Iceni, at such places at Colchester and Epping Forest. The second dealt with the legend of the seven kings, the kings of the Heptarchy, and the triumph of Christianity in Essex. Episode 3 depicted Tudor Essex (Henry VIII's hunting in the Royal Forest lands, his palace at New Hall, Boreham, and Anne Boleyn whose parents' home was at Rochford Hall), followed by Episode 4 which portrayed Queen Elizabeth I's review of her troops at Tilbury in 1588. Then followed the Siege of Colchester in 1648 during the Civil War; Dick Turpin, Fairlop Fair between 1775 and 1780, and Charles Dickens' Barnaby Rudge: and finally the ceremony at High Beech on May 6, 1882 when Queen Victoria declared the residue of Epping Forest open to the public for ever.

Valentines Park Shelter Tragedy

On August 21st 1939 Lightning struck a shelter in Valentines Park killing 7 people and injuring 19.

Commuting by train to London in the 1920's, and the opening of the Underground Railway December 1947

Before the Second World War there was no Tube or Underground Railway serving Ilford and relatively few people owned cars. Most commuters to London therefore travelled by rail – known then as the London & North Eastern Railway (L.N.E.R.) – from Ilford and the other stations within the area. With the local population steadily increasing as more houses were built travelling by train went from bad to worse with standing room only for many passengers in each narrow compartment. The journeys were made worse in those days by the thick yellow fogs – known colloquially as "pea soupers" – which occurred regularly every Winter, particularly in November. These fogs were undoubtedly due largely to the smoke emitted into the atmosphere by the many thousands of house chimneys – no gas or oil-fired Central Heating then – and to some extent by the chimneys of the several industrial buildings in the district and by the coal-fired steam locomotives on the railways. An Underground Railway to serve the northern part of Ilford, therefore, became a dire necessity. By 1935 after a great deal of public pressure over several years plans were completed for the extension of the Central London Line to the Ilford area and some time later a start was made on its construction. However the Second World War began on 3rd September 1939 and it was to be more than eight years later – on 14th December 1947 – before the Underground from Leytonstone to Newbury Park was opened. It was extended to Hainault on 31st May 1948. On the main Railway Line from Liverpool Street through Ilford to Shenfield, the first electric train ran on 26th September 1949.

World War II 1939-1945: death and destruction from the air: civilian and H.M. forces losses

During the Second World War – for which Germany under Hitler had been preparing for several years with the object of dominating Europe as well as other parts of the World – Ilford suffered heavily from the many Air Raids carried out by the Luftwaffe. In addition to the countless number of incendiary, phosphorous and oil bombs there were 618 High Explosive bombs, 25 parachute mines, and 69 Flying Bombs (V1's or Doodle Bugs) and Rockets (V2's) dropped within the Borough of Ilford. A map showing the location of these many "Incidents", as they were called by Civil Defence, published by the Ilford Recorder in its issue of 26th September 1946 is reproduced in this book.

According to the Ilford Borough Council Handbook 1949-1950 civilian casualties in the Borough were: Fatal 530, Seriously injured 854: Slightly injured 1786 – a total of 3170.

The names and addresses and other particulars of the Civilians killed are listed in a book which can be seen in the Local History Room of the Central Library. They were of all ages: children, women and men, and in many instances more than one member (sometimes several) of the same family died at the same time. It is indeed an extremely sad and poignant record.

I have already mentioned the number of Ilford men serving in the H.M. Forces who were killed during the First World War (which until the start of the Second World War was always referred to as the Great War) but just how many men and women who served in the Armed Forces and the Merchant Navy lost their lives during the Second World War? In the Central Library is a Roll of Honour which contains the names of Ilford men and women in the various branches of the Forces who have been officially notified as having lost their lives. The actual number, however, was not known when I enquired several months ago and, following my request to do so, I was afforded the facility of carrying out a physical count. The total number I found to be 538 made up as follows:

Army 219, Royal Marines 1, Royal Navy 68, RNVR 1, Royal Air Force 224, Merchant Navy 15, WAAF 2, ATS 1, Not Stated 7. It will be seen from these figures that the Royal Air Force suffered slightly more fatalities during 1939-1945 than the Army. Undoubtedly this would have been largely due to the number of RAF crews who were killed while carrying out raids over heavily defended parts of Germany and other enemy-occupied territories. The appalling casualties were not made known at the time but fairly recently it was disclosed that on one night alone no less than 108 planes failed to return. I must add that the Roll of Honour Remembrance Book mentioned is not necessarily a complete record of all fatalities for I know of one soldier and one airman who lost their lives during World War II whose names I was unable to find recorded.

Perusing the second part of the Roll of Honour I found that the names of Civilians killed in Ilford through enemy action (by Air Raids and V1's and V2's) during those years totalled 552. This is perhaps not surprisingly a slightly higher figure than the 530 published in the 1949/50 Handbook mentioned.

Thus the total number of recorded fatalities suffered by Ilford people during the Second World War is 1090, a figure which is slightly less than the 1159 Ilford men who were killed during the First World War.

It is, of course, impossible to quantify the suffering, the grief, the anxieties, sorrow, pain, hardship and loss (in more ways than one) that such conflicts bring to residents, relatives and friends as well as to those in the various Services both at home and abroad. Only those who have endured those terrible years can have any idea of what it was really like.

The damage to property in Ilford as a result of the Air Raids in the second World War was considerable. 313 houses were demolished, 9410 houses were badly damaged, and nearly 30,000 sustained minor damage. Apart from the Ilford Hippodrome and the Super Cinema already mentioned the Clock Tower which used to stand in Ilford Broadway and was transferred to the entrance to South Park was destroyed. The Second World War against Germany officially ended at one minute past midnight on 8th May 1945. The very next day King George VI and Queen Elizabeth (the present Queen Mother) accompanied by the two Princesses (Elizabeth and Margaret) paid a visit to Ilford to see the damage sustained and to meet the people.

Plessey's use of the underground tunnelling at Ilford during World War II

Playing a very important role during the Second World War was the Plessey Company and it was their Chairman, Mr. A.G. Clark (later to become Sir Allan Clark) who was instrumental in getting the five miles of uncompleted Underground tunnelling in the Ilford area used for manufacturing purposes during that time.

The General Election 1945: Labour elected

Very soon after the end of the Second World War against Germany a General Election was held. Ilford was divided into two Parliamentary Consituencies – Ilford South and Ilford North – and Labour took both seats, Mrs. Mabel Ridealgh and Mr. James Ranger being elected.

House repair and house building after World War II

Immediately after the end of the Second World War priority was given to the repair of the many houses damaged and to the replacement of those that had been destroyed. Additionally the building of new houses took place particularly in the Hainault area and in the Clayhall area but the supply of the limited building materials which became available was strictly controlled by the introduction of Building Permits which were in force for some years afterwards, as of course was the rationing of other commodities.

General Election 1951: Conservative government under Churchill elected

In the General election of 1951 the Conservatives took both Ilford South and Ilford North with Mr. A.E. Cooper (a local man) and Mr. Geoffrey Hutchinson (later to become Lord Ilford) being elected.

Office development resumed

In the late 1950's some office development took place and this continued in the 1960's with large office buildings being erected at Gants Hill and in Clements Road and, later, in the High Road and on Ilford Hill.

Ilford ceases to be a separate Borough

It was largely as a result of Ilford Borough Council in the early 1950's (*Continued on p. 99.*)

(*Above*) Spitfire fighter planes of the Royal Air Force which together with the Hurricane fighter planes and our anti-aircraft guns were responsible for bringing down or damaging many enemy planes during the critical Battle of Britain days of August and September 1940. These planes flew from Fairlop Airfield and from Hornchurch and North Weald and were frequently seen over Ilford during World War II. Ilford-born and resident Raymond Baxter flew one of these planes in Britain, in the Mediterranean and over the mainland of Europe. (Reproduction by kind permission of the RAF Museum, Hendon.) (*Below*) A German V1 (Flying Bomb) as used during World War II. Thirty-four of these weapons fell on Ilford from 16 June 1944 to 16 August 1944 killing 60 people and seriously injuring 242, besides causing widespread damage. Their approach was audible and some were even shot down in flight by our pilots. (Photo: Imperial War Museum.)

(*Left*) A German V2: Rocket Projectile. Thirty-five of these almost silent weapons fell without warning on Ilford from 26 October 1944 to 27 March 1945, killing 100 people and seriously injuring 435. Great damage to property was also caused. The launching of these rockets ceased when the territory on the continent from which they were fired was overrun by allied armies towards the end of the war. (Photo: Imperial War Museum.) (*Below*) Officially prepared drawing of a German V2 Rocket Projectile. The drawn figure gives an idea of the size of the weapon which is approximately 46ft long and 5ft 6ins in diameter. (Photo: Imperial War Museum.)

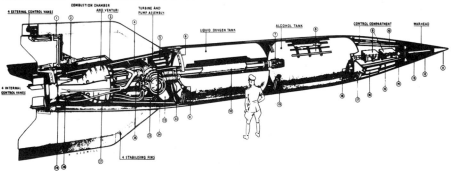

F.196 H.M.S. *Urchin* adopted by the citizens of Ilford during Warship Week March 1942. The ship's crest is mounted on the wall inside the Town Hall (Oakfield Road entrance). (Photo: National Maritime Museum.)

Crater caused by a parachute mine which fell in Clayhall Park. The late Basil Amps of the Ilford Recorder is standing in the crater. (Photo: lent to the author by the late Basil Amps.)

Going to work in the Underground Tunnel used by Plessey's in World War II. (Mr. A.G. Clark seated on "train".)

This photograph taken during World War II shows employees of the Plessey Company engaged on war work in a section of the uncompleted underground tunnelling at Ilford, where 2000 people on each shift worked deep below ground. (Photo: Local History Room, Central Library, Ilford.)

92

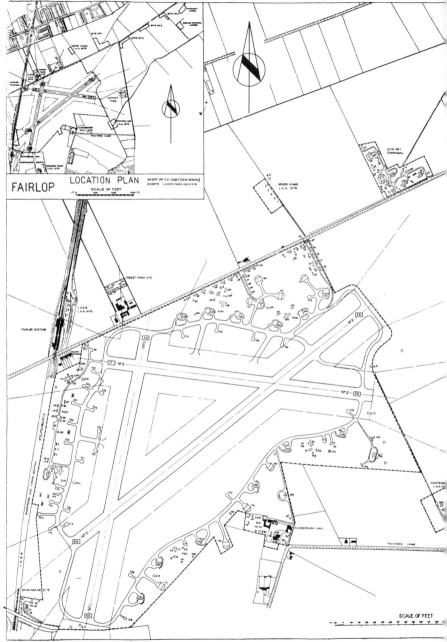

Fairlop airfield. Taken over by Air Ministry 26 Sept. 1940, three runways and ancillary buildings, etc. completed by 18 August 1941. Airfield fully operational – 1 Sept. 1941; opened as a satellite to Hornchurch – 12 Nov. 1941; among various operational duties, it provided air cover for the

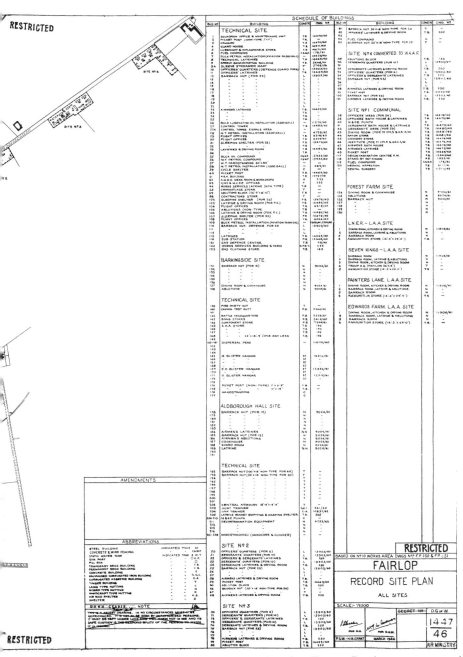

Dieppe landings – Sept. 1942; fighter cover to American Fortress Bombers, convoy patrols and attacks on flying bomb launching sites in Northern France. In use as a balloon centre – Sept. '44–Sept. '45. Closed 22 August 1946.

Flying Bombs (V1's) which fell on Ilford during World War II

No.	Date			South of High Road	Between High Road & Eastern Avenue	North of Eastern Avenue	Actual Location
1	16 June	1944		X			South Park (near South Park Terrace)
2	18	,,	,,			X	Padnall Road (off Billet Road)
3	22	,,	,,		X		Blackbush Ave, Chadwell Heath
4	23	,,	,,			X	Chase Lane, Newbury Park
5	24	,,	,,			X	Tunstall Avenue, New North Rd, Hainault
6	26	,,	,,	X			St. Mary's Road
7	,,	,,	,,			X	Oakleafe Gdns, (Longwood Gdns)
8	,,	,,	,,	X			Meadway (Longbridge Road)
9	27	,,	,,		X		Royston Gardens, Redbridge
10	,,	,,	,,	X			Gordon Field (Green Lane)
11	30	,,	,,			X	Dr. Barnardo's Homes
12	,,	,,	,,			X	Woodford Ave – between Lord Avenue and Herent Drive
13	,,	,,	,,			X	Otley Drive – near Sringfield Drive
14	1 July	,,				X	William Torbitt School Playing Field
15	5	,,	,,		X		Field rear of Shenstone Gdns. (Eastern Avenue), Newbury Park
16	,,	,,	,,			X	Geariesville Gdns/Woodville Gardens
17	,,	,,	,,	X			Allotments, Uphall Road
18	6	,,	,,			X	Atherton Road/Ewellhurst Road, Clayhall
19	7	,,	,,			X	Woodford Avenue/Woodford Bridge Road
20	9	,,	,,			X	Mossford Lane, Tomswood Hill
21	24	,,	,,		X		Beehive Lane – near Wanstead Lane
22	27	,,	,,		X		Cowley Road (Cranbrook)
23	,,	,,	,,			X	Fairlop Road
24	,,	,,	,,			X	Redbridge Lane East (near Redbridge Station)
25	29	,,	,,	X			Hampton Road (Ilford Lane end)
26	30	,,	,,		X		Huxley Drive, Goodmayes
27	3 August	,,				X	Eastern Avenue (north side), near Little Heath
28	,,	,,	,,			X	Windermere Gardens (Eastern Avenue), Redbridge
29	,,	,,	,,		X		Eccleston Crescent (junction Barley Lane)
30	,,	,,	,,			X	Fowler's Meadow, Forest Road, Fairlop
31	8	,,	,,		X		Coventry Road, junction Christchurch Road
32	10	,,	,,			X	New North Rd – between Beech Grove and Cyprus Grove
33	15	,,	,,		X		Allotments, Benton Road East
34	16	,,	,,			X	Beechwood Gardens (off Woodford Avenue)
	TOTAL (34)			6	9	19	

Rocket Projectiles (V2's) Which Fell on Ilford During World War II

No.	Date	South of High Road	Between High Road & Eastern Avenue	North of Eastern Avenue	Actual Location
1	26 Oct 1944		X		Courtland Ave (off The Drive)
2	4 Nov ,,		X		Ilford Golf Course
3	12 ,, ,,		X		Exeter Gdns (off The Drive)
4	,, ,, ,,			X	"Dick Turpin", Aldborough Hatch
5	22 ,, ,,		X		Allotments, Aldborough Road (Eastern Avenue end)
6	24 ,, ,,	X			South Park Road (Green Lane)
7	19 Dec ,,			X	Claybury Hospital Grounds (south side)
8	26 ,, ,,	X			Capel Gardens (Longbridge Rd)
9	30 ,, ,,			X	Collinwood Gdns (Woodford Ave)
10	4 Jan 1945	X			Levett Gardens
11	7 ,, ,,			X	Peel Institute Sports Ground (Woodford Avenue)
12	12 ,, ,,	X			rear of Ilford Hippodrome (near The Broadway)
13	14 ,, ,,		X		Abercorn Gardens, Goodmayes
14	26 ,, ,,			X	Fencepiece Road
15	3 Feb ,,	X			Goodmayes Park
16	4 ,, ,,		X		Wanstead Park Rd (York Rd end)
17	,, ,, ,,		X		Aldborough Road (near junction with Eastern Avenue)
18	7 ,, ,,			X	Stoke Avenue, New North Road, Hainault
19	8 ,, ,,		X		Ley Street (near Super Cinema)
20	13 ,, ,,	X			High Road, Goodmayes (burst in air, near Station)
21	17 ,, ,,			X	Claybury Hospital Grounds (by main buildings)
22	18 ,, ,,		X		Ley St (near "The Bell" PH)
23	19 ,, ,,	X			Kent View Gardens (New Road, Seven Kings)
24	20 ,, ,,	X			Uphall Road (Ilford Limited)
25	21 ,, ,,		X		Belgrave Road (between Kensington and Seymour Gdns)
26	,, ,, ,,		X		Cranley Dr/Westernville Gdns
27	26 ,, ,,			X	Hatley Avenue (near Dr. Barnardo's Homes)
28	27 ,, ,,		X		Goodmayes Hospital Grounds (near Eastern Avenue)
29	3 Mar ,,	X			Breamore Road (between Westrow and Gyllingdune Gardens)
30	6 ,, ,,		X		St. Albans Road, Seven Kings (High Road end)
31	7 ,, ,,	X			Allotments, Loxford Lane
32	8 ,, ,,		X		Endsleigh Gardens (Wanstead Park Rd end) see photograph
33	12 ,, ,,			X	Field off Forest Road, Hainault Forest end
34	26 ,, ,,	X			Oakfield Rd (near Town Hall): burst in air
35	27 ,, ,,			X	Atherton Road, Clayhall
	TOTAL (35)	11	14	10	

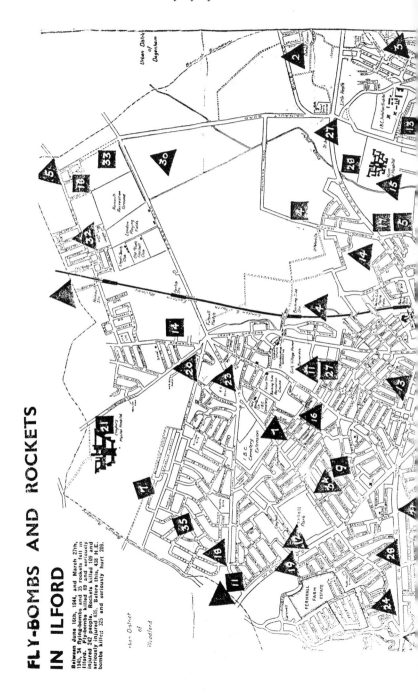

FLY-BOMBS AND ROCKETS IN ILFORD

Between June 16th, 1944, and March 27th, 1945, 34 flying-bombs and 35 rockets fell in Ilford. Fly-bombs killed 69 and seriously injured 242 people. Rockets killed 109 and seriously injured 435. Before this, 438 H.E. bombs killed 325 and seriously hurt 209.

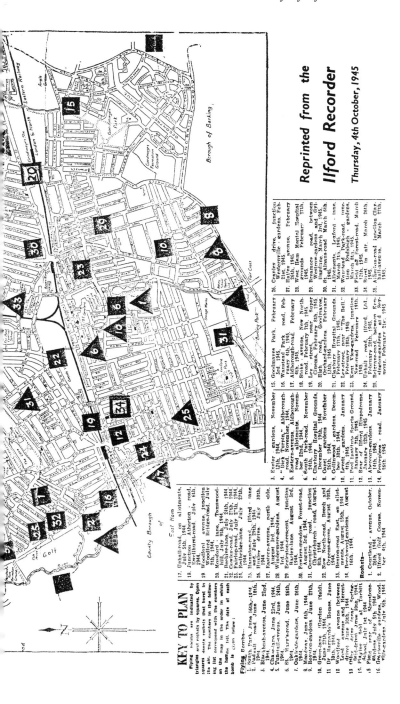

Reprinted from the

Ilford Recorder

Thursday, 4th October, 1945

KEY TO PLAN

Flying bombs are indicated by triangles and rockets by squares. Open squares denote rockets that burst in the air. The numbers in the following list correspond with the numbers on the map in the order in which the bombs fell. The date of each bomb is given below:

Flying Bombs:

1. South Park, June 16th—1944.
2. Redball road June 18th.
3. Blackbush-avenue, June 22nd, 1944.
4. Chadwell, June 23rd, 1944.
5. Tuberal-avenue, June 24th, 1944.
6. St. Mary's-road, June 26th, 1944.
7. Oakdale-gardens, June 26th, 1944.
8. Meadway, June 6th, 1944.
9. Roycroft-gardens June 27th, 1944.
10. Green-lane (Gordon field), June 27th, 1944.
11. Dr. Barnardo's Homes, June 30th, 1944.
12. Woodford avenue (between allotments and Horns-drive) June 30th, 1944.
13. Plaistow field at Torbitt-drive near Spring-gardens, July 1st, 1944.
14. Fielsel, July 1st, rear of Shentstone gardens July 5th 1944.
15. Glanville gardens, Wood-ville-gardens, July 5th, 1944.
16. ...gardens, July 5th, 1944.
17. Uphall-road, on allotments, July 5th, 1944.
18. Junction Alberton - road, Kewilhurst-road July 6th, 1944.
19. Woodford avenue, junction Woodford Bridge-road, July 7th, 1944.
20. Mowbford-lane, Tomswood-hill, July 9th, 1944.
21. Rochlee-lane, July 24th, 1944.
22. Goster-road, July 27th, 1944.
23. Fairlop-road, July 27th, 1944.
24. Redbridge-lane, July 27th, 1944.
25. Hamnton-road, Ilford Cemetery, July 29th, 1944.
26. Inactive drive, July 30th, 1944.
27. Eastern-avenue, north side, 1944.
28. Wintermere-gardens, August 3rd, 1944.
29. Roginston-crescent, junction Barley-lane, August 3rd, 1944.
30. Fowlders-meadow, Forest-road, August 3rd, 1944.
31. Coventry road, junction Christchurch - road, August 8th, 1944.
32. New North-road, Beech and Gwen-grove, August 16th, 1944.
33. Benton-road East, on allotments, August 15th, 1944. Beechwood-gardens, August 16th, 1944.

Rockets:

1. Courtland - avenue, October 26th, 1944.
2. Ilford Golf Course, November 4th, 1944.
3. Exeter - gardens, November 12th, 1944.
4. "Dick Turpin," Aldborough-road, November, 1944.
5. Eastern-avenue, Aldborough-road allotments, November 22nd, 1944.
6. South Park-road, November 24th, 1944.
7. Claybury Hospital Grounds, December 19th, 1944.
8. Capel gardens November 26th, 1944.
9. Golliwood - gardens, December 30th, 1944.
10. Levett gardens, January 4th, 1945.
11. Pool Institute Sports Ground, January 12th, 1945.
12. Rear of Ilford Hippodrome, January 12th, 1945.
13. Aberton-gardens, January 14th, 1945.
14. Fenriplace - road, January 26th, 1945.
15. Goodmayes Park, February 3rd, 1945.
16. Wanstead Park, road, February 4th, 1945.
17. Aldborough-road, February 4th, 1945.
18. Stoke - avenue, New North-road, February 7th, 1945.
19. Ley - street, near Super Cinema, February 8th, 1945.
20. High road, Goodmayes Orchard-gardens February 12th, 1945.
21. Claybury Hospital Grounds, February 17th, 1945.
22. Levett-street, near "The Bell," February 18th, 1945.
23. Kent View-gardens, junction New - road February 19th, 1945.
24. Uphall - road, Ilford, Ltd., February 19th, 1945.
25. Belrave-road, between Kensington-gardens and Seymour, February 21st, 1945.
26. Cranley drive, junction Westerville - gardens, February 21st, 1945.
27. Hatley avenue, February 26th, 1945.
28. West Ham Mental Hospital grounds February 27th, 1945.
29. Broxmore road, between Westrow-gardens and Gylingstone March 3rd, 1945.
30. St. Albans-road March 6th, 1945.
31. Allotments, Loxford - lane, March 7th, 1945.
32. Wanstead Park-road, junction Redsleigh - gardens, March 8th, 1945.
33. Field of Forest-road, March 12th, 1945.
34. Burst in air, March 26th, 1945.
35. Alfreton-road junction Clayhall-avenue, March 27th, 1945.

A V2 fell here. An aerial photograph taken in April 1945 of the scene where a V2 rocket fell at the junction of Endsleigh Gardens and Wanstead Park Road, Ilford on 8 March 1945. Nine people were killed, 15 seriously injured and 19 slightly injured. There were eight houses demolished, 16 had to be demolished, 33 uninhabitable and 116 very seriously damaged.

King George VI accompanied by Queen Elizabeth and the Princesses Elizabeth and Margaret visit Ilford on 9 May 1945 – the day after VE (Victory in Europe) Day. The Mayor of Ilford, Mrs. B. Harding JP escorts the Royal Party. (Photo: Local History Room, Central Library, Ilford.)

promoting a Bill in Parliament seeking County Borough status – as did such local government authorities as Ealing and Luton afterwards – that in 1957 a Royal Commission was set up to examine the system and working of local government in the Greater London area. Eventually in November 1962 a Bill was introduced in Parliament broadly in line with the Commission's many recommendations but reducing the number of Boroughs from the 52 proposed to 32, each with a maximum population then of about 200,000. The Bill received the Royal Assent in July 1963 and became law as the Local Government Act 1963. Under this Bill Ilford, which at that time had an area of 8404 acres, was to be combined with the neighbouring Borough of Wanstead and Woodford. It is, of course, often difficult to choose a name for a newly formed district which will have the approval of all residents but the name Redbridge was chosen as a compromise and so the London Borough of Redbridge came into existence and Ilford as a separate Borough ceased to exist from 1st April 1965.

Changes in the town: re-development of Ilford Town Centre etc.

Although it is now over twenty-five years since then the town of Ilford has not lost its separate identity any more than Wanstead and Woodford have. Changes have, of course, taken place in Ilford during that time and some old buildings have gone and new ones come. Among those built are the Kenneth More Theatre, the new Central library (at a cost of £4 Million), the new Fire Station, and Ilford's Railway Station Booking Hall and Entrance. The re-development of the north sde of Ilford Hill, which had become a very rundown section of main road, has been completed and further office buildings erected in Clements Road and at Gants Hill. There is a large Sainsbury's Supermarket where the premises of Ilford Limted stood, with another at Newbury Park, and where the Railway Sidings at Goodmayes were for many years a large Tesco Supermarket now stands. Additionally large D.I.Y. stores have been opened by B & Q near the junction of Eastern Avenue and Horns Road, and W.H. Smith's "Do It All" in the High Road, as well as others at Chadwell Heath. The year 1968 saw the opening of the Public Library and the adjoining Swimming Pool at Fulwell Cross, and in 1977 the Redbridge Magistrates Court at Barkingside was opened.

Further changes in the Town Centre have yet to be made for there is now being built a £100 million shopping Complex named "The Exchange" and financed by the Norwich Union Insurance and the Prudential Assurance Companies. This will extend from C & A in Ley Street and over the Railway, joining up with the High Road between Marks & Spencer and Littlewoods. It is due to be opened on 6th September 1991.

As part of the Ilford Town Centre re-development (something which has been planned over a good many years and in which Councillor Chris Annal has played a prominent part) new roads have been built, most importantly Winston Way which takes through traffic away from the main shopping Centre in the High Road. On 10th January 1987 a section of several hundred yards of the High Road was finally closed to traffic so that a safe and quiet pedestrianised shopping precinct could be created as now seen in many towns throughout Britain.

Further land lost to development: Ilford F.C. (1987), Ilford golf course, etc. threat to the P.L.A. ground

With the disappearance of Ilford Football Club as a separate Club in 1979 the ground at Lynn Road was sold for the building of houses and flats. Now the Leytonstone Ilford Club has disappeared following the sale of the Leytonstone ground for building purposes. A further merger with Walthamstow Avenue F.C. has taken place – the new Club playing under the name of Redbridge Forest. Thus the name "Ilford" would have disappeared from Senior Football had not a new Football Club with the name Ilford F.C. been formed in 1987 largely due to the efforts of Mr. Peter Foley, its first Chairman, and his son Michael. Although now in their fourth season as a member of the Greene King Spartan League, Division One, the permanent use of a ground within Ilford has not yet been procured and home matches are currently being played on Barking F.C.'s ground at Mayesbrook Park. Hopes that home matches could be played on the Cricklefield Ground have been dashed by Redbridge Council which contends that the ground would as a result be over-used. Another playing field that has unfortunately disappeared is that of the Peel Institute, near the junction of Woodford Avenue and Clayhall Avenue, and the former Kearley & Tonge Sports Ground in Wanstead Park Road like the Ilford Golf Club has been considerably reduced in size by the new main road running through it.

The 26 acre Sports Ground of the Port of London Authority situated off The Drive Ilford would also have disappeared since the local Council in September 1989 granted Planning Permission for the building of 345 houses and flats there. However, following a Public Inquiry the Department of the Environment rejected the Application on the grounds that the serious harm which would result to the character and appearance of this residential area would not be outweighed by the benefits to be derived.

Fairlop Plain and Fairlop Waters

Apart from small sites which developers and Councillors refer to as "infill" there are the larger areas and open spaces which must be conserved if the Green Belt is not to be further eroded. Since the last War England has lost farmland equal in size to the counties of Bedfordshire, Berkshire, Buckinghamshire and Oxfordshire combined. It is to be hoped that what farmland still remains in the Ilford area will be preserved as has the council-owned land at Fairlop Plain which at one time was all woodland forming part of Hainault Forest. During the Second World War Fairlop Plain was used as a Royal Air Force fighter base with Spitfires, Hurricanes, Mustangs and Typhoons and afterwards nearly became a Civil Airport for London or another Council Housing Estate. Vigorous protests by many local organisations including the Ilford Ratepayers' Association were made against the proposed Airport and in 1950 the Government under Prime Minister Attlee decided it could not be used for housing as it was zoned as an open space in the County Development Plan.

The proposal to use Fairlop Plain as a Civil Airport was finally laid to rest in 1953 during the 1951-55 Government of Sir Winston Churchill. The then Minister of Transport and Civil Aviation, Mr. Lennox Boyd, in February 1953 notified the City Court of Common Council that Fairlop was unsuitable. The reasons given were that there was more fog on the north and east sde of London, that Fairlop got more smoke than any other part of the London area and was usually under a smoke haze from London factories. Additionally aircraft would have to fly in and out of densely populated areas such as Stoke Newington and Walthamstow and across other air routes.

In 1955 Ilford Council purchased the land for £360,000 from the City of London Corporation which in 1937 had purchased it for £310,000. Since then huge quantities of sand and gravel which had been discovered under the soil have been excavated – at a rate of 300 tons a day at one time – and in turn as much as 300 tons of rubbish daily was tipped into the pits to restore the land to its former level. Today part of it has become a vast 360 acre Leisure Park, called Fairlop Waters, with a lake of 38 acres for sailing, another of 6 acres for angling, and an 18 and a 9 hole Golf Course, etc. Credit for this is in no small measure due to Councillor R.A. Dalton who played such an important part in its concept.

The "Flying Scotsman" at Ilford

During 1988 the famous steam locomotive the "Flying Scotsman" was at Ilford's British Rail Engineering Depot having work done to it prior to the locomotive being shipped to Australia where it went on tour, but has now returned. Nicknamed the "Flying Scotsman" but officially then known as the Special Scotch Express, this was originally the name of the train which well over 100 years ago ran from London to Edinburgh in 10 hours including a 30 minute stop at York. The Flying Scotsman locomotive is a Gresley Pacific engine No. 4472 and was chosen for exhibition at the British Empire Exhibition at Wembley in 1924. The train became a legend with its high reputation for fast, smooth and punctual running. By 1939 it was running non-stop in the summer between Kings Cross and Edinburgh in 7 hours. (With the change to diesel-traction and a load of 11 coaches weighing about 400 tonnes the journey is now accomplished in approximately four and three quarter hours). Note: While on its year-long tour in Australia the "Flying Scotsman" set up a world record by steaming non-stop for 422 miles and won the hearts of thousands of railway enthusiasts.

Recent changes

During the past few years Ilford has seen the introduction of buses run by private Contractors replacing some of the familiar red buses of London Transport. The Ilford Maternity Home has become offices for the Redbridge Health Authority and, at the rear, an Old Peoples' Home, and the days of King George Hospital within the National Health Service appear to be numbered now that a larger Hospital is being built within the grounds of Goodmayes Hospital (which at one time was the West Ham Mental Hospital). The opening of large Supermarkets for Groceries and Provisions etc. has resulted in many of the traditional shops of the past (Butchers, Bakers, Greengrocers, Fishmongers and Dairy Shops, as well as the small Grocery shops) closing down. In their place we now have numerous branches of Banks, Finance Houses and Building Societies, Estate Agents, Solicitors and Accountants' Offices, Restaurants, Fast-food Establishments and "Take-aways", Launderettes, Betting Shops, Travel Agencies, Charity Shops and Ladies' Hairdressers. The M11 Motorway, opened a few years ago to the Cambridge area from Redbridge roundabout, has now been joined to the new section of the A406 southward to the A13 at Barking.

Modern Living and a glimpse into the future

We are now living very much in an electronic age, with Computers and Screens or Visual Display Units (VDU's), with Word Processors, and with highly technical and sophisticated means of communication using satellites and dish aerials, as well as "in car" and portable (cordless) telephones and facsimile transmission (fax) machines. Even as I write scientists in America are racing to build record-breaking computers which will carry out one million million operations per second – 1,000 times faster than today's fastest. The use of Video Recorders for home entertainment etc. is now quite commonplace and the Camcorder (with sound recording) has replaced the home cine-camera. The printing of Newspapers using the latest technology has been revolutionised over the past four or five years. More and more robots are now being used in industry especially in the manufacture of motor vehicles and even some trains such as are in use on the Docklands Light Railway now operate without a driver.

We are also living at a time when the natural resources of the World as a whole, both on land and in the sea, are rapidly diminishing but simultaneously the total population is increasing at an alarming and dangerous rate – by nearly one quarter of a million people every day! Clearly this cannot continue indefinitely without it having a catastrophic result. Already in south-east England we are experiencing the effect of over-crowding, resulting in frequent congestion on public transport and on the roads into and out of London (especially during peak periods) and on space generally. The price of many houses and flats has doubled in four years (1986-1990) putting them now out of reach of two-thirds of the population, and having its effect on rented property which in turn has been responsible, partly, for unprecedented homelessness. At the same time there is increasing pressure to take more land both within the Green Belt and beyond it, as well as any other open space which becomes available for the building of more houses and more roads etc. Pollution of our rivers and of the oceans and seas (many of which are now being over-fished), of the land and of the Earth's atmosphere itself – affecting the all-important ozone layer – is another problem which currently confronts us, as well as the problems of countering the increase in anti-social behaviour in the form of serious crime, of burglary, violence, muggings, rape, vandalism, hooliganism etc., and the illegal dumping of toxic and other waste, and litter. Happily at last, there is a growing awareness among people (but by no means all) of the ecological damage which mankind has caused to the environment for so long. However, there is still a real danger that mankind through its indifference, shortsightedness and general lack of caring, wisdom, and understanding will eventually bring about its own destruction.

In Ilford the new £100 million no-doubt excellent shopping complex named "The Exchange" now under construction and nearing completion, will mean more shops which will attract more people and vehicles – causing more congestion – into our already bustling and litter-strewn Town Centre. We can only hope there will be significant off-setting benefits.

Ilford's Post Code

In the 1970's Post Codes were introduced by the Post Office and the Ilford & Barking Postal District was allotted the letters "IG". The use of the letter G may be difficult to understand but it was considered that the more appropriate letters IB, ID, IF or IL could be confused with IP for Ipswich and LL for Llandudno so it was decided to use I for Ilford, with G, being the last letter in the name Barking. This Ilford/Barking Post Code area extends from the "Wake Arms" (Epping Forest) in the north to the Thames (Barking Reach) in the south.

Hopes for a better future

It is interesting to note that the old Borough of Ilford's motto IN UNITY PROGRESS has been retained in the new Redbridge Borough's Coat of Arms. According to the Oxford English Dictionary Progress is advancement, or continuous improvement. Let us hope that the Progress made will be of real and lasting benefit to its citizens of today and in the years to come.

Part of the Watson Hornby collection of photographs of old Ilford on public display prior to their being presented to the Central Library, 1965.

(*Above*) The cedar tree in Valentines Park. (Photo: Author.) (*Below*) The new Fairlop Oak: Fulwell Cross. (Photo: Author.)

Aircraft Carrier H.M.S. *Ark Royal* (Commanded by Ilford-born and former Ilford County High
School pupil, Admiral Sir Raymond Lygo 1969–71). Laid down: 3 May 1943 Launched: 3 May
1950 Completed/commissioned: 25 February 1955. Length: 803′ 9″. Beam: 164′ 6″. Tonnage
53,060 (Standard Displacement 43,340). Complement: 2,637 (including Air Group personnel).
Aircraft: 36 Close-in Defence System (1969). 4 Sea-Cat Launchers (Guided Weapons). Paid off:
December 1978 (Devonport). Broken up: 1980 Since replaced by a carrier of the same name.
Note: This is the ship which was featured by the BBC in its long-running series "Sailor" televised
several years ago.

The Flying Scotsman. (Photo: National Railway Museum, York.)

The Flying Scotsman at Ilford during 1988. (Photo: E.W. Birchler.)

The Flying Scotsman at BR's Ilford Depot. (Photo: E.W. Birchler.)

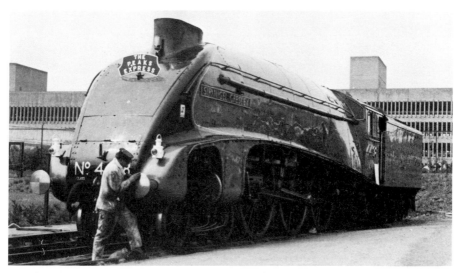

The Sir Nigel Gresley at Ilford, May 1989. (Photo: M. Landers.)

These photographs show the extensive damage sustained following the second Harrison Gibson fire which occurred on the night of March 16, 1959 and which also affected the nearby (but not adjoining) store of Moultons, where the Boots store now is.

The fire was fought by approximately 200 firemen with 40 appliances one of which was brought from Harwich some 68 miles away.

Chronicle of Events

PRE-HISTORY (B.C.)

4,500,000,000   Estimated age of Earth

2,000,000,000   (Part of Proterozoic Era: Pre-Cambrian period) life on Earth first appears: primitive sea creatures (crustaceans, molluscs, and sea urchin)

400,000,000-350,000,000   (Devonian period) fishes, primitive land plants

350,000,000-270,000,000   (Carboniferous period) primitive amphibians, tree ferns, first insects. Coal starting to form

270,000,000-180,000,000   (Permian period) first mammals, early reptiles

180,000,000-135,000,000   (Jurassic period) dinosaurs, plesiosaurs, sharks, cuttlefish, earliest flying animals

70,000,000-2,500,000   (Tertiary period: warm climate) birds, mammals, modern plants and tropical forests

1,750,000   Ice Age Begins: ice-sheet in places more than 300 feet thick. Mammoths, woolly rhinoceros, reindeer, musk ox, arctic fox, lemmings

400,000   Beginning of Lowestoft glaciation followed by Inter-glacial period: (part of middle Pleistocene Era) Homo erectus stage (warm Hoxnian interglacial period) estimated date of Swanscombe (Kent) skull – oldest British human fossil belonging to ancestor of modern man

170,000-100,000   Fossil mammal remains unearthed in Ilford estimated to date from this, the Pleistocene, period

40,000   Homo sapiens (modern man) first appears in Europe

15,000-10,000   Domestication of animals for food and transport, invention of ox-drawn plough and wheeled cart: domestication of the dog: basketry, weaving, and metallurgy (middle East)

10,000-8,000   Britain becomes an island (land connection with mainland of Europe severed by melting ice-sheets)

5,000 and earlier   Early Stone Age people inhabiting Britain

EARLY CIVILISATION

3,700   Knowledge of farming reaches Britain from Europe and Middle East

3,000   Flint implements (arrow heads etc.) found at Uphall could have been made at this date

1,900-500 approx   Early, middle, and late Bronze Ages

500   Celtic immigrants from the Rhineland begin to settle in southern and eastern England

300   Main wave of Celtic immigrants (the Trinovantes) from northern France and Brittany settle in southern England including Essex

200-100 or earlier   Iron Age fort and encampment covering about 48 acres at Uphall

100   Third wave of Celtic people (Belgic Tribes) retreating from advancing Roman Conquerors of Gaul, settle here

55   Julius Caesar's first British expedition

54   Caesar's second British expedition (returns to Rome)

INVASIONS AND OCCUPATION; AND THE DARK AGES (A.D.)

43   Roman invasion of Britain under Aulus Plautius. Occupation lasts approx 360 years. Road from London (Londinium) to Colchester (Camulodunum) passing through Ilford constructed: some Romans living hereabouts. In the year 265 Constantine the Great was born in Colchester

406   Roman forces in Britain withdrawn, ending Roman military occupation here

5th, 6th & 7th centuries   Invasion of and settlement in much of Britain by the Angles, Saxons, and Jutes from north west Europe, Essex being occupied mainly by the Saxons

527 (approx)   The Kingdom of the East Saxons (Essex) established

666-670 (approx)   The building of Barking Abbey by the Saxons begins (first of three built over many years)

685 (approx)   St. Erkenwald, Bishop of London dies at Barking Abbey: the place-name Barking appears on records as "Berecingas"

673-735   The lifetime of "the Venerable Bede", historian and scholar

8th, 9th, 10th and early part of 11th centuries   Attacks on Britain, and settlement in parts by the Vikings from Scandinavia, and the Danes. Essex and East Anglia annexed by Offa, King of Mercia (757-796). Canute (a Dane) King of England (1016-1035)

1041   Saxon supremacy restored: Edward the Confessor king

1066   Harold II, the last Saxon King of England (succeeding Edward the Confessor in January) defeats the King of Norway at Stamford Bridge, Yorkshire on 25th September, but is in turn defeated at the Battle of Hastings on 14th October by William, Duke of Normandy who is crowned King William I of England in Westminster Abbey on Christmas Day

1066/67   Barking Abbey and adjoining land used as Winter Quarters by William ("the Conqueror") and his army

MIDDLE AGES

1085/86   Survey of most of England, and the compiling of the 2-volumed "DOMESDAY BOOK" – a detailed inventory of land, buildings, stock, equipment, and people. Ilford included with Barking: the separate parish of Little Ilford appearing as ILEFORT

1145 (approx)   Hospital (with Chapel) built on Ilford Hill by Adeliza – Abbess of Barking specifically for accommodating and nursing 13 lepers. (Adeliza was followed by Mary, sister of Thomas a Becket)

1171   The name of Ilford appears on a document as "Yleford"

1203   The name of Clayhall on record

1233   Cranbrook on record as "Cranebroc"

1234 The name of Ilford appears on a document as "Hileford"

1239 Hainault appears on record as "Hyneholt"

1248 Gaysham appears on record

1272 The name "Hyleford" appears on a document

1285 Seven Kings appears on record as "Seofingas"

1292 Earliest known mention of Gaysham Hall

1303 Padnall on record as "Padenhole"

1310 The Abbess of Barking authorised to fell trees in Hainault to rebuild Loxford following a fire

1321 (25 26 Nov) King Edward II spends two days in Ilford and issues seven documents from here. (A local farmer claims compensation for the cost of 50 hurdles burnt by soldiers to keep warm)

1327 Aldborough on record as "Albo(u)gh"

1339 Green Lane on record

1339 John Godemay, holder of land at Goodmayes

1346 New rules drawn up by Ralph Stratford, Bishop of London for inmates of Ilford Hospital

1347 Manor farm and mansion of Cranbrook held by John Malmaynes from the Abbess and Convent of Barking at a quit rent of 2 shillings per annum

1348 Newbury on record in Court Rolls

1348-1350 The Black Death reaches England from Europe: one tenth of London's population wiped out

1349 Land "near Craynebroke Lane" given to Barking Abbey

1379 (21 Apr) John Tanner found guilty at Brentwood of stealing a horse at Ilford: his lands and properties taken into the King's possession

1381 The Peasants' Revolt: local men join marchers

by 1400 Only one surviving leper inmate at this date at Ilford Hospital

RENAISSANCE AND REFORMATION

1456 Ley Street on record as Leestrete (mention of a tannery here)

Early 1500's The River Hile re-named the Roding

1532 Dorothy Barley, the last Abbess of Barking

1536-1540) The Dissolution of the Monasteries by order of Henry VIII. Ilford Hospital and Chapel sequested by the Crown

1541 (12 Sept) Uphall – previously in the possession of the Abbess of Barking – purchased by one Morgan Phillips, alias Wolfe

1545 Stone Hall "given" by Sir John Raynsforth to King Henry VIII

1550 Earliest known mention of Clayberry (Claybury Hall)

1553-1558 Reign of Queen Mary I
300 Protestants including 73 from Essex burnt at the stake (20 at Stratford)

1557 Loxford Hall given by Queen Mary to one Thomas Powle

1558 Name of "Barking side" first appears on a map

1558-1603 Reign of Queen Elizabeth I; at least 200 Catholics executed over the years

1572 Ilford Hospital and Chapel, and its lands, granted by Queen Elizabeth to Thomas Fanshawe on conditions, including the maintaining of six poor men at the Hospital (no longer a Leper Colony): the Chapel used regularly for public worship from this date

1576 First map of Essex (drawn by Christopher Saxton) shows Ilford Bridge over R. Roding

1579 Queen Elizabeth makes a royal progress through Essex visiting various houses and lasting more than a month

1585 Cranbrook Manor purchased from the Earl of

Leicester by Sir Horatio Palavicini, living there until his death in 1600

1587 England threatened by invasion by Spain: great activity through Ilford (movement of militia)

1588 Spanish Armada defeated July/August. Four Spanish noblemen held captive at Cranbrook Hall pending ransom or exchange

1588 Richard Nightingall found guilty of stealing six lambs at Ilford – probably hanged

1599 Will Kemp (an associate of Shakespeare) dances from London – through Ilford where he stopped for refreshment – to Norwich in 9 days

1600's Claybury Hall owned by the Malmaynes family

1608 (25 Feb) John Clifton of Ilford branded for stealing

1608 Sir Ferdinande Fairfax marries Mrs. Mary Sheffield in the Hospital Chapel, Ilford

1608 (Nov) Sir Christopher Hatton, resident for several years at Clay Hall (situated near Woodford Bridge Road) builds a Chapel for the mansion there

1617 Great Gearies the seat of one William Finch

1617 Fulwell Hatch (mansion) the seat of one Sir Edward Wilde

1617 The paternal grandparents of Dr. Edmond Halley married in St. Margarets Barking: the grandmother (Katherine Newce) resident at Hedgeman's Farm, Ilford

1625 Sir Charles Montague, brother to the first Earl of Manchester dies at Cranbrook

1634 (9 July) Phillipa Smith charged at Chelmsford with keeping a bawdy house at Ilford

1647 John Saltmarsh, Chaplain at Hospital Chapel, dies at Ilford two days after rebuking Cromwell at Windsor

1648 (June) Royalist troops fight rear guard action through Ilford against the Parliamentarians on their way to Colchester

THE COMMONWEALTH PERIOD

1650 (approx) Waltham Forest at this time 60,000 acres in extent – extending along main Romford Road from Bow to Chadwell Heath and northwards to Roydon and Harlow

1650 A robbery on the highway between Chadwell Heath and Ilford on record: the victim, a Rector of Hutton who had a bag and £16.10s stripped from him by "a poulterer and two women"

1650 Ilford and Barkingside made separate Ecclesiastical divisions of the parish of Barking

1650 Mention made of Little Gearies in the Forest

1649-1655 John Evelyn, the Diarist, visits his manor at Great Warley travelling through Ilford from his home at Sayes Court, Deptford

1653 Ilford village – in the vicinity of the Broadway – comprises about 50 houses in all

1658 Death of Oliver Cromwell

1658 A large whale caught in the Thames: some of its bones set up at Chadwell Heath

1660 66 houses in Ilford. Population between 200 and 300

RESTORATION OF THE MONARCHY:

1660 Reign of Charles II begins

1662 (18 Aug) Samuel Pepys' first recorded visit to Ilford with the King's master ship builder: they have dinner here

1665 (13 June) Samuel Pepys rides out by coach to Ilford with Sir John Minnes to meet the Duke of York on his way to London from Harwich

1671 (26 July) Alex Greene summoned at Brentwood for erecting a penthouse over the King's Highway at Ilford: John Hockley summoned for having an unlicensed tippling house here

1683 Mr. Daniel Day born

1690 "Valentines" (Mansion) built by James Chadwick

son-in-law of Archbishop of Canterbury Tillotson who visited here

1690 A new Cranbrook Hall built

Late 1600's Presbyterians holding meetings at Aldborough Hatch

Early 1700's Queen Anne (1702-1714) visits the ancient Fairlop Oak. Farlop Fair which was held annually over the next 180 years originated from Daniel Day's bacon & bean feast to his tenants and friends: Fair firmly established by 1725

1720-1730 Dick Turpin, burglar-turned-highwayman (executed 1739) active in this area. His wife, formerly a Miss Palmer, lived at Aldborough Hatch

1722 London born Daniel Defoe (author of Robinson Crusoe, A Tour of Great Britain, and other books) observes the development taking place in Leytonstone, Ilford, & Barking

1724 "Valentines" (Mansion) enlarged

1724 A Roman stone-coffin (containing a human skeleton) unearthed at Valentines

1725 The Fairlop Fair a public event by this date

1730 (approx) Aldborough Hall re-built (Chapel attached to it)

1735 Earliest surviving plan of the Uphall earthworks made by a John Nobel at about this time

1735 The name Red Bridge appears on Jean Rocque's plan of Wanstead House and Parkland

1737 An Act of Parliament passed for the improvement of the River Roding for river traffic from Barking to Ilford Bridge

1739 Sir Crisp Gasgoyne (Lord Mayor of London in 1752) the owner of the Hospital and Chapel

1740 Daily Stage Coach service from Ilford to London

1746 A Roman urn (containing burnt bones) discovered at "Valentines"

1746 The name "Red Bridge" appears on a map (Jean Rocque's)

1758 (Apr) The Valentines Vine planted

1759 The medieval Ilford Bridge demolished

1760 Death of Mr. Smart Lethieuller (local historian and man of literature)

1767 (19 Oct) Death of Daniel Day

1768 "Cranbrook Castle" built by Mr. Charles Raymond of "Highlands"

1768 Rateable value of Great Ilford (according to Morant) estimated at £2,502.3s.0d.

1769 A cutting (one of several over a period) taken from the Valentines Vine planted at Hampton Court to become the Great Vine there. Further work carried out on "Valentines"

1770 Revd. Philip Morant, Essex historian (born 1700) dies

1771 Mark Gibbard, a plasterer and bricklayer granted a lease by Bamber Gascoigne, Patron of the Hospital on Ilford Hill to develop Spittel Field, Ilford Lane as a brickfield

1777 John Chapman and Peter Andre publish their map of Essex which shows the extent of Hainault Forest at that time

1774 Mr. Charles Raymond (owner of Highlands and Valentines) knighted

1774 The name of Toms Wood first appears

1778 The Valentine Vine producing 4 cwt of Grapes annually at this date

1785 (25 May) William Grace hanged at Chelmsford for stealing a horse at Aldborough Hatch

1786 Daily Stage Coach service from Ilford to London increased to two coaches

1786 Remains of pre-historic animals discovered in south Ilford brick-earth pits

1788 Transportation of offenders to Australia begins

1789 The stem of Valentines Vine 13 inches in circumference

1790 The old Claybury Hall demolished

1791 Cage or lock-up behind the "Angel" replaced by larger one at entrance to Roden Street (Back Lane)

1791 Hospital Chapel restored by Mr. Bamber Gascoigne (Patron)

1793 Hainault Forest 17,,000 acres in area, of which 2939 acres are the King's Woods, at this date

1794 (8 Dec) James Martin, a King's messenger robbed and shot dead by five footpads on the main road at Goodmayes

1795 The Prince of Wales (later George IV) reviews troops raised locally (Napoleon menacing Europe)

1796 Ilford Village comprises 149 houses (plus 78 in Cranbrook Lane)

1796 "Beehive" – a farmhouse in the forest, recorded (formerly a Mansion here by that name)

1796 Uphall Camp and fortifications described by Daniel Lysons in his "Environs of London"

1796 Baptists holding open-air meetings in Ilford

1797 (8 Apr) Ilford sub-division of Yeomanry Cavalry muster on Wanstead Flats (fear of French invasion)

1800 Ilford noted for its potato-growing at this time

1801 First Baptist church in High Road founded. Six Ilfordians baptised in the River Lea at Old Ford

1801 Population of Ilford now 2041

1803 Clements Farmhouse and land purchased by Mr. John Thompson

1804 A new Claybury Hall built

1805 (June) The Fairlop Oak severely damaged by fire

1806 (5 June) Bare-knuckle Prize-fighting at Padnall corner (one purse of 100 guineas, another 40 guineas)

1806 An army of 10,000 men reviewed by King George III on Wanstead Flats

1808 (approx) Aldborough Hall demolished but Chapel there continues to be in use until 1863 when St. Peter's Church built

1809 Ray House (on corner of Ilford Lane and Roden Street) demolished

1810 (approx) Direct road from Barking to London constructed

1811 Further repairs and alterations carried out at "Valentines"

1812 The fossil remains of oxen, stags and other animals unearthed in a brickfield attached to Clements House (near the Broadway), also teeth and bones of elephants and hippopotami in a field near the Roding

1812 Bare-knuckle Prize-fighting at Ilford (a purse of 20 guineas)

1820 The ancient Fairlop Oak (previously damaged) blown down in heavy gale but the annual fair, as popular as ever, continues

1821 Funeral cortege of Caroline of Brunswick (estranged wife of George IV) passes through Ilford on its way from London to Harwich for burial of body in Germany

1823 Nearby Wanstead House demolished

1824 Ilford House Academy (at foot of Ilford Hill) marked on map of this date

1824 The skeleton of a mammoth unearthed at Ilford

1826 Rail link between London and East Anglia first proposed

1826/27 Green Lane diversion into the High Road by Mr. Thompson angers local residents resulting in pitched battle; Riot act read

1830 Prospectus issued for proposed London and Essex Railway

1830 (approx) A new Loxford Hall built by Sir Charles Hulse

1830/31 St. Mary's Church built: consecrated 9 June 1831 (land given by Mr. John Scrafton Thompson of Clements)

1832 National Schools adjoining St. Mary's built, accommodating 500 children

1834 (approx) Mr. Antonio Brady (knighted 1870) commences a 40 years' part-time exploration of the prehistoric animal remains in central and south Ilford

1834 Henry Sayer, a Surveyor, revives plea for a Railway from London to Norwich, and Great Yarmouth

1835 Municipal Reform Act passed, revising local government and giving Ratepayers the right to elect their own municipality

1836 An Act of Parliament authorises the Eastern Counties Company to build a railway line from London to Colchester and Norwich

1836 Work on the Railway (to serve Ilford) begins

1836 Ilford becomes a separate Ecclesiastical parish: St. Mary's the Parish Church

1837 Accession of Queen Victoria: passage of Stage Coach traffic through Ilford at its busiest at about this time

1839 Ilford Gas Company formed: Ilford Gas Works built (at a cost of £1500)

1839 (20 June) The coming of the Railway: Eastern Counties Railway opened from Devonshire Street, Mile End through Ilford to Romford. Many of the bricks used in its construction made in Ilford. Appprox. 60 houses demolished to make way for Ilford Station

1840 The Railway extended to Brentwood

1840 (3 July) An estimated 200,000 people at Fairlop Fair

1840/41 Holy Trinity Church in Mossford Lane, Barkingside built

1841 (Apr) Barkingside made a separate Ecclesiastical Parish

1841/42 National Schools adjoining Holy Trinity Church built

1842 The Railway extended to Chelmsford

1843 (May) The Railway extended to Colchester

1846 The Railway extended to Ipswich

1849 (11 June) A Cricket match played between an Ilford XI and Chelmsford, won by Chelmsford

1849 An outbreak of Cholera in Ilford: many die

1850 and earlier The "Angel" being used on alternate Saturdays for Petty Sessions

1850 Mail Coaches still running through Ilford to and from London and elsewhere

1850/51 Present surviving houses in Park Avenue (south side) built at this time

1851 Present surviving cottages in Tanners Lane built

1851 Census of Ilford shows population at 4,523

1851 Further disafforestation authorised by the Government by Act of Parliament clearing some 3 1/2 square miles of forest land at Fairlop

1851 Further illegal enclosure of parts of Epping Forest in progress

1853 (Feb) On the main road near Goodmayes John Toller of Chadwell Heath robbed and murdered by a tramp who was caught and executed at Chelmsford

1854 Fenchurch Street Station opened giving rail passengers direct access into the City

1855 Buildings at Forest Farm Fairlop bear this date

1855 The Railway extended to Harwich

1856 High Road lighted by Gas

1857 Tusk (over 9 feet in length) of pre-historic mammoth excavated in south Ilford

1858 The Thompson Rooms (where Centreway now is) built and presented by Miss E. Thompson to Ilford

1861 Ilford's population 5405

1862 The Great Eastern Railway (incorporating the Eastern Counties Railway) formed

1862 Mr. Sherman, Captain of Ilford Amateur Cricket Club for nine years presented with a watch

1862/63 St. Peter's, Aldborough Hatch built: stones used from the first Westminster Bridge which was built between 1737 and 1749, and demolished 1861

1863 Aldborough Hatch made a separate Ecclesiastic Parish

1863 Skull of mammoth with 8'8" tusk discovered in the Uphall brick-earth pits

1863 The Railway extended to Wivenhoe

1864 Transportation of offenders to Australia ended

1866 The Railway extended to Brightlingsea

1866 St. Mary's Church enlarged: tower and spire added

1867 The Railway extended to Walton on the Naze

1868 Carlton House (Redbridge Lane East) – one of the oldest surviving houses in Ilford – built

1870 Education Act passed: puts elementary education within reach of all British children

1871 Population of Ilford 5,947

1872 Secret ballot system introduced in Britain

1872 20 trains in each direction in daily service to and from Fenchurch Street

1872 The Drill Hall (at rear of Thompson Rooms) built: another gift of Miss E. Thompson

1874 Doctor and Mrs. Barnardo start the homes for destitute and orphaned girls at Barkingside with a house (Mossford Lodge) on a 21 year rent-free Lease from a well wisher, Mr. Sands

1874 Liverpool Street Station opened

1875 (approx) Ilford Paper Mills (Mill Road) founded

1876 90 trains running through Ilford Station daily

1877 Diocese of St. Albans formed, taking in Ilford – previously within Diocese of Rochester

1879 Mr. Alfred Hugh Harman (founder of Ilford Limited) sets up home in Cranbrook Road where he manufactures photographic plates in the basement

1879 The Clements Estate (from Ilford Lane to St. Mary's Church) owned by the Thompsons sold for house building

1879 Ilford Cricket Club founded

1880 Mr. Harman commences manufacturing from Roden Street premises under the name of Britannia Works Company

1880 Ilford Gaol (with treadmill) situated in Romford Road demolished

1880 St. Mary's Church again enlarged, and improved

1881 Ilford no longer a village: population 7,645: 1400 houses

1881 Ilford Cemetery and Mortuary in Buckingham Road first used

1881 Ilford Football Club founded

1881 (approx) Ilford Conservative Club founded

1882 The Railway extended to Clacton

1882 (6 May) Surviving portion of Epping Forest officially opened by Queen Vctoria, the forest land having been saved by the Corporation of London after a Court Case lasting three years (1871-1874) against 17 defendants who had been accused by the Master of Rolls of appropriating it to their own use.

1882 (1 Aug) Wanstead Park – a small portion of it within Ilford Parish – opened to the public

1883 Ilford Lodge Estate sold for house building

1884 St. Chad's Church, Chadwell Heath, built

1886 The Salvation Army sets up in Ilford

1887 Town Pump – to commemorate the 50th year of Queen Victoria's reign – installed in the Broadway

1887 Claybury Asylum built. The Cairns Memorial Cottage (in memory of Earl Cairns, Lord Chancellor of England) built at Dr Barnardo's, Barkingside

1888 By Act of Parliament Ilford becomes a separate administrative Parish (no longer part of Barking)

1888 (1 Oct) First meeting of the Overseers of Ilford

1888-1895 Mr. E.J. Beal Ilford's sole representative on Essex County Council

1889 Claybury grounds and mansion taken over by London County Council from the Middlesex justices

1889 Hospital Chapel restored

1889 The building of St. Clement's Church begins: foundation stone laid by the Marchioness of Salisbury, wife of the then Prime Minister, the Marquess of Salisbury

1890 (8 Oct) Ilford constituted a Local Government district: first meeting of the Local Government Board

1890 (14 June) Mr. John Bodger opens his first shop in the High Road

1890 (June) Lord Rosebery lays foundation stone of the Claybury Mental Hospital

1890 Swimming in the River Roding becoming popular with Ilford residents at this time

1891 Population of Ilford 10,913: approx 2000 houses

1891 Fire Station in Oakfield Road opened

1892 Doctor Barnardo's Church in Tanners Lane built

1892 Congregationalists hold meetings in the Thompson Rooms

1893 The Birkbeck Estate, Newbury Park sold for house building

1893 The Town Hall site purchased. Ilford's first Fire Station opened there

1893 The Girls' Village Homes at Barkingside enlarged by a gift of buildings by Mr. & Mrs. John Newberry

1893 Fragments of Roman pottery discovered at Hatton Corner (near St. Swithins Farm, Woodford Bridge Road)

1894 Ilford becomes an Urban District with a council of 9 members (subsequently increased to 12) and a Clerk

1894 Grange Estate (north of Ilford Station) sold for house building

1894 Ilford Railway Station re-built

1894 (approx) Ilford Ratepayers Association formed

1895 The first Board School built (the Horns school, accommodating 264 children)

1895 The Britannia Works Institute opened

1895 First Swimming Bath opened (situated off Uphall Road near R. Roding)

1895-1901 Mr. W. Ashmole replaces Mr. E.J. Beal as Ilford's sole representative on Essex County Council

1896 Mr. A.W. Green opens the first of his many Grocery & Provision shops at No.86 High Road

1896 Cleveland Road School built

1896 Cranbrook Lodge becomes a private school (Cranbrook College)

1896 Sports Ground between Wellesley and Coventry Road comes into use

1897 The Angel P H (in High Road) re-built. J. Sainsbury's first Ilford shop – at No.114 High Road – opened

1897 Site of the Uphall Iron Age Camp including Lavender Mount purchased by Mr David Howard of "Howards Chemicals"

1897 Loxford, Uphall and Cranbrook Estates sold for house building

1897 Ilford Cricket Club obtain from Mrs. Ingleby a lease on their present ground

1898 Downshall (Seven Kings) and Mayfield (Goodmayes) Estates sold for house building

1898 Isolation Hospital at Chadwell Heath opened

1898 The Ilford Improvement Act passed by Parliament: Mr. Henry Weeden mainly responsible for its promotion

1898 Barkingside Football Club founded

1898 (4 May) Foundation stone of S.S. Peter and Paul RC Church laid

1898 The Ilford Guardian and the Ilford Recorder commence publication (27 August, and 17 September respectively)

1898 Council meetings held at Ilford Hall until Town Hall built: now 18 members

1898 Ilford divided into three Wards for local Electoral purposes: South, Central (or North), and Hainault

1899 Seven Kings Station opened

1899 S.S. Peter and Paul RC Church built: enlarged in 1906 and 1909

1899 (Mar) Attempt by Ilford Council to compulsorily acquire Ilford Gas Company defeated in Parliament: Council decide to go for Electricity

1899 The last Fairlop Fair held

1899 The building of West Ham Mental Hospital (now Goodmayes Hospital) – in grounds covering 110 acres begins

1899 Howards & Sons Ltd., manufacturing chemists, move part of their operations from Stratford to newly built works at Uphall

1899 (16 Sept) Central Park (first section of Valentines Park) comprising 47 1/2 acres including the lake of 7 acres, opened

1899 Town Pump removed from the Broadway and installed in the Park

1899 Land for South Park (32 acres) and Barkingside Park (14 1/2 acres) purchased by Ilford Council

1899 (10 Oct) Boer War begins

1899 (12 Nov) South Essex Recorders Co. Ltd. (then at No.3 Cranbrook Road) incorporated

1900 Rateable value of Ilford £197,000

1900 (1 Feb) Christchurch Road School and the adjoining Park Higher Grade School (later to be known as Ilford County High School) opened

1900 First portion of Seven Kings Park presented to citizens of Ilford by Mr. A.C. Corbett

1900 (17 Mar) Foundation stone of Ilford Town Hall laid

1900 (May) Foundation stone of St. Alban's Church laid

1900 (17 May) Ilford's residents celebrate Relief of Mafeking

1900 (June) Occupation of Pretoria celebrated by exuberant Ilfordians

1900 (25 Aug) Foundation stone of Ilford's Electricity Station laid

1900 Valentines Lake first used for swimming and boating

1900 In Parliamentary Election Mr. L. Sinclair, Conservative, elected with 3000 majority

1900 Bandstand erected in the Park

1900 Britannia Works Company changes its name to ILFORD Limited (following approval being sought and obtained from Ilford Council)

1900 Cranbrook Hall demolished, the Estate having been sold for house building

1900 The Royal Arms of George I dated 1718 used in the Court Room at The Angel presented to Ilford by the proprietor

1900/01 Vine Congregational Church built

1900/06 St. Alban's Church built

1901 Ilford's Population 41,234

1901 (1 Jan) "Ilford Past and Present" published by Mr George E Tasker

1901 (22 Jan) Queen Victoria dies

1901 (30 Mar) Electricity generated from Ilford's own Station illuminates some of Ilford's streets

1901 Ilford's representatives on Essex County Council increased from 1 to 3

1901 Clock Tower (and Drinking fountain) the gift of Mr W.P. Griggs erected in Ilford Broadway

1901 Goodmayes Station opened

1901 West Ham Mental Hospital built at Goodmayes

1901 Ilford Town Hall opened (loan of £25,000 raised to cover its cost – to be spread over a period of 50 years)

1902 Mr. John Harrison Gibson opens his first shop in the High Road

1902 (31 May) Boer War ends: celebrations by Ilford's residents

1902 (14 June) Foundation stone of Ilford Presbyterian Church (now the Mildmay Youth Centre) laid by Mr. A. Cameron Corbett MP

1902 St. Clements becomes the Parish Church of Ilford (replacing St. Mary's)

1902 School Boards abolished

1902 Downshall School built

1902 The building of St. John's Church begins (completed 1913)

1903 (14 Mar) Ilford's electric tramway system opened

1903 Railway loopline serving Hainault and Woodford built

1903 St. Paul's Church, Goodmayes, built

1903 Loxford Junior School built

1903 (15 June) Parts of Ilford and Seven Kings flooded after three days of continuous rain

1903 Ilford Recorder moves from Cranbrook Road to No. 169 High Road, opposite the Town Hall

1903 The present Hainault Forest (approx 800 acres in area) purchased from the Lord of the Manor by London County Council and local authorities

1904 Loxford Boys and Girls school built

1904 Newbury Park Boys and Girls school built

1904 Vine Congregational Church organises its own labour exchange for members

1904 Over 40 gipsys' vans encamped off Gordon Road

1905 Purpose-built Fire Station in Ley Street opened

1905 Highlands School built

1905 Branch of Workers Educational Association opened in Ilford

1905 The Ilford Hospital Saturday Fund inaugurated the series of Carnivals which continued for several years to raise funds for a local Hospital

1905 (19 Sept) Death of Doctor Barnardo (aged 60)

1906 (3 Jan) Mrs. Sarah Ingleby dies (aged 82) at Valentines

1906 (July) Hainault Forest opened to the public

1906 Mr. Holcombe Ingleby presents to the people of Ilford 12 acres of the grounds of "Valentines" in memory of his mother. Ilford Council purchase a further 37 1/2 acres

1906 In Parliamentary Election Mr. J.H. Bethell, Liberal, elected with nearly 9000 majority

1906 Goodmayes School built

1906 St. Andrew's Church Hall built

1906 Wycliffe Congregational Church built

1906/07 Ilford Football Club are Champions of the Isthmian League completing the Season without losing a League match

1907 Edward Tuck – a great Ilfordian – dies

1908 (Mar) Motor bus service from Ilford to the Elephant & Castle starts

1908 Memorial to Dr Barnardo unveiled at Barkingside

1908 Public Library and Hall in Seven Kings built

1908 South Park School built

1908 Ilford's first Baptist Church in High Road (built 1801) demolished: 600 bodies in the adjoining burial ground exhumed and re-interred

1908 Mr. G.J. Fairhead opens his shop in Cranbrook Road

1908 Railway loopline to Hainault etc. closed

1909 Uphall School built

1909 Ilford Hippodrome opens

1909 (Oct) Ploughing Match (the largest in the south of England with 69 ploughs competing) held at Forest Farm on Fairlop Plain

1910 (Jan) Foundation stone of Ilford Emergency Hospital laid

1910 Biograph Cinema on Ilford Hill and Cinema-de-luxe Picture Palace at No. 98 High Road open

1910 London Penny Bazaar (fore-runner of Marks & Spencer) opens at No.76 High Road (opposite "The Angel")

1910 Ursuline High School for Girls opens in Morland Road

1910 Two General Elections held (January and December). Lloyd George speaks at Town Hall for Sir John Bethell. Mr. W.P. Griggs has an audience of 7000 at the Ilford Roller Skating Rink on Ilford Hill. Sir John Bethell re-elected

1910 (6 May) King Edward VII dies

1911 Ilford's population 78,188

1911 Mr. A.C. Corbett MP created Lord Rowallan

1911 (22 May) Dunn & Co. open their shop by Ilford Broadway

1911 Another Ploughing Match at Fairlop. A record 76 ploughs, of which 63 came from Ilford, competing

1912 Ilford Emergency Hospital opened

1912 Valentines Park extended

1912 Ilford Chamber of Trade started

1913 Woolworth's comes to the High Road

1913 Empire Kinema (Ilford Lane) opens

1914 Women's Suffragette demonstrations in Ilford

1914 Bodger's Arcade opened

1914 St. Margaret's Church built

1914 All Saints Goodmayes built

1914 (4 Aug) First World War (the Great War) begins. More than 10,000 Ilford men answer the call to arms during the War

1914 (onwards) Some Belgian refugees housed at "Valentines"

1915 (1 Jan) Rail crash outside Ilford Station 10 killed, over 80 injured

1915 (October) Airfield at Hainault Farm begins operations in defence of London

1915 St. Luke's Church built

1916 (3 Sept) Ilford residents witness the shooting down of the German airship SL11 – the first to be brought down on British soil

1916 Kelvin Hughes factory in New North Road commences operations

1916 Mr. W.P. Griggs knighted – becomes Sir Peter Griggs

1917 (19 Jan) The Silvertown Explosion: 69 killed, 72 seriously injured; Ilford Fire Brigade render assistance

1918 (11 Nov) First World War ends: 1159 Ilford men are fatal casualties

1918 (Dec) Ilford (hitherto in the Southern Parliamentary division of the County of Essex) is made a separate Parliamentary Constituency: Sir Peter Griggs elected in General Election

1919 (July) All Ilford Council workmen out on strike

1919 (27 Sept) National Railway strike affects Ilford

1919 (Dec) Airfield at Hainault Farm reverts to farmland

1920 (11 Aug) Sir Peter Griggs dies: Mr. Frederic Wise elected MP in By-Election

Early 1920's Perth Road extended from Quebec Road to Gants Hill: the end of Stringer's (Middlefield) farm

1921 Ilford's population 85,194

1922 Local resident Revd. Herbert Dunnico elected Member of Parliament for Consett (Durham)

1922 (Oct) Ilford Super Cinema opened

1922 (4 Oct) Mr. Percy Thompson murdered: Mrs. Edith Thompson and Mr. Fredk Bywaters found guilty and hanged in January 1923

1922 (11 Nov) Ilford War Memorial unveiled
1923 (1 Jan) Railway serving Ilford etc. taken over by the L.N.E.R.
1923 (12 June) King George V stops at Ilford Town Hall on his way to see the new Becontree Housing Estate
1923 Cranbrook Castle demolished; Ground having been puchased by Port of London Authority
1923 Cranbrook Lodge demolished
1923 Clock Tower in Broadway removed to South Park
1923 St. Andrew's Church built
1923-1924 The Plessey Company commences manufacturing operations in Ilford
1924 Cinema-De-Luxe Picture Palace in High Road closes: replaced by ABC (Acrated Bread Company) Restaurant: J. Lyons open their first Tea shop at No.165 High Road
1924 (22 July) The first Harrison Gbson fire
1924 Cranbrook House (parade of shops in Cranbrook Road with offices over) built by Mr. C. Prentis
1924 Mr. Frederic Wise (Ilford's MP 1920-1928) knighted
1924-1927 Mr. Emmanuel Shinwell MP resident locally (Goodmayes)
1925 The former Red Bridge replaced
1925 (25 Mar) Eastern Avenue opened by H.R.H. Prince Henry
1925 (23 Sept) Death of Mr George Tasker (Author etc)
1925 Valentines Mansion used for Public Health offices
1926 The first portable radio to be sold in Britain made by Plessey's at Ilford
1926 Ilford Maternity Home opened
1926 (4 May) General Strike in Britain begins: lasts about 10 days
1926 (21 Oct) Duke & Duchess of York (the latter our present Queen Mother) bring Royal Charter, dated 24 August, to Ilford: Sir Frederic Wise is Civic Mayor
1926 Mr. Frederick H. Dane Ilford's first annual Mayor
1927 The People's Dispensary for Sick Animals purchase
St. Swithine Farm

1931 (24 Aug) Beal Modern School in Ley Street opened
1932 (2-11 July) Pageant of Essex held in Valentines Park (Melbourne Field)
1932 St. George's Church (Woodford Avenue) built
1933 (1 July) London Passenger Transȯrt Board takes over responsibility for passenger movement
1933 (16 Oct) Foundation stone of Ilford County High School for Boys (at Barkingside) laid by the Bshop of Chelmsford
1934 Marks & Spencer (formerly the London Penny Bazaar) at No. 76 High Road closes
1934 Ilford County Court in Buckingham Road opened
1935 Ilford Borough Council's first attempt to purchase 1000 acre Fairlop Plain: City of London Corporation express their desire to develop it for a Civil Airport
1935 After years of public pressure plans are completed for an Underground Railway to serve North Ilford etc.
1935 Ilford celebrates Silver Jubilee of King George V's reign: a temporary arch built across High Road
1936 (20 Jan) King George V dies
1936 (3 May) Former Wimbledon champion Fred Perry and other top players attract 1600 people to watch a series of exhibition matches at North Ilford Tennis Club, Beehive Lane
Mid 1930's The former Roller Skating rink on Ilford Hill in use by Football Pools firm McLaughlan's
1936 Ilford F.C. again reach final of Amateur Cup: lose to Casuals 2-0 at Upton Park after 1-1 draw at Selhurst Park (Crystal Palace)
1936 (11 Dec) King Edward VIII abdicates
1936 (12 Dec) The Duke of York succeeds as King George VI
1936 Beehive Lane (Valentines Hall) Synagogue opened
1937 (12 May) Coronation of King George VI and Queen Elizabeth (our present Queen Mother)
1937 The City of London Corporation purchases Fairlop Plain for £310,000 to develop an Airport there
1938 Population of Ilford estimated to be 166,900
1938 (6 Feb) Ilford's trams replaced by trolley buses
1938 Vera Lynn sings with Ambrose and his Orchestra at Ilford Hippodrome
1938 Gants Hill Public Library opened
1939 St. Laurance's Barkingside built
1939 Mr. Joseph Pates retires after 60 years at Parish Clerk (evacuated at the outbreak of War he dies 6 October 1939)
1939 (Aug 21) 7 people killed and 19 injured by Lightning in Valentines Park
1939 (5 Nov) Tram Service from Ilford to Aldgate replaced by trolley buses
1939 (Sept 3) Second World War begins after the invasion of Poland by German forces (Sept 1)
1940–1945 During the "World War II years" many thousands of incendiary bombs etc. and 618 High Explosives, 25 Parachute mines, and 69 V1's and V2's were dropped or fell on Ilford. There was also some machine gunning of civilians from enemy aircraft. During these raids 530 Civilians were killed and over 2,600 injured, 313 houses were destroyed and nearly 40,000 damaged. The Ilford Super Cinema, The Hippodrome, and the Clock Tower were also destroyed or extensively damaged. Fatal casualties of Service personnel (including Merchant Seamen) totalled at least 552. Between 1940 and 1944 the Plessey-developed naval radar was made in Ilford, and from March 1942 five miles of the unfinished underground tunnelling here was used by Plessey's for manufacturing purposes. In Warship week March 1942 the Citizens of Ilford adopted H.M.S. Urchin. From June 1942 Fairlop Plain was used by Fighter Squadrons, and in 1944 as a Balloon Centre. In 1943/44 Dr. Barnardo's

ADDENDUM

29 (9 May) Second visit to Ilford of the Duke of York who is made the first Freeman of the Borough: a silver casket and scroll presented to him.

33 (2 Feb) Oakfield Road extension to the Town Hall opened by the Duke of York: a gold-mounted engraved walking stick presented to him.

J

Homes at Barkingside were used to house some refugees, or displaced persons, from N. Africa

1944 (21 Nov) Mrs. Barnardo dies, aged 96

1945 (8 May) VE Day (end of the War of Europe)

1945 (9 May) King George VI and Queen Elizabeth accompanied by the two princesses, Elizabeth and Margaret, pay visit to Ilford

1945 (July) Ilford divided into two Parliamentary constituencies – Ilford North and Ilford South in preparation for General Election: Voting Day 5 July. Result announced on 26 July after all Service personnel votes counted surprisingly gives Labour victory, and Clement Attlee replaces Winston Churchill as Prime Minister. Mr. James Ranger is elected for Ilford North and Mrs. Mabel Ridealgh for Ilford South (both Labour)

1945 (14 Aug) VJ Day (end of the War against Japan)

1945 In local Council Elections Labour wins majority on Ilford Borough Council taking 8 out of the 9 wards

1946 Chess player Mr. Barry Wood, Editor of "Chess" Magazine for 52 Years (1935-1987) conducts chess games simultaneously with 127 people at Ilford (Note: Mr. Barry Wood died April 1989)

1946 Ian Thomson joins Ilford Cricket Club (In 1953 he was capped for Sussex and in 1964/65 played for M.C.C. in five Test Matches to become first ex-Ilford cricketer to play for a side representing England)

1947 (Jan/Feb) Ilford experiences a very severe Winter

1947 Last steam trains through Fairlop etc.

1947 Gants Hill Station built

1947 (Nov) Local Council elections: Conservatives win 10 out of 12 seats to regain control of Ilford Borough

1947 Beal Grammar School formed

1947 (14 Dec) First tube trains to Newbury Park and Woodford

1948 (May) Canon Patrick Palmer dies

1948 (31 May) Railways nationalised. Underground system extended to Hainault

1949 First Electric trains in public service on main Railway

1949/50 New entrance and bus stand at Newbury Park Station built

1950 Labour Government announces its decision not to allow Fairlop Plain to be used for housing

1950 General Election: Mr. A.E. Cooper (a local man) wins Ilford South and Mr. Geoffrey Hutchinson Ilford North

1951 Festival of Britain: plaque commemorating unearthing of Pleistocene Mammalian remains at Uphall etc. placed by Ilford Council on church wall in Ilford Lane

1951 Festival of Britain awarded to Newbury Park bus stand etc. for architectural merit

1951 Population of Ilford 184,706

1951 (27 Mar) Death of Mr. A.W. Green

1952 Death of Revd. W. Sparrow Simpson, Chaplain at Ilford Hospital Chapel for 50 years

1952 (6 Jan) Mr. C.W. Burnes dies

1952 (6 Feb) King George VI dies in his sleep

1952 (May) Ilford Schoolboys win the English (Football) Shield

1953 Death of Revd. Sir Herbert Dunnico

1953 Conservative Government announces that Fairlop Plain not suitable for use as Civil Airport

1953 (2 June) Coronation of Queen Elizabeth II; street parties in Ilford

1954 (3 July) The end of 14 years of rationing: meat the last item to go

1954 (11 Nov) The Ilford Guardian newspaper changes its name to Ilford Pictorial

1955 Ilford Council purchases the 1000 acre Fairlop Plain from City of London Corporation for £360,000

1956 Tenders invited for gravel extraction at Fairlop: Council accepts offer of P.T. Read and grants a 13 year lease

1956 A crypt discovered at Hospital Chapel in which are found to be buried some very early battle victims

1957 Beal High School in Woodford Bridge Road opened

1957 Government sets up Royal Commssion on local government in Greater London (affecting Ilford)

1958 Ilford F.C. are Amateur Cup Finalists at Wembley: lose to Woking 3-0

1958 Death of Mr. Owen Waters, Senior, aged 80

1959 Ilford Palais modernised

1959 (March 16) Second Harrison Gibson fire

1959 (Dec) C.W. Burnes Store in Cranbrook Road sold to Chiesmans of Lewisham

Late 1950's-1960's Office development (now permitted by the Government for the first time since the end of the War) in progress at Gants Hill, in Clements Road and on Ilford Hill (north side)

1960's Part of the Uphall earthworks and Lavender Mount excavated by staff of the Passmore Edwards Museum

1960 Ilford Lodge (off Balfour Road) demolished

1961 Census shows Ilford's population now 178,024

1961 Howards & Sons Ltd. (Chemicals) taken over by Laporte Industries Ltd.

1961 Kelvin Hughes becomes a Division of S. Smith & Sons (England) Ltd.

1961 Plessey and Ericssons and the Automatic Telephone & Electric Company merge to become the largest single manufacturing unit in the British Telecommunications Industry

1961 A new Vine Congregational Church built in Richmond (now Riches) Road following the sale of their distinguished church in the High Road

1961 Ilford Recorder moves into purpose-built premises at 539 High Road

1962 (30 June) Sir Allen Clark, Chairman of Plessey's dies

1962/63 Ilford experiences another severe Winter (late December to early March)

1963 (1 July) London Government Bill passed

1963 Ilford-born John Carmel Heenan becomes RC Primate Archbishop of Westminster

1963 "Ilford's Yesterdays" published by Mr. George Caunt

1963 John Lever joins Ilford Cricket Club (playing regularly for 1st XI from 1965)

1963 New Pavilion at Ilford Cricket Club built

1963 (21 Nov) The Ilford Pictorial (formerly Ilford Guardian) changes its name to Ilford & Redbridge Pictorial and Guardian

1964 Alderman Mrs. L. Fallaize becomes Ilford's last Mayor

1964 General Election: Labour wins power by small majority: Mr. Wilson Prime Minister

1965 (24 Jan) Death of Sir Winston Churchill

1965 More than one million cubic yards of gravel extracted to date from Fairlop

1965 (1 Apr) Ilford (population 175,490) ceases to be a separate Borough becoming, with Wanstead & Woodford, the London Borough of Redbridge

1966 (14 Dec) Topping out of 18-storey office building on Ilford Hill – subsequently occupied by North Thames Gas and British Telecom

1967 (14 Oct) Foundation stone of Ilford Lane Methodist Church Hall laid

1968 (20 Mar) Fulwell Cross Swimming Pool and the adjacent Library opened by Field Marshall Sir Gerald Templer K.G

Samuel Pepys. In his famous Diary covering events from 1 January 1660 until 31 May 1669, Samuel Pepys recorded two visits to Ilford (in 1662 and 1665).

This National Maritime Museum painting by A. Storck entitled "The Four Day Battle 1–4 June 1666" – between the English and the Dutch – shows the type of ships which were being built when Samuel Pepys came to Ilford with Mr Anthony Deane, the King's Shipbuilder, in August 1662. Much of the timber used at that time came from the forest hereabouts and was taken by wagons to Barking and then by barges to the shipyards at Woolwich (and possibly Chatham).

During the Commonwealth period (1649–1660) Oliver Cromwell paid a great deal of attention to the Navy and much new building took place then. King Charles II, with all his extravagances and dissolute court also had a real regard for ships and the sea (which his father did not) and was fortunate to have Mr. Pepys and others at the Admiralty. (Ernle Bradford: "The Great Ship". Published by Hamish Hamilton.)

The Queen's House at Greenwich. See page 219 for explanation.

The Great Vine at Hampton Court Palace. See page 219 for explanation.

1969 National School at Barkingside demolished: Trinity Hall built on its site

1969 Graham Gooch joins Ilford Cricket Club (playing regularly for 1st XI from 1971)

1969 (21 July) Widespread interest as American astronauts Neil Armstrong and Buzz Aldrin set foot on the Moon

Late 1960's-early 1970's Post codes being introduced by the Post Office: Ilford & Barking postal district allocated letters "IG"

1970 (19 June) General Election: surprise win for Conservatives – Mr. Heath, Prime Minister

1970's Work on the M11 through North Ilford to Redbridge roundabout in progress

1971 (15 Feb) Decimal currency replaces centuries of £.s.d.

1972 (1 Jan) Clayhall Ward transferred from Ilford North Parliamentary Constituency to Wanstead & Woodford

1972 Australian touring Cricket team makes their first appearance on Ilford C.C.'s ground (Valentines Park) against Essex: match drawn

1973 (16 Oct) Topping out ceremony at Kenneth More Theatre performed by Kenneth More

1974 Ilford F.C. again at Wembley in last Final of the Amateur Cup – lose to Bishops Stortford 4-1

1974 (11 Oct) General Election: Labour wins power from the Conservatives with an overall majority of 3 seats

1974 Beal Girls Grammar and Downshall Secondary Schools are merged to become Seven Kings High School

1975 Explosion at Howards (Laporte's) Chemical Works: 1 killed, 2 injured

1975 (7 Nov) Death of (locally born) Cardinal Heenan

1976 Demolition of part of Ilford Limited's works at Roden Street begins

1976 Beal Grammar School becomes a mainstream comprehensive school for boys and girls

1977 (14 Apr) First section of the new M11 – from Redbridge roundabout to near Harlow – opened

1977 (Oct) Death of Mr. George Caunt, local historian

1977 (11 Nov) Redbridge Magistrates Court (Barkingside) opened by the Duke of Gloucester: a semi-mature Canadian Maple planted to commemorate the occasion

1978 (2 Mar) Mr. Vivian Bendall elected MP for Ilford North in a By-election

1979 (3 May) General Election: Conservatives win power from Labour with an overall majority of 43: Mrs. Thatcher, Prime Minister. Mr. Vivian Bendall re-elected for Ilford North, Mr. Neil Thorne wins Ilford South

1979 Ilford F.C.'s ground at Lynn Road sold for housing. Club merges with Leytonstone F.C.

1980 Howards (Laporte's) Chemical Works at Uphall closes down

1980 "Ilford's Yesterdays" re-published (by Mrs. Rose Caunt)

1980 Work in progress on part of Fairlop Plain to provide a 360 acre Country Park and Leisure Centre

1980 Construction work on Ilford Town Centre (Winston Way, Griggs Approach, etc.) in progress: further prehistoric animal remains unearthed by contractors during excavations

1981 Wedding of the Prince of Wales and Lady Diana Spencer at St. Paul's Cathedral: Ceremony watched on Televison by many Ilfordians, and in all an estimated 790 million viewers

1982 (21 May) British troops land in the Falklands

1982 (14 June) Argentinians in the Falklands surrender

1983 (10 June) General Election: Conservatves back with an increased majority (144 seats): Mr. Vivian Bendall and Mr. Neil Thorne re-elected

1983 Further excavation work at Uphall carried out by Passmore Edwards Museum staff. Finds include pieces of pottery belonging possibly to the late Bronze Age, 400-600 years earlier than Middle Iron Age (approx. 200-100 BC). Pottery also found there

1984 (July) Water Festival held at Fairlop (sailing, windsurfing, water-skiing, etc.)

1985 Winston Way opened – taking traffic around Ilford's Town Centre

1985 A new "Angel" P.H. built in Station Road, replacing the old "Angel" (built in 1897) in High Road which becomes a Wimpey Restaurant

1985 Demolition of Ilford Limited's premises in Roden Street completed

1985 (12 Nov) Sainsbury's Supermarket and car park (built mainly on the former Ilford Limited's premises) opened

1986 (25 Feb) New Central Library (built at cost of £4 million) in the extended Clements Road opened by the Duke of Gloucester

1986 (18 Mar) Sainsbury's Supermarket at Chase Lane, Newbury Park opened

1986 Ilford Railway Station Entrance and Booking Hall re-built

1986 (31 Mar) Greater London Council abolished: London Borough of Redbridge Council takes over responsibility of certain local functions hitherto performed by the G.L.C.

1986 (12 Oct) Michael Pinner and Daren Lee of Ilford Golf Club win London Amateur Matchplay Foursomes at the Berkshire Golf Club – teams from 64 Clubs competing

1987 (10 Jan) Section of the High Road ceremonially and permanently closed to through traffic after many centuries of use: main shopping area to be paved and "pedestrianised"

1987 (21 Jan) New Fire Station – built at a cost of £1.2 million opened in High Road (replacing the Fire Station in Ley Street)

1987 (12 June) General Election: Conservatives win a third term of office with 100 seat majority. Neil Thorne and Vivian Bendall re-elected for Ilford South and Ilford North respectively

1987 "Fairlop Waters" including 18 hole Golf Course now in use

1987 Cutting from the famous Hampton Court Vine (grown from a cutting of the Valentines Vine) planted at Valentines by pupils of Christchurch Junior School

1987 (15/16 Oct) The night of the "Big Blow": Winds gusting up to 110 mph across southern and south-east England cause casualties and widespread damage especially to trees. Many of Ilford's trees blown down

1987 (20 Oct) Tesco's Supermarket at Goodmayes opened

1987 (Feb) Further excavations in progress at the Uphall Iron Age Camp site by staff of the Passmore Edwards Museum. In addition to traces of round houses and pieces of Middle Iron-Age pottery a very early arrow head and fragments of a Middle Bronze Age urn are found: also some pre-Roman metal coins

1988 Woodford-Barking Relief Road (cutting through west Ilford including Ilford Golf Course) – now part of the A406 – opened

1988 "Flying Scotsman" locomotive at Ilford's Railway works prior to its shipment to Australia on tour

1988 Paved shopping precinct in Ilford Town Centre completed

1989 (Jan) Preliminary work commenced on a new £100 million shopping complex to be called "The Exchange" (from C & A in Ley Street over the Railway, and linking up with High Road between Marks & Spencer and Littlewoods) – planned to open in 1991 and being

1989 *(cont'd)*

financed by Norwich Union Insurance and Prudential Assurance

(Jan) Buildings of the one-time Ilford Roller Skating Rink (Ilford Hill) demolished

(27 Feb) Excavations of the Uphall Iron Age Camp site by Passmore Edwards Museum staff cease, prior to re-development of the land for housing

(24 Mar) Beginners' (9-hole) Golf Course at Fairlop Waters officially opened by the Mayor of Redbridge, Councillor Keith Axon (additional to the 18 hole full sized course already in use there)

(April) The building of the £41.5 million – 372 bed General Hospital at Goodmayes which was to have started this month deferred until the autumn

Public petition for a local Museum at Valentines Mansion presented to the Council by Reference Librarian Mr. Peter Wright

(20 April) Ilford architect Mr. Jack Lewis dies, aged 73: he was responsible for the design of several of the modern commercial buildings in Ilford including Mill House and Valentines House on Ilford Hill

(21 April) Kelvin Hughes Ltd. awarded their fourth Queen's Award – (Navigational Aids)

The Plessey Company also receive Queen's Technological Award for a battlefield radio system

(23 April) Ilford Athletic Club man the 19th mile station on the Isle of Dogs during the ADT London Marathon in which there were 23,700 registered runners (including several from Ilford) of which a world record 22,587 finished

(26 April) Raiders snatch £712,500 from Security Van outside Allied Irish Bank in High Road

(29 April) Cricketer John Lever (nearing the end of his career with Essex F.C.) takes 4 wickets for his former Club, Ilford C.C. to give Ilford victory by 79 runs at Chelmsford

(29 April) Leytonstone-Ilford Football Club become Champions of the Vauxhall Opel League, Premier Division and thus become eligible for promotion to the G.M. Conference League. Plans to share Leyton Orient's ground next season, however, have had to be abandoned and it now seems that their temporary home will be at Dagenham – their home ground at Green Pond Road, Walthamstow having been sold

(4 May) Hot air Balloon (blown off course from Loughton) makes forced landing on Ilford Golf Course

(12 May) G.M. Conference League Committee announce that Leytonstone-Ilford Football Club will not be admitted to their League next season because the agreement with Dagenham FC to share their ground has not been approved by Dagenham's landlords, Barking & Dagenham Council

(17 May) Southport-based 24-year old Wonder horse "Red Rum" – 3 times Grand National winner – at opening of a new betting shop adjacent to "The Cauliflower" P.H.

(20 May) 15,000 people attend Brtish Rail Engineering Depot at Ilford raising more than £15,000 for Charities – to celebrate the 40th Anniversary of the Depot

(21 May) Boxer Nigel Benn of Ilford – undefeated in 22 previous professional bouts loses his British and Commonwealth Middleweight titles to Michael Watson at Finsbury Park

Ronnie O'Sullivan aged 13, of St. Andrews Road, Ilford becomes the youngest winner of the Great Britain under-16 Snooker Championship played at Dudley, West Midlands

John Lever takes 7 wickets for 63 runs in Ilford's win by 66 runs over Southend. His book "A Cricketer's Cricketer" now published

(22 May) Ilford South MP Neil Thorne agrees to sponsor British Rail's controversial Private Bill on the Channel Tunnel link through south London and Kent the first reading of which is set for November 1989

Plessey's announce a record £195 1/2 million profit before Tax for the 12 months ending 31 March 1989

(1 June) Building work now proceeding on the first of 839 houses on the former Laporte (Howards) site off Uphall Road

Under draft proposals published by the Local Government Boundary Commission many homes in the south of Ilford and 2000 on the Padnall Estate could be transferred to neighbouring Barking & Dagenham while some to the north of Ilford could be gained

Council give the go-ahead to a 6-months trial waste paper re-cycling scheme but only at one Depot to which paper will have to be taken. A house-to-house collection scheme being considered

Council give green-light to an £18,300 scheme to install traffic lights at junction of Chapel Road and Ilford Hill

Community Charge (dubbed the Poll Tax) Registration forms being sent out by local council to all householders etc. in the Borough. Replacing the present Rates system it will be effective from 1st April 1990

(3 & 4 June) Ilford A.C.'s walkers 1st 2nd & 3rd in Essex 20 kilometres (just over 12 1/2 miles) Championship at Colchester. Ilford veterans win the 4 x 100 and 4 x 400 metres relays in the Southern Counties Veteran Championships

(5 June) Second A.G.M. of Ilford Football Club held at Central Library and attended by Mr. Neil Thorne and the Mayor of Redbridge Councillor Geoffrey Brewer

Ilford-born and former resident John Lyall – 32 years with West Ham F.C. and the longest serving Manager in the Football League – is informed that his contract with the Club will not be renewed when it expires on June 30th.

(6 June) A Private Bill enabling a Market to be set up in Ilford – over-riding a Charter of 1247 granted by King Henry III in respect of Romford Market given a second reading in the Commons by 157 votes to 88

(8 June) The building of the 372-bed General Hospital at Goodmayes now scheduled to begin in January 1990

(17/18 June) An estimated 40,000 people attend Show and Carnival in Valentines Park. Regular entrant 89 years-old Mr. Fred Bines of Henley Road wins trophy for best local trader with his horse and cart

(18 June) Following the Polling on June 15, Ilford resident Miss Carole Tongue (Labour) re-elected to European Parliament for London East (comprising Redbridge, Havering, Barking & Dagenham and part of Newham) with majority of 27,385

(20 June) Council agree to bear the cost of clearing overgrowth at St. Mary's Churchyard and to maintain it annually

Mrs. Mabel Ridealgh, Ilford North's first MP (1945-1950) dies, aged 90, at Eastwood Lodge Residential Home, Goodmayes

Ilford Rotary Club (founded 1928) decide to admit women members

Miss Carole Tongue MEP elected Deputy Leader of the 45-strong British Labour Group of European MP's

(21 June) The Port of London Authority announces its intention to apply for planning permission to build 345 homes on its 26-acre Sports Ground situated off The Drive

(21-27 June) In Ilford's Cricket Festival week at Valentines Park Essex win all three matches beating Warwickshire (twice) and Hampshire

1989 *(cont'd)*

(1 July) Ilford A.C.'s 46 year-old Bob Dobson wins European Veterans 30 Kilometres Road walking Championship in Bruges, Belgium

(2 July) Mock disaster Exercise involving Police, Fire and Ambulance Services held at Gants Hill

Building work for the planned £41.5 million Goodmayes General Hospital now out to tender

(3 Aug) Proposals announced for the building of Offices (currently being used to store wrecked cars) situated by the Roding on the corner of Ilford Hill and Mill Road

(3 & 4 Aug) 21 yr-old cricketer Nasser Hussain of Mayfair Avenue formerly with Ilford C.C. plays for Essex plays for England XI in two matches against Rest of the World XI at Jesmond, Newcastle-upon-tyne

(4 Aug) The Anglo-German consortium GEC-Siemens makes an improved offer of £2 billion for Plessey and announce they now have 29.9% of the Company

(5 Aug) John Lever, away from Essex duty, takes 6 wickets from 29 for Ilford C.C. against Wanstead (all out for 56)

(10 Aug) More than 10,000 protesters have now signed a petition against developing the P.L.A. ground

Ilford's Citizen Advice bureau to set up home in the Hospital Chapel

Final reminder given by Redbridge Council for the return of local Community Charge forms

(31 Aug) To commemorate the 50th anniversary of the start of the Second World War (3 Sept 89) Ilford Recorder published extracts from the diaries of former Editor Basil Amps covering the years 1939-1945

(14-16 Sept) Exhibition of "The Exchange" Ilford Shopping Complex being held at the Central Library

(7 Sept) London Transport announces plans to spend £300 million on replacing its 85 Central Line trains between 1991 and 1995, and a further £400 million on other improvements, both benefiting local passengers

(7 Sept) Ilford Football Club to play this season's home fixtures at Coppermill Lane, Walthamstow

(8 Sept) The GEC-Siemens consortium announces that it now has a controlling interest in the Plessey Company. Under the terms of the bid Siemens will own Plessey's military communications empire which includes the Vicarage Lane plant

(14 Sept) Contractors P.J. Read having exhausted the gravel supplies at the 300 acre Fairlop Plain site after 35 years work mark the end by bulldozing to the ground their Staff Canteen

Safety improvements at the Fulwell Cross roundabout at a cost of £50,000 approved by Highways Committee

Cricketer John Lever appointed P.E. instructor at Bancroft's School

The Duke of Gloucester visits the Fairlop Oak Playing Fields – 80 years after his Grandfather (King George V) opened them in 1909

(21 Sept) Redbridge Council give planning permission to the P.L.A. to build 183 houses, 91 flats and 40 sheltered housing units on the sports ground at The Drive, Ilford a part of the ground to be given to the Council for a primary school, sports complex and a doctor's surgery

Redbridge Tree Fund totals £26,000. Many hundreds of trees now planted to replace the 3000 trees destroyed in October 1987

(24 Sept) Ilford A.C.'s Stuart Phillips wins Southend AC'S open 5 mile walk at Thorpe Bay in 36 mins 46 secs.

(25 Sept) A "Planning Blueprint" for the next decade announced by Redbridge Council. It envisages the provision of 9,000 extra homes by the year 2001, also office development and light industry, and a new park on the site of Claybury Hospital

The London Tourist Board awards Hainault Forest Country Park one of its 14 trophies for work done in restoring the area following the hurricane of October 1987

(29 Sept) The £900,000 John Telford Clinic in Cleveland Road officially opened

The cost of getting Parliamentary approval for a street market in Ilford may now exceed £50,000

(5 Oct) Transport chiefs announce it is now unlikely that Ilford will get an Underground British Rail link

A programme of major improvements to local leisure facilities given the go-ahead by Redbridge Council

Ilford Football Club given permission by Redbridge Council to stage a floodlit match at Cricklefield, probably on October 25th

Almost £200,000 pledged towards an appeal for an extension to the Jewish Youth and Community Centre in Woodford Bridge Road, Ilford

(10 Oct) The new Environment Minister, Mr. Christopher Patten announces that the proposed P.L.A. sports ground development is to be the subject of a Public Inquiry

Problems being encountered in disposing of thorium (radioactive) waste from part of the Uphall Road Laporte site now being developed for housing

(12 Oct) Controversial plans by Redbridge Council to transfer 2000 homes on the Becontree Estate to Barking & Dagenham look set to go ahead but 1500 homes on the Padnall Estate are expected to be retained. (Up to 10,000 people in Chigwell, Grange Hill, Buckhurst Hill, Wanstead and Woodford could also transfer to Redbridge). The new boundaries, if agreed by the Local Government Boundary Commission would take effect in 1992

(Dec) Majority of tenants in local Council's 7500 houses and flats vote against plan to sell their homes to a specially formed Oakbridge Housing Association

Council agree to establish a professionally staffed archive service in Valentines Mansion at an initial cost of £56,000

Bert Halford a former music hall entertainer and now a long stay patient at Chadwell Heath Hospital celebrates his 105th birthday

Alteration and refurbishment of the former Wycliffe Church in Cranbrook Road into a 4-storey office building now named Wycliffe House completed at a cost of £3.5 million

Redbridge team, including 10 boys from Ilford schools, progress to last 16 of the English Schools Trophy beating Worksop 3-2 at Cricklefield

Ilford Wanderers Rugby Club beat Thames Polytechnic 40-0 to make it three wins in succession in their last matches of 1989

1990 (Jan 2) Redbridge Councils Recreation and Amenities Committee decide to permit part use of Cricklefield by Ilford Football Club next season

Inspector Sharon Lemon after gaining the highest marks in the 1989 Metropolitan Police exams for Inspectors, joins Ilford Police Station where she will be responsible for one of the four shifts

(Jan 13) Redbridge team, including 10 Ilford schoolboys, progress to the last 8 of the English Schools Trophy beating Havant 1-0 at Cricklefield

(Jan 18) MP's Neil Thorne (Ilford South) and Vivian Bendall (Ilford North) abstain in Poll Tax vote cash support for local authorities but Government push through proposal with a majority of 36

(Jan 21) 35-strong local Jewish Lads and Girls Brigade wins London Regimental Brass Band contest at Picketts Lock Centre, Edmonton for the third time since 1981. (Runners-up 5 times)

(Jan 22) 16 yr-old Valentines High School Pupil Gul Khan of Empress Avenue who plays for Ilford C.C. and named

1990 *(cont'd)*
south England's most promising batsman of 1989, awarded a cricket bat at a Surrey factory for his outstanding performance for Essex (116 against Middlesex) in the 1989 Texaco under-16 County Cricket Championship – 39 Counties competing

(Jan 25) A daytime gale (similar in intensity to the October '87 gale) causes widespread damage

(Feb) Local council reveals that the Community Charge will be £290 for 1990/91. Though £52 higher than the Government's figure it will be one of the lowest in the Greater London area. Total expenditure will be just over £157 million which after receival of Government grants will leave approx. £50 million to be collected from local residents

Announced by local council that during recent gales 500 trees in Hainault Forest and nearly 200 others in open spaces and roads destroyed or damaged

(Mar 2) Livestock killed and equipment destroyed in barn fire at Hainault Forest Country Park

(Mar 3) New £600,000 library in Goodmayes Lane on target for June completion

(Mar 6) Announced that 554 tonnes of glass collected by contractors last year from 16 local bottle bank sites resulting in £6,000 for council and reducing cost of waste disposal. (Glass taken to United Glass factory at St. Albans for recycling)

After a wait of nearly seven years a £52 million contract signed for building by Wimpey Construction Ltd. the new 450 bed District General Hospital at Goodmayes. Including 18 special care cots in the baby unit, an accident and emergency department, a cancer scanner and therapy department it will replace the present King George Hospital. Work will commence in April, and is due to be completed by October 1992, opening in Spring 1993

Council tenants in protest at 43% rent increase

(Mar 8) Veteran left-winger Tony Benn speaking at Fulwell Cross Library advocates non-payment of the Community Charge

Ilford Jewish lads and girls brigade officially adjudged the smartest and   brightest in the London area

Gants Hill residents launch campaign to oppose the building of a 14-storey office block on Ray Powell's premises near Beehive Lane

(Mar 13) Ilford ambulance crews return to work after nationwide dispute lasting six months

18 local councillors announce that they will not be standing for re-election and residents protesting against plans to develop the P.L.A. Sports Ground propose to adopt prospective candidates in the May elections

Eight children from Eastcourt Independent School, Goodmayes chosen to appear at Covent Garden opera being attended by members of the Royal Family

(Mar 16) More than 1500 pupils from local schools sing at the Royal Albert Hall in Redbridge Schools choral festival to mark 25th anniversary of the Borough of Redbridge

(Mar 23) Sotheby's experts at Fairlop Waters value local residents' antiques in aid of London Chest Hospital Appeal

400 pupils of Ursuline High School knit for 40 minutes to raise money for the Catholic Fund for overseas development

(Mar 24) Granada Bingo and Social Club in High Road, Ilford (one time Regal Cinema) closes to make way for an office complex

(Mar 25) Fire at Wimpey bar in High Street fought by 30 firemen from Ilford, Stratford, and East Ham stations

(April 2) 18-year old pianist Zoe Mather of Ilford reaches semi-finals of the Young Musician of the Year competi-

tion (600 entering nationwide) : performs on BBC2 television

(Apr 5) Announced that a squad of 17 Redbridge boys under 14 years old, mostly from Ilford shools, are to complete in Southern California in August challenging for the Ken Aston Cup

Ilford-based Filofax Plc announce a trading loss of £959,000 for 1989

60 Aldborough Hatch residents collect 40 cubic yards of rubbish in local anti-litter campaign

Barnardo's to receive more than £50,000, and Gants Hill Methodist Church £10,000 in will of 86 years old Mrs. Daisy Webb of Northwood Gardens who died last year

Announced that the large department stores of Owen Owen is to take 105,000 sq.ft. in the Exchange Shopping development now under construction in Ilford Town Centre

Cost to local ratepayers of Parliamentary Bill – now at the Lords stage, to permit Ilford to have a market – now estimated at £130,000

A total of 140 candidates in the 15 Ilford wards to contest the council elections on May 3

New (replacement) toilets built at The Wash, Cranbrook Road at a cost of £122,000 now open

(Apr 19) Director of Finance, Maurice Tilley, estimates cost of collecting the Community Charge of £2,500,000 compared with about £1,000,000 it cost to collect Rates

New organ installed at St. George's Church, Woodford Avenue at a cost of £12,000 raised in just over a year

(Apr 22) Over 80 runners from Ilford take part in the 10th London Marathon which had an official entry of 24,871 runners. Douglas Graham, 11, of Leicester Gdns., Seven Kings, was the youngest competitor in the 2.1 mile Junior Wheelchair mini-marathon finishing 9th in 18 minutes

(Apr 26) 66 yr-old Margaret Evans, former headmistress at Seven Kings High School wins 4 gold medals for swimming at the Invitational Masters Sports Exchange Challenge Championships

Ilford's MP's Neil Thorne and Vivian Bendall vote against, but fail to defeat, the Government in the British Nationality Bill which could mean a quarter of a million people coming to Britain from Hong Kong

(Apr 28) Stuart Phillips and Bob Dobson of Ilford Athletic Club finish 1st and 2nd in 20-mile Walking Championship held at Enfield

(Apr 29) Ilford-born Nigel Benn wins a World Mddleweight boxing title in Atlantic City, USA

(May 3) Retail site at Newbury Park which houses B & Q, Dansk, and Charlie Brown's Auto Centre changes hands for £5,580,000

27 Conservative and 18 Labour Councillors elected in the 15 Ilford wards. Local Council now comprises 42 Conservatives, 18 Labour and 3 Lib. Democrats

Junior Health Minister Virginia Bottomley takes the controls of a mechanical digger to cut the first turf to mark the start of building work on the £55 million Goodmayes District General Hospital

Governing body of Ilford County High School considering the possibility of "opting out" of local Council control as now permitted by the Education Reform Act

Imperial Cancer Research Fund shop in Cranbrook Road receives from Fund President, Sir Angus Ogilvy, a commemorative certificate for raising £250,000 to date. Certificate presented by Trevor Brooking who opened the shop three years ago

(May 6) Code for local telephone numbers changes from 01 to 081

(May 12) Redbridge Schools, including 9 boys from Ilford schools, share Welsh Shield with Waltham Forest follow-

1990 *(cont'd)*

ing 1-1 draw after extra time in final at Leyton Orient's ground

In Parliament a clause in Local Authority Bill which would permit mini-cab drivers to operate the same as black-cab drivers (of whom there are an estimated 4000 resident locally) is blocked

(May 17) Team from Ilford's Ursuline High School wins the Rotary Youth Speaks debating contest held in Kensington, W. London, teams from all over the London area competing

(May 19) Team of 10 girls, aged 8-11, from Hainault Girls Brigade (celebrating their 50th anniversary this year) wins National Team Games Championships at the Royal Albert Hall, more than 20 teams competing

Ilford Jewish lads and girls Brigade wins national contest, and Ancill Trophy, by beating provincial champions, Liverpool, at Beal High School for drill and P.E.

Newly-built £8 million Countryside Properties Office development Clements Court (near Clements Rd) officially opened by the Mayor of Redbridge, Councillor Geoffrey Brewer

Essex Water Company and Thames Water warn of possible water shortage this summer after worst drought for many years

Sunday Trading Bill (which would allow all shops to open between noon and 6 p.m.) "talked out" in the Commons after an hour's debate

Goodmayes Rotarians donate £2000 for multiple sclerosis sufferers at Chadwell Heath Hospital

(May 24) Local firemen provided with improved protective clothing and helmets etc. after rigorous 9-month trial period

30 Japanese politicians visit Ilford as part of a fact-finding tour of Europe: received by Councillor Geoffrey Brewer on his last day as Mayor of Redbridge 1989/90

Planning permission to build a 43-bedroom Travel-Inn at The Red House PH being opposed by nearby residents

Salvation Army veteran Henry Mayers receives award for exceptional service to the Corps over 66 years from the age of 15

(June) Veteran Cancer Research fund-raiser Mrs. Dorothy Bates, 86, of Fairmead Gardens receives a Certificate on her retirement after over 30 years work for the Charity

(June 3) On Ilford's C.C.'s ground in Valentines Park Essex beat Glamorgan off the last ball of the match

Stuart Phillips of Ilford A.C. wins the Essex 20-kilometres Road Walk at Colchester

A girls' team from Clayhall wins the annual St. John Ambulance 5-a-side football tournament at Walthamstow, twenty London divisions taking part

(June 6) Marks & Spencer open a third floor which has taken 10 months to complete adding 27,000 sq.ft. of display space

(June 7) Two old people's Homes and a house for the mentally ill are set to close in a re-deployment of resources proposed by local council's Social Services Committee

(June 8) An application to build 20 flats on the Hill View Crescent site of Valentines Tennis & Social Club refused by the Department of the Environment on appeal

(June 12/22) Public Inquiry into the P.L.A.'s application to permit the building of 345 houses etc. on their Sports Grounds off The Drive being held at the Town Hall

(June 14) Bodgers celebrate their 100th Anniversary since Mr. John Bodger JP opened his first shop on 14th June 1890

Recreation & Amenities Committee of the newly elected Redbridge Council vote against Ilford F.C. 1987 being granted part-use of the Cricklefield Ground

(June 16/17) Record crowds attend the 22nd Redbridge Carnival and Show held in Valentines Park

(June 23) Ilford C.C. go top of the Paladin Plastics Essex League after a 9 wkts. win over Walthamstow

(June 30) Ilford C.C. re-inforce their lead with a 2 wickets win over Fives and Heronians off the penultimate ball of the match, climaxing a superb game of cricket

(July 5) Local Council give go-ahead for a 43-bedroom motel at The Red House

(July 7) A 350-strong local team win the 13th annual London Youth Games at Crystal Palace – 33 teams competing

(July 9) Announced by the Department of the Environment that Claybury Hospital, built in 1890, due for closure in 1993 has been designated a listed building and therefore to be preserved

(July 12) Appeal launched for £15,000 to enable structural repairs to the Hospital Chapel to be carried out before the winter

(July 15) The first of the 4 Tower cranes at the new Exchange shopping complex being dismantled

(July 19) Thames Water and Essex Water again warn of possible water shortage as temperatures stay high and demand soars

Ilford Police announce that serious crime in the Ilford area last year increased by 18%, from 381 to 431 recorded offences

(July 21) Former Morgan Crucible Sports field off Grove Road, Chadwell Heath, due to open today as a public park postponed because of vandalism to trees etc. estimated at £30,000

(July 31) Post Office announce that its Cameron Road, Seven Kings branch may close and be replaced with an Agency (sub post office)

(August 2) Kuwait invaded by Iraq

Former Fire Station (built in 1905) in Ley Street demolished

(August 9) £18,000 of uninsured electrical equiipment stolen in break-in at Goodmayes Hospital

(August 10) Ban on hose pipes and sprinklers imposed by Thames and Essex Water Companies, with possible fine of £400 for noncompliance

Basil Amps, Ilford Recorder journalist, dies aged 85

(August 16) Local Council set to issue Summonses to many thousands of Community Charge non-payers

Vicar of St. Laurance's Barkingside Revd. John Walmsley, and Gants Hill Method. Minister Revd. Alan Jenkins arranging to drive to Romania with essential supplies for child relief collected locally

Ilford Round Table collect £4000 for King George Hospital children's ward

Ilford F.C. 1987 arrange with Barking F.C. to play home matches on Barking's ground in Mayesbrook Park from September 1st.

(August 19) Nigel Benn wins in 1st round defending WBO middleweight title against Iran Barcley in Las Vegas

(August 23) Claybury Hospital in process of being run-down. Once having 2500 patients from over a wide area it now has less than 900 beds

TSB take a 25-year lease on the newly built Clock Tower House overlooking Valentines Park at an all-time local high of nearly £19 per sq.ft.

Conversion of Wycliffe Church into Offices wins a Redbridge Merit Award

Concern being felt for Ilford residents held in Iraq and Kuwait

(August 30) More than one-third of the new Exchange Shopping complex handed over to Department stores Owen Owen for fitting out

Stuart Phillips of Ilford A.C. wins the annual 19.4 miles walk event in Guernsey in 2 hrs. 44 mins.

1990 *(cont'd)*

(Sept 1) Ilford C.C. knocked off top of Paladin Plastics Essex league after losing to Wanstead

(Sept 8) Ilford-Liverpool Street rail link being closed for 5 weekends for repairs to track

Ilford C.C. back on top of table with a 1 point lead over Brentwood following a 9 wkts. win over Westcliff

(Sept 9) Lord Sieff, President of Marks & Spencer opens a £1.1 m. 20-bedroom extension to the Vi and John Rubens Residential Home in Clarence Avenue, the money being donated by Mr. Alan Sugar

Church of St. John the Evangelist, Seven Kings (Curate the Rev. Rosemary Enver) re-dedicated by the Bishop of Barking and other notable clerics after a £500,000 refurbishment programme

Department of the Environment rejects plans for a housing development of 253 flats on the former Wangye Works at 950 High Road on the grounds that the proposed development was too cramped

(Sept 20) Call for Rent Review after Dept of Environment confirms that local Council Rents, averaging £51.58 p.w. are the highest in Britain. Council Rent arrears now total £1.7 M.

Four lorry loads of essential supplies leave St. Laurence's Church Barkingside on a 3250 mile mercy mission to Romania

Pupils at Ursuline High School for Girls achieve a 97 percent pass rate at 'A' level and a 90 percent pass rate at GCSE

(Sept 22) Ilford C.C. are Champions of the Paladin Plastics Essex League after defeating Brentwood by 6 wickets at Valentines Park

Mr Percy Hope, a resident of Gable Court Nursing Home, Roxy Avenue, Chadwell Heath celebrates his 100th birthday

(Sept 24) Thames Water warns of a drought order likely to be imposed unless there is a significant fall of rain soon

(Sept 29) BBC Theatre Organist Nigel Ogden visits St. John Vianney Church in Stoneleigh Road, Clayhall to perform in concert, playing the Compton Organ which used to be in the Ritz Cinema in Nuneaton

The re-formed Ilford F.C. – bottom of the Greene King Spartan League Div.1 last season – now playing their home matches on Barking F.C.'s ground at Mayesbrook Park win their third successive match this season beating Metropolitan Police, Chigwell 8-1. Previous wins were 6-0 versus Pheonix Sports and 4-0 versus Catford

The planned closure of Claybury Hosptal delayed indefinitely following a budget review by regional health chiefs

(Oct 4) During their recent American tour the Redbridge Schools' Under-14 squad, mostly from Ilford schools, remained unbeaten winning 5-1 against San Clemente coached by former West Ham striker Clyde Best

Local Council gives outline planning permission for the building of a £50 m. 13-storey office block on the Ray Powell site at Gants Hill

BT announces plans to phase out the Ilford manual operator centre, employing 170 people, by 1995

(Oct 18) The former Downshall School, Seven Kings built in 1902 and closed in April, now being demolished

The last of the giant cranes at The Exchange development now being removed, following completion of the exterior. With most of the internal work yet to be done it will be almost a year before the shopping complex opens its doors to customers

Labour's deputy leader Roy Hattersley speaks at a meeting in Ilford South

Pupils of Ursuline High School collect 200 pairs of old spectacles for Kenya Vision Aid

Corporation of London make £10,000 available in the current financial year for work to historic Wanstead Park

(Oct 22) Cattle, allowed to graze under the Epping Forest act of 1878, mingle with traffic at the busy Gants Hill roundabout

(Oct 25) Development on former British Rail land at rear of Kinfauns Road Goodmayes for 120 houses and 150 flats approved by local Council

Display of Essex Regiment memorabillia on display at Central Library

(Oct 31) DIY giant Do-It-All decide to sell off its Ilford High Road store but will keep it open until a buyer is found

(Nov 1) Announced that local Council is to close Seven Kings Library (opened over 70 years ago) by April 1, 1991: also Aldersbrook and Woodford Bridge libraries

(Nov 6) Miss Dorothy Harding of Cowley Road celebrates her 100th birthday

(Nov 18) Nigel Benn loses his WBO Middleweight title to Chris Eubank at Birmingham

(Nov 22) Plans to build 345 houses on the PLA Sorts Ground off The Drive (aproved by local Council) are rejected by the Department of the Environment whose Inspector concludes that the serious harm which would result to the character and appearance of this residential area would not be outweighed by the benefts derived

(Nov 27) Mrs. Thatcher resigns as Prime Minister and is replaced by Mr. John Major

(Nov 29) Barkingside F.C. record their tenth win in 13 games in their match against Croydon Athletic

(Dec 6) Marks & Spencer purchase for £4.25 million from local Council 4 1/2 acres of the former Barnardo's site at Cranbrook Road, Barkingside, 20,000 sq.ft. of which will be for a food store and 40,000 sq.ft. as an office village and restaurant

(Dec 10) Two Ilford residents arrive home from Iraq after their extended (enforced) stay

Local traders who defy Sunday trading law are warned by Council that court action will be taken if repeated

A 60-hectare site (approx.24 acres) of overgrown scrubland in Hainault Forest to be thinned out, starting this winter

Announced by local Council that the cost of collecting the Community Charge from the 178,000 liable people in Redbridge is £3.3 million plus an estimated £2.6 million in bad debts etc. (Previously Rates were collected from 75,000 people throughout the Borough)

(Dec 17) 50 pooper-scooper bins in use in local parks installed at a total cost of £5,000

In Parliament Ilford's MP's vote for capital punishment but the proposal is defeated 367 to 182

Former well-known Ilford musical conductor Fred Waggott dies, aged 90

(Dec 29) On the last Saturday of 1990 Redbridge Forest lead the Vauxhall Premier Division after beating Marlow 5-1. Other matches: Barkingside 2 Halstead Town 1 Swanley Town 1 Ilford F.C. 4

Origin of Ilford and surrounding district Place-names

ALDBOROUGH   Aldborough was first recorded as Albo(u)gh in 1327 and is a manorial name from the family of Alborough. Hatch is a small gate for foot passengers, usually leading into a forest.

ALDERSBROOK   appears as Alderbroke in 1531: the brook along which the Alder (related to the Birch tree) grew.

BARKING   on record as Berecingas in 695 AD it appears as Berchingas in Domesday 1086/1087 and means "the settlement of Berica's people" (Note: the element "ing" is found in over forty Essex place-names: e.g. Barling, Epping, Fobbing, Havering, Mucking, The Rodings, Wakering, and in most cases means 'the people (or the sons, dependants, or descendants) of.' These names date mainly from the 5th, 6th and 7th centuries and owe their origin to the invasion and settlement by the Saxons from Saxony who gave their name to Essex, and to Middlesex, Sussex and the one time Kingdom of Wessex in the same way as the Angles from an angular-shaped district of Schleswig-Holstein gave their name to East Anglia and finally to England.

BARKINGSIDE   so named because when an early map was being drawn in the year 1558 (the first year of the reign of Queen Elizabeth I) some cottages there were marked on the map as being on the "Barking side" of the forest (then known as the Forest of Waltham). Ilford was part of Barking ecclesiastically until 1836 and administratively until 1888.

BARLEY LANE   appearing as Barley Lane in 1609 it was Berdelevestrete in the 15th Century – the lane running between barley fields.

BENNETT'S CASTLE   from Adam Beneyt 1327 who held land on lease from the Abbess of Barking.

BRENTWOOD   Brendewode 1274 ("Burnt wood").

BUCKHURST   from Old English Boc-hyrst meaning Birch Grove: was Bochurst c.1135.

BUNTING BRIDGE   in 1456 the northern part of the Cran book was called Bunton's Brook after a local family.

CHADWELL HEATH   from "cald wielle" meaning cold spring, or from St. Chad's (or Cedd's) Well. The heath was a noted place for highwaymen.

CHELMSFORD   Celmerefort (Domesday). Chelmeresford 1190.

CHIGWELL   appears as "Cingheuvella" in Domesday and as "Chiggewell" in Pipe Rolls dated 1187. The first element may be from "Cica", a personal name, or the Old English "ceacge" meaning gorse, or influenced by nearby Chingford.

COLLIER ROW   from the row of cottages in which lived the colliers (makers of wood charcoal which was used extensively as fuel).

CRANBROOK   appears in 1233 as Cranebroc meaning Crane brook. Cranes, which are similar to Herons, were formerly abundant in Britain but are now extinct here.*

CRICKLEFIELD   on record as Crikelwode in 1291, it was referred to as Crickleywood in the 16th century and later. Its origin is probably in the ancient word "crue" indicating a "barrow" or gravemound.

DAGENHAM   on record as early as 692 AD as Daeccanhaam – Daecca's ham. (Note: "ham" is from Old English and generally means homestead, village, manor or estate, though in the case of East Ham and West Ham it means a piece of enclosed land or meadow. The element appears in over twenty Essex placenames: e.g. Boreham, Cranham, Dedham, Elsenham, Henham, Langham, Rainham, Witham and Castle Hedingham).

DUNSPRING   probably from a spring that is down a slope or hill. The name appears as Downspring in 1777.

EPPING   apears as "Eppingas" in Domesday: the people of the upland. It is a derivative of "yppingas" from the Old English "yppe" – a raised place, or a look-out place.

ESSEX   appears as East Seaxe ("the East Saxons") in the year 604, and as Excessa in Domesday.

FAIRLOP   appears in 1738 when the Fair which grew from the annual outing and bean-feast started by Daniel Day of Wapping was already well established. A "lop" is a lopped tree or part thereof. The ancient and immense Fairlop Oak was cut down in 1820 after having been damaged previously by fire and storm.

FENCEPIECE   the map published in 1777 by John Chapman and Andre Petre shows a large fenced piece of land within Hainault Forest to the west of where Fencepiece Road is now. (The map also indicates that there was a brick kiln here).

* Surprise, surprise! In the Daily Telegraph of 25th April 1990 appeared a report that cranes were not only now flying over Britain but several had settled down to breed in this country for the first time in 400 years. Their nesting ground, however is being kept secret in order to protect them. The report goes on to say that breeding cranes in this country were hunted to extinction by falconers in medieval times and were a favourite main dish for banquets, 200 of them being served at a time.

FOREST GATE   the gate to the forest was on the north side of the Great Essex Road by which name the road was known for several centuries.

GANTS HILL   from the le Gant family. Gantesgrave appears as early as 1291. In 1321 Ralph le Gant was steward of Barking Abbey, and Richard and Gilbert le Gant were stewards in 1456.

GAYSHAM   appears as early as 1248. Gayesham Hall in the year 1360 stood in the forest and was the property of Thomas de Sandwitch, a steward to the household of the Black Prince (1330-1376).

GEARIES   from John Gery 1327, holder of land on lease from the Abbess of Barking.

GOODMAYES   from John Godemay 1319, holder of land on lease from the Abbess of Barking. It has been recorded as Goodmaistrete (15th Century) and Goodmath (1777).

GREEN LANE   goes back to 1339, and probably earlier. It originally ran from Hornchurch through Becontree Heath to Ilford village, joining Barking (Ilford) Lane where Winston Way is now.

HAINAULT   Hyneholt 1221. Hineholt 1323: from "higna" and "holt" meaning the wood of the community (of Barking Abbey to which it belonged).

HAVERING   appears as Haverings in Domesday: the settlement of Haefer's people. It appears as Haverynge Bure in 1305. The Bower House is close to Havering.

HORNCHURCH   recorded as Monasterium Cornutom in 1228 and as Hornedcherche in 1331 – church with horn-like gables.

HORNS ROAD   from Richard Horn 1547.

ILFORD   originally Yleford, then Hileford and Hyleford: the ford through the River Hyle or Hile (former name of the River Roding until the 16th century) meaning "trickling stream". The first known recording of the name Hile (ealden hilae) appears as early as 958 AD. The name Hileford appears in 1234 AD. The ILEFORT in Domesday refers to the separate parish of Little Ilford which was owned by a minor Norman "lord" Goscelinas Loremarius, unlike (Great) Ilford which was part of the manor of Barking. The "bridge at Ilford" was mentioned in 1321. Before the Dissolution of the Monasteries (1532) this bridge and the smaller one over the Aldersbrook nearby were maintained by a hermit living in Back Lane (Roden Street) who collected alms for the purpose.

INGATESTONE   Ginges ad Petram 1254. Gynges Atteston 1283. (Settlement of) Ingas's people at the stone (~~possibly Roman milestone~~).⚹

LEY STREET   recorded in 1456, it appears as Lee Street in 1609. The name is derived from the stretch of open land (pasture or field) which bordered it.

LEYTON   the "tun" (originally a fenced enclosure by the River Lea). Appearing as Lei(n)tuna in Domesday it is also on record as Lygatun (1065) and Luitan (1201).

LEYTONSTONE   part of Leyton by the high stone.

⚹ *most probably one of the large boulders brought down from the north during the last Ice Age.*

LONDON   Londinium 115-117. Londinion c.150. Lundonia c.730. Lundenne 839. Lundin 1205.

LOUGHTON   Lukinstone 1062: "Luca's tun" (a fenced enclosure).

LOXFORD BRIDGE   existing in 1456 it carried the lane to Barking across Loxford Water.

MOSSFORD GREEN   is Mossfoot Green on John Chapman's and Peter Andre's detailed map published 1st October 1777.

NEWBURY PARK   Newbury appears in Court Rolls in 1348. "Bury" is a manor house.

NEWHAM   A new name, originating as recently as 1965 following the re-formation of the London Boroughs, and being a combination of East Ham and West Ham. (There was, and still is, a town called Oldham). See also Dagenham.

REDBRIDGE   the name appeared as "Red bridge" on Jean Rocque's map of 1746 and referred to the old red brick and stone bridge over the Roding and linking Ilford and Wanstead where it is now crossed by Eastern Avenue. The old bridge, which was sometimes known locally as "Hockley's bridge" from a nearby house was built in 1650 and demolished in 1759. The name "Red house" (no doubt built also of red brick) appears on the same map of 1746. Note: As a result of research recently carried out by Mr. Brian Page of Wanstead it has been found that Jean Rocque first used the name "Red bridge" on his plan of Wanstead House and its Parkland, published in 1735.

RODING   the present name of the river (formerly "Hyle" until the early 1500's) is from the seven Roding villages between Ongar and Dunmow which take their name from the Saxon "Hrodingas", the settlement of Hroda's people. The source of the Roding is just north of Dunmow. In olden times it was very clean and fish were abundant. It is probable that the upper stretches of the Roding went by the name, whilst the lower stretches were still called the R. Hyle.

ROMFORD   although an old market town (holding a Royal Charter dated 1247 AD – reign of Henry III) the name does not appear in Domesday, it being part of Havering. The name "Rumford" first appeared in 1200 AD and probably means "roomy ford".

SEVEN KINGS   most probably from the Saxon "Seofecingas" meaning the "settlement of Seofeca's people". The earliest known recording of the name Seven Kings is in approx.1285 AD. The name Seven Kings Water (which rises near Hog Hill) first appeared in 1609. This stream becomes Loxford Water before joining the Roding. There is, of course, the legend of the seven kings meeting here by the stream to water their horses, and this would have its origin in Saxon times when chosen leaders were regarded as "minor kings". It is possible that they were out hunting from nearby Havering. Unfortunately there appears to be no documented evidence of this legendary meeting.

SHENFIELD   Scenefelda (D.B.) Shenefeld 1165 – "Beautiful field".
SOUTHEND-ON-SEA   Sowthende 1481. Originally part of Prittlewell of which it was the southern end.
STONEHALL   appears in documents as Stonehale (1327), Stone Hallye (1496) and Stone Hall (1545).
STRATFORD   street ford: ford by which the Roman road crossed a river. The river in this instance is the Lea which for centuries formed the western boundary of the County of Essex. There are several Stratfords and they are all on Roman roads.
TOMSWOOD   first appears in 1777, from Thom at Woodeshill 1590.
UPMINSTER   Upmynster 1062. Upmunstra (D.B.). Upper church.
VALENTINES   owes its origin to Christopher Valentine who resided there in an earlier house during the reign of Queen Elizabeth I. A subsequent resident there was a John Valentine. The present house (known now as Valentines Mansion) was built in the 1690's by James Chadwick, son-in-law of Archbishop Tillotson. At the time the house was within Hainault Forest, which then extended to Ilford.
WANSTEAD   the name "Waenstade" can be traced back as far as the year 824 AD. The first element is probably from the Old English "waegn", "waen" or "wain" meaning waggon. "Stead" probably means "place" or the site of a building, or possibly dairy farm. Wanstead Flats was so named because it was "the flat part of the Forest". Here many years ago a great mart for cattle from Wales, Scotland and the north of England was held annually from the end of February to the beginning of May. A great part of the business between dealers was transacted at the Three Rabbits public house.
WHIPPS CROSS   appears as Phypp(y)s Cross, from John Phippe, 1374.
WOODFORD   appears as Wudeford in 1062 AD: ford by a wood

Notable Old Houses, Mansions, Halls and Manors at one time in Ilford

Aldborough Hall
Beehive
Castle Rising
Claybury Hall
Clay Hall
Clements
Cranbrook Hall
Cranbrook Lodge
Downs Hall
Dunsprings (Downspring)
Forest House
Fulwell Hatch
Gaysham Hall
Goodmayes
Great Gearies
Great Newbury
Highlands
Ilford Cottage

Ilford Hall
Ilford Lodge
Little Gearies
Little Newbury
Loxford Hall
Padnall Hall
Rayhouse
Red House
Roden House
St. Swithins
Spratly Hall
Stone Hall
The Grange, Aldborough Hatch
Tyne Hall
Uphall (Upper Hall)
Valentines
Wangey Hall

Farms in Ilford
towards the end of the last century

Aldborough Hall Farm, Aldborough Hatch
Aldborough Hatch Farm, Aldborough Hatch
Asylum Farm, Tomswood Hill
Barley Hall, Little Heath
Beehive Farm, Beehive
Bennett's Castle, Bennetts Castle Lane
Buntingbridge Farm, Newbury Park (Bunters Bridge)
Castle Rising Farm, Ley Street
Claybury Farm, Roding Lane North
Clay Hall
Cranbrook Farm, Cranbrook Hall
Downshall Farm, Seven Kings

Dunsprings, Dunsprings Lane, Barkingsde
Fencepiece Farm, Fencepiece Road, Barkingside
Fernhall Farm, Roding Lane South
Forest Farm, Forest Road, Fairlop
Forest House, New North Road, Hainault
Fulwell Hatch Farm, Fulwell Hatch
Gaysham Hall, Barkingside
Goodmayes Farm, Goodmayes
Great Gearies, Barkingside
Great Newbury, Aldborough Road
Grove Farm, High Road, Chadwell Heath
Hainault Farm, Hainault Road
Heavy Waters, Green Lane, Goodmayes
Hedgemans (located near where Longwood Gardens runs through to Moss-
  ford Green)
Highfield Farm, Barkingside
Highlands Farm, Cranbrook (near where the Cathedral Estate is today)
Hope Farm, New North Road, Hainault
Huntings Farm, Green Lane
Ley Street Farm, Ley Street, Ilford
Lttle Gearies, Barkingside
Little Heath Farm, Little Heath
Little Newbury, Ley Street
Loxford Hall, Loxford Lane
Middlefield Farm (located around where Perth Road is today)
Padnall Hall, Chadwell Heath
Primrose Farm, Barley Lane
Red House Farm, Billet Road
St. Swithins, Woodford Bridge Road
Seven Kings Farm, Seven Kings
Shackmans Farm (located near where Falmouth Gardens is today)
The Grange, Aldborough Hatch
Uphall Farm, Uphall Road
Wangey Hall Farm, Chadwell Heath
Whites Farm, Oaks Lane

(List by courtesy of Mr P J Wright, Late Reference Librarian and Present
Chairman, Ilford & District Historical Association)

Notes: (1) Before the end of the Century some farms, notably Clements
           Farm had already disappeared for house building.
       (2) Some farms were more frequently known locally by the names of
           the occupants, e.g. Clayhall (Brown's) and Middlefield (Strin-
           ger's).

Ilford's Oldest Roads –
from Ordnance Survey Map of 1873-1881

PRESENT NAME	PREVIOUS NAME where Different
ALDBOROUGH ROAD NORTH ALDBOROUGH ROAD SOUTH	ALDBOROUGH HATCH LANE
ASHURST DRIVE (part only)	BLIND LANE
BARLEY LANE	BERDELOVE STRETE (15th Century). BARLOWE STREET (1540)
BEEHIVE LANE (part only)	SILVER STREET. (The keeping of bees in this locality was first mentioned in 1609).
BILLET ROAD	—
CAMERON ROAD	was one of two Southern ends of ALDBOROUGH HATCH LANE
CHADWELL HEATH LANE	BRICKHILL LANE
CHASE LANE	—
CRANBROOK ROAD	CRAYNEBROKE LANE, BARKING-SIDE LANE
DUNSPRING LANE	—
EASTERN AVENUE	HATCH LANE (small part only)
FENCEPIECE ROAD	—
FOREST ROAD	—
GOODMAYES LANE	GOODMAISTRETE (15th Century). GOODMATH 1777
GOODMAYES ROAD	STOOP LANE

(Note: Until recent times some old roads or lanes did not have names)

GREEN LANE	GREEN STREET
GROVE ROAD	CAT LANE
HAINAULT ROAD	—
HAINAULT STREET	CAUCOTS LANE 1728. CALCUTT LANE. CORKERS LANE
HIGH ROAD (including ILFORD HILL)	part of ROMAN ROAD, the GREAT ESSEX ROAD, or the ROMFORD ROAD. The section passing through the main part of Ilford was previously named HIGH STREET
HIGH STREET, BARKINGSIDE	—
HORNS ROAD	was part of LEY STREET (Lee Strete)
ILFORD LANE	BARKING LANE
LEY STREET	LEESTRETE
LONGWOOD GARDENS	(Follows the farm road from Beehive Lane to Hedgemans Farm which was located near where the Doctor Johnson P.H. is now)
MEADS LANE (part)	—
MILL ROAD	(was part of the track to Barking Abbey continuing where Uphall Road is now)
MOSSFORD GREEN	MOTTES LANE/MOSSFOOT GREEN/MOTT STREET
NEW NORTH ROAD (HAINAULT)	—
NEW ROAD (SEVEN KINGS)	—
OAKS LANE	—
PAINTERS ROAD	—
PARK AVENUE (CRANBROOK)	SOUTH PARK/SOUTH PARK AVENUE
REDBRIDGE LANE EAST	REDBRIDGE LANE
RODEN STREET	BACK STREET (or BACK LANE)
RODING LANE NORTH RODING LANE SOUTH	RODING LANE
TANNERS LANE	—
THE DRIVE	(from CRANBROOK ROAD (Barkingside Lane) to CRANBROOK HALL and HIGHLANDS FARM)
TOMSWOOD HILL	TOMSWOOD LANE

UPHALL ROAD (including RIVER DENE and LOWERBROOK ROAD)	This was an alternative track to Barking Abbey along the River Roding
VICARAGE LANE	CAULIFLOWER LANE
WANSTEAD LANE	—
WARDS ROAD (EAST & WEST)	WARDS LANE
WATER LANE	—
WOODFORD AVENUE (small part only)	(extension of Beehive Lane)
WOODFORD BRIDGE ROAD	—

Note: The long straight roads named Forest Road, Hainault Road, and New North Road were made following the destruction of a large part of Hainault Forest authorised by an Act of Parliament of 1851 and therefore date from the 1850's or 1860's.

The road built by the Romans which passes through Ilford remained for many centuries the main route from London to Colchester and beyond, and to parts of the East Coast. However, when Eastern Avenue was opened in 1925 much of the through-traffic was taken away from the High Road. Further through-traffic was reduced when on January 10th, 1987 a section of the High Road from the Broadway to near Green Lane was closed to such traffic after Winston Way had been opened. The following thought-provoking Poem by Dorothy M. Hobbs (who also wrote the words for the song entitled "In Unity Progress" in 1926) describes the association of the earlier track and the centuries-old Roman Road – or Great Essex Road as it was later called – with some of the many people who throughout its history have travelled along its way.

THE ROMAN ROAD
By Dorothy M. Hobbs

Citizen, what of the road you tread
On the way to your morning train?
Do your feet alone make the undertone
Or is it a far refrain,
A melody cast from the dim, dim past
On the granite sets of your street,
An echo that sings of far off things
To the time of your moving feet?

Do you ever attend, on the way you wend,
To the voice of the years gone by?
Or are you too worried, too bored or too hurried
To hear this insistent cry?
Do you sometimes muse on the road you use?
Do you know how the road came there?
Whose hard brown feet on your old High Street
Wore the first thin footpath bare?

Who followed the track with his native pack
Of ivory, skins and jet,
While the cambered road that the Romans strode
Was an unthought thing as yet?
Who, shod with leather, in windy weather
Went trudging along to the coast?
Who carried the corn one July morn
To provender Caesar's host?

Their days have flown with their names unknown
And even their bones are gone,
But rod by rod, on the track they trod
The Road to the Coast goes on.

Through a clearing made in a forest glade,
Through the ford that the Romans paved,
Came the Saxon thane and the raiding Dane,
And the Norman banners waved.
With pennoned lances and lofty glances
The Templars rode to Town:
In the dust and mire walk the preaching friar
And the pedlar and priest and clown.

A maid rides pillion, a boy postillion
Whistles an old world air:
The turnpike swings and the mail coach brings
Its load to the market square.
While yet we wonder, the steam puffs under
An arch, and a train appears,
In the rush and flurry of crowds that hurry
We join the fleeting years.

One brief bright meeting, one swift short greeting,
We nod and our steps are gone;
But day by day, the Roman Way,
The Road to the Coast goes on
Through the hopes and fears of the unknown years
To carry its untold load,
While the rhythmic beat of a thousand feet
Still move to the Song of the Road.

Some Notable Local Residents and Associates

Basil E.H. AMPS. Born in Caversham, Reading on 3rd November 1904 he began his journalistic career in 1920 with the Reading Standard earning half-a-crown a week. In 1924 he joined the staff of South Essex Recorders rising from junior reporter through to chief reporter, sports editor, acting editor, editor, group editor and editor-in-chief until 1961, when he returned to his home town and resumed working for the local newspaper. During the 37 years he was with the Recorder in Ilford, working from their premises above a shop opposite the Town Hall, Basil Amps reported on much of the life and happenings in Ilford, including countless council and other meetings, and events of all kinds, travelling mostly by bicycle. During the World War II years he compiled an astonishingly detailed account of Ilford and the surrounding district and served as honorary secretary of the local branch of the Soldiers, Sailors and Airmen's Families Association. From 1961 he continued to write a weekly article for the Recorder, drawing on his vast and

The late Basil Amps: "The Voice of Ilford".

probably unique knowledge of the town and its inhabitants, during his residence here. His last article appeared in the Recorder of August 16th 1990, written a few days before his death at the age of 85 on August 10th, at Reading. For many years he lived at 94 Glenwood Gardens, Ilford. In a tribute to him a fellow journalist wrote that his was the voice of reason and of common sense for Basil was truly possessed of wisdom, and was the finest of men and the best of journalists.

Ken ASTON JP. Born in Colchester in 1915 he came to Ilford at an early age and was educated at Ilford County High School. In 1935 he joined the staff of Newbury Park School where in addition to his teaching duties he ran the school football team. In 1936 Mr. Aston qualified as a football referee and took part in local league games until the outbreak of the Second World War during which he served with the Royal Artillery. In 1953 he was appointed Head of Newbury Park School and in the meantime, having resumed his refereeing, progressed to Senior F.A. League Matches. In 1960 he refereed the first Club World Cup Final in the Real Madrid Stadium where there were 140,000 spectators; he refereed the European Nations Cup Final in 1961, and was a referee in the World Cup Series in Chile in 1962. The following year (1963 May 25) Mr. Aston refereed the F.A. Cup Final at Wembley when Manchester United beat Leicester City 3-1. For 8 years a member of the all-important International Federation (F.I.F.A.) Referees committee he was also its chairman for 4 years, and in charge of World Cup referees for the years 1966, 1970, 1974. He is currently senior lecturer of the F.A. Referees Panel, and Chief Instructor for the American Youth Soccer Organsation necessitating a stay of one or two months in the States each year. (In Southern California in August 1990 a Redbridge team of under 13 yr olds competed – the first overseas team to be invited to this 5 year old tournament – in the Ken Aston Cup in which teams from Southern California, Arizona, New Mexico, Utah and Hawaii took part.) For 14 years Mr. Aston also served as a JP on the Inner London Bench.

Benjamin BAILEY JP, 1857-1929. A member of the Ilford Urban District Council from 1896, and Chairman in 1901 when he opened the Town Hall, he was a genial man of great ability, wit and foresight and played a leading part in the development of the town in the late 1890's and early 1900's. He was particularly associated with Ilford's own Electricity works, its Tramway system (he drove one of the trams at its opening), the Ilford Emergency Hospital, of which he was founder and Chairman, the Ilford Football Club, of which he was President, and (in spite of opposition from some Councillors to the expenditure) the acquisition of land for what is now part of Valentines Park. He served on the Bench at Stratford's Magistrates Court, was a dedicated Liberal, and a staunch supporter of Sir John Bethell who eventually won the Southern Parliamentary Division of Essex (of which Ilford was then a part) in 1910. Following the collapse of the Liberator Permanent Building and Investment Society with debts of £8 million – in respect of which Jabez (*Continued on p. 140.*)

Long-time Ilford resident Ken Aston JP (former headmaster Newbury Park School).

Changes in Association Football (Senior and International Level) which Mr Ken Aston has been responsible for bringing about.

(1) In 1946 Mr Aston was the first referee in League Football to wear the now almost universally worn black uniform.
(2) In 1947 he introduced the bright orange linesmen's flags – household dusters were used on the first occasion – to replace the hitherto traditional flags in the home club's colours which because they were sometimes drab and visibility was sometimes poor (no floodlighting then) could not always easily be seen. (The linesmen's flags now are usually orange and red quarters.)
(3) In 1966, following the England v Argentina World Cup match when there was a language problem between the Argentine captain and the German-speaking referee, Mr Aston's proposal for the use of yellow and red cards was adopted. (The idea came to Mr Aston next morning whilst driving his car and being halted in quick succession by traffic lights.)
(4) Again in 1966, Mr Aston "invented" the practice of appointing (before the match) a substitute referee – the senior linesman – in the event of the match referee being unable, during the match, to continue – as seen in a televised football match recently.
(5) Also in 1966, when for 103 years no-one had given consideration to the pressure of the ball Mr Aston proposed that this omission in the Laws of the Game be rectified and the pressure specified. (This is now $0.6 - 0.7$ atmosphere equalling $9.0 - 10.5$ lbs/sq.in at sea level.)
(6) In 1974 he introduced the number board for substitutes in order to ensure that it was perfectly clear which player (who might be reluctant to come off the field of play) was being substituted.
(7) During Mr Aston's Chairmanship of the FIFA Referees' Committee the problem of determining the winner of a match which had ended in a draw after extra time was considered. It was Mr Aston's proposal that the side which had had the fewer free-kicks, and yellow and red cards, given against it should be declared the winner. However, when this proposal was defeated in favour of the system of penalty goals Mr Aston was responsible for writing the Regulation governing this.

* * *

Photo—W. Martin.
Councillor B. Bailey.

This reduced copy of a pen and ink drawing (dated 1896 and costing 100 guineas) by Thomas Raffles Davison is of the former Hotel Cecil in the Strand which Mr. Ben Bailey, in 1892, was made responsible for completing after the collapse of the Liberator Permanent Building and Investment Society (the rear of the building is now occupied by Shell-Mex House but the buildings fronting the Strand are still there).

The following is an extract from an article about Mr. Bailey published in the Ilford Guardian of 10th September 1898 which pays tribute to his work on this important and prestigious undertaking:

"In 1892 Mr. Bailey was engaged under the Official Receiver's Department of the Board of Trade to complete various important properties which came under their control owing to the failure of what is today known as the 'Balfour Group of Companies'. Chief among these properties may be mentioned the Hotel Cecil, Whitehall Court, and Hyde Park Court. It was on receiving this responsible and prominent appointment that Mr. Bailey came to Ilford to reside in December 1892.

It may be interesting here to make special reference to the pre-eminent feature in Mr. Bailey's career up to the present, namely his masterly carrying to a successful issue of the building of the Hotel Cecil in London. It was he who took in hand the business of completing that superb building when things were in a chaotic state due to the Balfour failures. He has been connected with the Hotel from the time that the first foundation stone was laid, and with the site of the building from an even earlier period. When Salisbury Street and Cecil Street had to be demolished to make room for the new structure, the management of the work was entrusted to Mr. Bailey, and it was under his supervision that the old sloping streets were replaced by the present building and the level courtyard which is supported on arches of solid masonry.

All the materials used in the building, except those provided by sub-contractors, were chosen and controlled by Mr. Bailey in person and he can tell you the exact number of bricks used for any particular part, the amount of wood and marble that was required and the number of tons of cement consumed. His staff consisted of something like 1500 men, their number increasing as the building neared completion, till at last the Cecil was crowded with men working day and night to finish their allotted tasks.

It seems almost incredible that one man should have controlled so vast an undertaking but Mr. Bailey not only did this but did it successfully, as is obvious to all who are acquainted with the Cecil. Perhaps its success may be explained by the fact that he has been connected with great building works all his life and the extent of his knowledge renders its application simple and easy. No wonder, after this, that minor difficulties are like water on a duck's back to Mr. Bailey.

As evidence of the high esteem in which he was held by the many men by whom he was brought in contact during the building of the Cecil they right royally entertained him to a banquet at the Hotel at the end of 1896 and presented him with some valuable plate etc. of the value of about £500, Mrs. Bailey also receiving an Erard Grand piano."

Balfour was in 1895 sentenced to 14 years penal servitude – Mr. Bailey was in 1896 appointed Official Receiver of the Society's assets. These included Whitehall Court (for many years the Headquarters of the Liberal Party), the Hotel Cecil (in the Strand) which Mr. Bailey had the responsibility of completing and which in its day was considered the finest Hotel in Europe, and the Ilford Park Estate (extending from Cranbrook Road to beyond Perth Road). He also started the Ilford Laundry which had the Hotel Cecil as its first customer. He lived variously in Coventry Road, The Drive, and Bute Road, Barkingside.

John Logie BAIRD 1888-1946. British electrical engineer and pioneer of television. Born at Helensburgh, Scotland he studied electrical engineering in Glasgow and was working on television possibly as early as 1909 taking out his first provisional patent in 1923. In the middle and late 1920's Baird came to Ilford and worked in a small wooden workshop on the roof of Plessey's Vicarage Lane works perfecting his brainchild. The Plessey Baird Television was on sale to the general public by the late 1920's at a price of £30. About 200 of these early televisions were produced many of which were exported. One was purchased by the German Post Office for their Berlin headquarters and used in early experimental transmissions in 1920-30. Baird went on to pioneer fibre optics, radar, and infra-red television and developed video recording, colour television and in 1944, facsimile television, the fore-runner of Ceefax, as well as demonstrating the world's first electronic colour and 3D Colour receiver.

Stanley John BAIRSTOW. Born in Leyton where his father was a dentist Mr. Bairstow served with the 4th Essex Regiment during the First World War and was badly wounded on the beach during the Gallipoli landings in April 1915 when many casualties were sustained. He was to spend the next three years in hospital at Lytham St. Annes but the bullet which crippled him stayed in his body for the rest of his life. In spite of his disability, in 1923 after starting in business in the Minories he set up as an Estate Agent in Clements Road, Ilford where he practised successfully up to and through the Second World War. With the return of peace and with Mr. Eric Earey as his partner the old-established firm of C. Eves & Son was purchased, Mr. Earey subsequently managing the Goodmayes office. Both offices continued to operate successfully and in 1954 the two were amalgamated under the name of Bairstow, Eves & Son. Further offices were opened in Brentwood, Shenfield, Billericay, Chelmsford and Colchester etc. bringing the total to nine up to the time of Mr. Bairstow's death in May 1967. Mr. Bairstow, who had lived at 25 Seven Kings Road and, later, at 38 Canterbury Avenue was a keen angler and kept a boat on the Norfolk Broads. He was a member of Ilford's Rotary Club for nearly 30 years.

The business of Bairstow Eves, directed by Mr. Bairstow's son John BAIRSTOW who had become a partner in the firm, and Mr. Earey continued to expand until eventually there were approximately 100 offices in all and in

Stanley John Bairstow. The founder of estate agents Bairstow-Eves.

John Bairstow. (Photo: Bob Dear.)

1982 the major step was taken to float the Company on the Stock Exchange, the first Estate Agency to do so. Three million 5p. shares were offered at 46p. each. They were over-subscribed two-and-a-half times and closed on the day at 54p. The business of Bairstow Eves plc has since been taken over by the Hambros Group. (From Obituary in Ilford Recorder 4 May 1967, and details kindly furnished by Mr. E.R. Earey)

John Bairstow, who was born in Ilford on 25 August 1930 and is a former resident of Ilford was educated at the City of London School leaving at 15. It was in 1967 after the death of his father that John Bairstow and his wife perceiving that, apart from the principal cities and a few tourist and seaside towns, the provinces were poorly served with hotels of a high standard, decided with a loan of just £45,000 to convert and extend their fine well-timbered Tudor home in Brentwood into a hotel and restaurant. It was soon to become the first 4-star hotel in Essex. This was the beginning of Queens Moat Houses plc. The house, known as the "Moat House", situated on what used to be called the Great Essex Road, and some 9 miles from Ilford, is reputed to have been built for Catherine of Aragon, the first wife of Henry VIII who spent some time there. In 1512, three years after Henry came to the throne and his marriage to Catherine, the house was re-designed as a hunting lodge.

Mr. Bairstow's Company, of which he is currently Chairman and Joint Managing Director – and which uses the Tudor rose on its logo – specialises in the commercial provincial market and has become the largest U.K. based hotel owner and operator in Continental Europe. Operating 175 hotels with over 20,000 bedrooms in all throughout Britain and in western Germany, Holland, Belgium, France and Switzerland its pre-tax profits for the year 1990 were £94.1 million. Mr. Eric Earey is a non-Executive Director.

Thomas John BARNARDO. Was born in Dublin on 4 July 1845 into what is described as a comfortable cosmopolitan family whose origins can be traced back to the aristocracy of 15th century Venice. According to Arthur Mee's book on Essex the young Thomas, when only two years old, was pronounced dead by two doctors; it was the undertaker who found that there was still a flicker of life! A member of a Protestant household, he grew up at a time of evangelical revival in Ireland, and when many people were suffering as a result of the potato blight (which led to a large-scale emigration to the United States). At an early age he decided that he wanted to be a medical missionary in China and he came to London for training at the London Hospital and the Mission training school in Stepney. The now almost unimaginably bad conditions which existed in London's East End then – particularly those of children, some of whom were homeless – had such a profound effect on him that he realised that he did not have to go to China to fulfil his desire to be of service. Barnardo left medical school as soon as he could (only later did he become a fellow of the Royal College of Surgeons of Edinburgh) and set up a home for destitute boys in Stepney.

It was in 1874 (Barnardo was not then 30) that a friend offered him the rent-free lease of a house, Mossford Lodge, in Barkingside where with the aid of his wife Syrie, whom he had married the previous year, was started a Home for Orphaned and Destitute Girls. From that small beginning the Village Homes at Barkingside grew. Other Homes followed and when Barnardo died, worn out at 60, on September 19, 1905, some 60,000 children had been educated and trained so that they could live a useful and purposeful life. Some went abroad to such countries as Australia and Canada. Through his strenuous efforts Dr. Barnardo managed to raise the enormous sum of £3 million to enable him to carry out his work but on his death there was still a debt of almost £¼ million – a large sum of money in those days.

The full story of Dr. Barnardo's life would fill several books; indeed there are no less than thirteen that have been written about him.

Justifiably acknowledged as one of the foremost social reformers of his time – as were Lord Shaftesbury, Charles Dickens and William Booth (founder and first General of the Salvation Army) Dr. Barnardo's ashes were buried in the grounds of the Village Homes at Barkingside and in 1908 nearby was unveiled a memorial which can still be seen there.

Mossford Lodge has since been demolished and the Redbridge Magistrates Court now occupies the site but many of the village buildings including the Children's Church, Queen Victoria House and Cairns House remain for Barnardo's (as it is now to be known) is still very much involved in the care and welfare of children and young people.

Mrs. Thomas BARNARDO (nee Syrie Elmslie) was the daughter of a City of London business-man and first met Dr. Barnardo when he was invited to speak at a large meeting and entertainment for poor boys in Richmond, Surrey. Syrie was an evangelical who was running a ragged school – a free school for the children of very poor parents – in Richmond.

Doctor Tom Barnardo (1845–1905).

She met Dr. Barnardo again in 1873 and they were married in the same year when she was 26 and he was 28. Syrie became dedicated to her husband's interest and helped him in setting up and running the first Home for Orphaned and Destitute Girls at Mossford Lodge. In all Dr. and Mrs. Barnardo had seven children but some died in infancy and the youngest, born in 1890 when Syrie was 43, was mentally handicapped.

After the death of Dr. Barnardo in 1905 Mrs. Barnardo published her biography of her husband's work and she addressed many meetings pleading the cause of the children in the care of the various Barnardo homes. She also started Sunday afternoon teas and meetings for children in the East End. She died on 21st November 1944 at the age of 96 and her ashes were interred with those of her husband's at Barkingside. (Surprisingly there is no mention of her nor tribute to her on the grave.)

To paraphrase Winston Churchill surely it can be said that "Never in the field of children's welfare was so much care, dedication and devotion given to so many by these two". What a truly wonderful couple they were.

Doctor Barnardo and his wife Syrie.

Mrs. Barnardo (she died 21 November 1944 aged 96 outliving her husband by 39 years).

The memorial to Doctor Barnardo at Barkingside erected 1908.

Raymond (Frederick) BAXTER. Broadcaster and Television Personality, writer, Farnborough Air Show Commentator and one of the original presenters of "Tomorrow's World". Born 25 January 1922, he lived at No. 168 Wellesley Road, was a choirboy at St. Margaret's Church and attended the Ilford County High School in Melbourne Road and the newly built one opened in 1934 at Barkingside. He joined the R.A.F. in 1940 (when only 18 years of age) and flew Spitfires with 65, 93 and 602 squadrons in Britain, the Mediterranean (including Malta at the time of its incessant bombing by the Luftwaffe) and in Europe. Was with the BBC until 1966. Director of Motoring Publicity BMC 1967-68. Member, Committee of Management RNLI from 1979. Air League 1980-85. Hon. Freeman, City of London 1978. Liveryman 1983. Hon. Admiral of Association of Dunkirk Little Ships from 1982. Now lives at Henley-on-Thames.

Edmund John BEAL JP 1843-1929. The first Chairman of Ilford Urban District council in 1895 (by which time he had played an important part in the separation of Ilford from Barking) he was in public life for nearly 60 years and was regarded for many years as the father of the Council. Among other offices and appointments he was first Chairman of the Ilford Conservative Association, a County alderman, a Magistrate, manager of the National Schools, a Poor Law Guardian and a lay preacher. He was at one time the only chemist in Ilford. The Beal School (Woodford Bridge Road) is named after him, as is Beal Road.

Vivian Walter Hough BENDALL MP Member of Parliament (Conservative) for Ilford North since March 1978, he was born 14 December 1938, and educated at Coombe Hill House Croydon and Broad Green College Croydon. Surveyor and Valuer LRVA 1976. Member of Croydon Council 1964-78. Member of GLC 1970-73. Contested Hertford & Stevenage Constituency February and October 1974. Chairman or Vice-Chairman of Various Committees. Recreation: Cricket.

John Adams Guy BODGER JP. Born in Clerkenwell, London 14 October 1846. A representative for Pawsons & Leafs Ltd., City of London Wholesale

Raymond Baxter (*left*)

Vivian Bendall MP (*right*)

Councillor John Bodger JP, ECC.

Haberdashers and Drapers, he acquired his first shop in Ilford (No.113 High Road) which was opened at 6 pm Saturday 14 June 1890. In 1903 two further shops adjoining (Nos. 114 & 115) were opened, and a further two (Nos. 116 & 117) in 1906. In 1914 the well known Bodger's Arcade was opened by Mr. W.P. (later Sir Peter) Griggs. During the years 1921-1926 premises in Station Road were acquired and developed to become the present large Department Store which replaced the High Road Shops. A local Councillor for many years including Chairman of Ilford U.D.C. 1906-7, he was also an Essex County Councillor and a Justice of the Peace, besides being Chairman of the Early Closing Association. He lived at a house named "Hainault" then numbered 73 Cranbrook Road and died 17 November 1924. (Details kindly given by Mr. Bodger's grandson Mr. John Burchell). The Bodgers store is now part of Morley's Stores Ltd. whose head office is at Brixton and whose Chairman Mr. B.H. Dreesman, has recently informed me that the good name of Mr. John Bodger on the Ilford store is something they do not intend to change.

Sir Antonio BRADY JP, FGS. Born in Deptford on 10 November 1811 he was educated at Golfe's School, Lewisham and entered the Civil Service when aged 17. He progressed to become eventually the first Superintendent of the Admiralty's new contract Department on a salary of £1000 a year. After his retirement in 1870 when he was knighted by Queen Victoria at Windsor Castle he devoted himself to social, educational and religious reform and played a leading role in the long drawn-out but successful campaign for the preservation of Epping Forest particularly when in 1871 the Trustees of Lord Cowley enclosed a part of Wanstead Flats. From about 1834 he was for many years engaged in the unearthing of the remains of prehistoric animals which were first discovered in 1786 off Ilford Lane and in the Uphall Brick-earth pits. A catalogue of his collection printed in 1874 listed nearly 1000 specimens found here. These formed the nucleus of the prehistoric animal exhibits at the Natural History Museum in South Kensington. He lived in Forest Lane, Maryland Point (Stratford) where he died on 12 December 1881.

Frederick Joseph BRAND 1857-1939. An outstanding local and Essex historian (one of the greatest), an archaeologist, painter, photographer, collector of books, author, publisher and organist. He was a founder member of the Barking and District Archaeological (now Historical) Society and was Chairman of the Essex Pageant Historical Committee 1932. He lived at No.26 Oakfield Road (now demolished) for many years. The Brand Collection of books and papers on Essex is now the property of the Redbridge Council.

Cecil William BURNES, born 15 June 1884, was the grandson of Mr. Benjamin Burnes who in the year 1848 opened a small furniture shop in Maldon, Essex, and the son of Mr. G. Burnes, who continued the business. On 15 June 1921 Mr. C.W. Burnes, having entered the family furnishing business in 1898, set up the firm of C.W. Burnes Ltd. in Cranbrook Road, Ilford (where McDonald's now occupy the ground floor). In addition to building up a thriving house-furnishing trade, the result of giving good service and value for money for quality goods Mr. Burnes won contracts for furnishing ocean-going Passenger Liners and Cargo Vessels, the first of which he furnished in the year 1910. In a souvenir booklet issued by the firm in 1953 to commemorate the Coronation of our present Queen no less than 52 ships (42 new and 10 re-conditioned) were listed as having been furnished by the Ilford store and its fitters, etc. in the seven years from 1946 to 1952 inclusive. These ships were in various yards in Scotland and Northern Ireland as well as England including the London Docks. A Freeman of the City of London and a founder member of Ilford Rotary Club Mr. Burnes lived for some years at No.4 Argyle Road. He died 6 January 1952 at 31 Falmouth Gardens the home then of his daughter and son-in-law. In December 1959 the business of C.W. Burnes in Canbrook Road which had been carried on by his two sons was sold to Chiesmans of Lewisham, the sale being necessitated to a large extent by the heavy death duties payable on Mr. C.W. Burnes' estate.

George L. CAUNT OBE 1908-1977. Author of "Ilford's Yesterdays", first published in 1963, and republished in an enlarged edition by Mrs. Rose Caunt in 1980. He wrote also "Essex Blood and Thunder" and "Essex in Parliament". A great researcher and authority on the history of Ilford, of Essex and of London, he gave many interesting talks to the Workers Educational Association and others. He was an Ilford Borough Councillor for ten years and in 1954 joined the staff of the Secretariat of the Parliamentary Labour Party being awarded the OBE in 1970 for his services. A conservationist (he fought to save Ilford Town Hall from the bulldozers believing there was not another building like it in the country) and Founder and one-time Chairman of the Ilford and District Historical Society. He wrote many articles for the local Press and for Essex Countryside magazine. Because of his incomparable knowledge of local history he was for many years known as "Mr. Ilford". Among his researches was a lengthy one into the de Vere family as a result of which Mr. Caunt became convinced that Edward de Vere, 17th Earl of Oxford (to whom Cranbrook Hall at one time belonged) was the author of the plays attributed to Shakespeare. Himself, in his younger days, a good amateur boxer, his ancester Ben Caunt was several times Boxing Champion of England in the 1830's and 1840's. Mr. Caunt lived at No.28 Ingleby Road where Mrs. Rose Caunt – his devoted wife and helpmate for over 40 years – still resides.

Air Vice-Marshall Sir Bernard CHACKSFIELD KBE, CB. Born 13 April 1913 at No.28 Khartoum Road. Like several other local residents who have distinguished themselves he was educated at Ilford County High School, though he went first to Uphall Road and then Christchurch Road Schools. He then joined the Royal Air Force and went on to the R.A.F. College at Cranwell before serving on the N.W. Frontier 1934-37, and later in India, Burma and Singapore. Air Ministry 1945-48. Western Union (NATO) Fontainebleu 1949-51, R.A.F. Staff College 1951-53. Fighter Command 1954-55 Director, Guided Weapons (trial) Ministry of Supply 1956-58. Recreations: Scouting (Chief Commissioner for England 1968-77), sailing, fencing, gliding, model aircraft, shooting, swimming, youth works, and amateur dramatics. Describing himself in a letter to me as an enthusiastic Ilfordian he now lives in Buckinghamshire.

Sir Allen CLARK. Allen George Clark was born in Massachusetts (USA) in 1898 and when his family moved to England he was educated at Felsted School, Essex. Early in the First World War he volunteered to serve with the London Scottish when still not 17, was wounded at Cambrai, and in 1918 was commissioned in the Royal Flying Corps. In 1920 he teamed up with Mr. W.O. Heyne and together started The Plessey Company, first in an attic in Highgate with a contract to make crystal sets for Marconi, then in 1924 in a little factory off Vicarage Lane, Ilford. (The name Plessey was chosen because it was the birthplace of Mr. Heyne's wife and also the first name of their Solicitor, Mr. Plessey Parker. Plessey is a small village near Blyth in Northumberland.)

Mr. Clark and Mr. Heyne worked seven days a week, ploughed back every penny into the business and gradually built up from a small contract shop to substantial manufacturers of radio telephones and all types of electronic components. "A.G." as everyone knew him, made a series of licensing deals with American companies in the 1930's and had diversified into aircraft connectors, starters, hydraulics and communications equipment when in 1939 the outbreak of War brought about a considerable expansion. The Company was trebled in size with additional factories started up from Essex to Cardiff. Additionally "A.G." obtained permission for 5 miles of uncompleted Underground railway tunnelling at Ilford to be converted into a highly secure factory where 2000 people on each shift worked deep below ground.

Peacetime brought wholesale cancellations of contracts and the challenge of starting again. It called for great foresight and clear thinking but through hard work and with dynamic enthusiasm and attention to detail, by reorganization and the merging of two of the most important telephone manufactur-

Sir Allen Clark – the Plessey Giant (1898–1962).

ing companies in Britain in 1961 Plessey became the largest telecommunications organizations in the country, an organization which "A.G." – a big man both physically and mentally – had built from nothing. An Olympic clay pigeon shot before the war (he was considered one of the ten best game shots in England), and a rare raconteur – drawing on his many experiences – he was

Offices and works of the Plessey Company, Vicarage Lane, Ilford. (Photo: Author.)

(*left*) A. Cameron Corbett, MP, later Lord Rowallan.

(*right*) Alderman F.H. Dane, MBE, JP, CA (ECC) Chairman of the Urban District Council 1912–1913. First Mayor of the Borough, 1926–1927.

highly regarded in London, Paris and New York. He died 30 June 1962. (Details kindly supplied by the Plessey Company and printed with their permission.)

Sqdn. Leader Albert Edward COOPER MBE, MP. Born on 23 September 1910 (son of Albert Fredk Smith and Edith Alice Cooper) he was educated at the London College for Choristers and in Australia and entered politics in 1935 when he was elected to Ilford Borough Council. Chairman, Electricity and Lighting Committee Education (Finance) and Legal Parliamentary Committees, Alderman 1947. Enlisted in R.A.F. in 1940 and served as Navigator in Coastal Command during World War II. Elected Member of Parliament (Conservatve) for Ilford South 1950-66, and 1970 to Feb. 1974. PPS to President of the Board of Trade 1952-54. Lived at 65 Highwood Gardens and later in London. He was an exceptionally good after-dinner speaker. Died 1984.

Archibald Cameron CORBETT MP (Lord Rowallan). Born in Scotland 23 May 1856. Mr. Corbett first contested the North Warwickshire constituency in 1884 and was in 1885 elected Member of Parliament for the Tradeston Division of Glasgow, holding that seat until 1911 when he was created 1st Baron Rowallan. Mr. Corbett was one of the two principal builders of houses in the Ilford area building over 3000 in all on the Grange (from 1894), Downshall and Mayfield Estates (both from 1898). Cameron Road is named after him as also is Rowallan House, Little Heath. Apart from his gift of land for the original Seven Kings and Goodmayes Parks, and the Westwood Recreation Ground (Goodmayes) he gave financial help for the building of a Baptist Church in Cameron Road, Seven Kings and a site for a hall. Died 19 March 1933.

Frederick Hopper DANE MBE, JP 1872-1955. Chartered Accountant. Elected to the Ilford Urban District Council 1906, he was Chairman from 1912-1913. When Ilford became a Borough in 1926 he was made Ilford's first Mayor. He was also an Essex County Councillor and a President of Ilford Football Club. The Dane school was named after him (now the Dane Remedial Centre). He lived at No.10 Chelmsford Gardens.

Daniel DAY, who was born in 1683, was a ship's block and pump maker at Wapping. His association with the Ilford district began on his acquiring some cottages in the vicinity of Fairlop Oak. Being a benevolent though prodigal man he conceived the idea of inviting his tenants and friends to a feast of beans and bacon after the collection of his rents on the first Friday of each July. The annual picnic soon attracted public attention as well as that of other landlords and employees using the same day and venue of the ancient Fairlop Oak. Subsequently booths and tents were added as was the annual procession of waggons and mounted boats decorated with flags and streamers from the East End to Fairlop. It became a real day out for thousands of people. Daniel Day ("Good Day") retired to his small estate near Fairlop Oak where he died on 19 October 1767, aged 84. The Fairlop Fair, as it had become known, continued for many years after his death and in fact for some years after the tree, this king of the forest, had been cut down in 1820.

Mrs. Maria Elizabeth DICKIN CBE. Born 22 September 1870 she was the daughter of the Revd. Wm. George Dickin, a Minister in Whitechapel. In 1899 she married her cousin Arnold Francis Dickin, a banker. There were no children. A philanthropist and social worker, it was during the First World War that as a result of visiting the families of soldiers she became aware of and was appalled by the condition and suffering of their animals. Realising that it was ignorance and lack of money for veterinary fees which contributed to the animals' suffering she started in 1917 with the help of a knowledgeable veterinary person an animals' dispensary and treatment centre in a whitewashed cellar in Whitechapel, offering free veterinary treatment. Thus was founded the People's Dispensary for Sick Animals (P.D.S.A.).

In 1927 St. Swithin's Farm – then a 30 acre estate – in Woodford Bridge Road, Ilford was purchased and became the first animal hospital and was the first to have an operating table for horses. (For many years previously the land had been used for the grazing of horses belonging to costermongers and gypsies). During the last war part of the 30 acres was acquired by the Government and subsequently Beal School and Sinclair House etc. were built thereon. The small cemetery for animals which adjoins the treatment centre is under the care of the P.D.S.A.

Mrs. Dickin was the author of "The Cry of the Animals", and other humanitarian works. She died on March 1st 1951, aged 80.

The DICKIN MEDAL, popularly known as "the animals V.C." was instituted by Mrs. Dickin. It was awarded upon official recommendation to any animal displaying conspicuous gallantry and devotion to duty associated with, or under the control of, any branch of the armed Forces or Civil Defence during World War II and its aftermath. Of the 53 Dickin Medals awarded 18 were to dogs, 3 to horses, 1 to a cat and 31 to pigeons. Besides carrying and safely delivering important messages – often under fire or in similar difficult conditions and on occasions over long distances and some-times wounded – these pigeons were responsible for saving many lives. The citations accompanying the award of these medals make heartfelt reading.

Joseph DINES. Born in 1886 he came to Ilford from Kings Lynn in 1910 to take up an appointment as a teacher at Highlands School. An outstanding amateur footballer he had played for Kings Lynn, was in the Norfolk team which won the Southern Counties Championship in 1908, and played for Norwich City Reserves, Woolwich Arsenal Reserves and Queens Park Rangers before joining the then famous Ilford Football Club of which he was later made Captain. In 1912 he played for Great Britain in the Olympics held at Stockholm when Great Britain beat Denmark 4-2 in the final and between 1910 and 1914 he was capped no less than 25 times for England. One of four brothers to volunteer for Army service when the First World War was declared he served in the Ordnance Corps, the Middlesex Regiment, the Machine Gun Corps and the Tank Corps. Upon being commissioned he was

Mrs. Maria Dickin 1870–1951. The founder of the P.D.S.A.

posted to the Liverpool Regiment but tragically was killed shortly after returning from home leave in Ilford and just a few weeks before the cessation of hostilities in 1918. He lived at No.12 Toronto Road.

Reverend Sir Herbert DUNNICO LL.D, JP, MP 1876-1953. Born in North Wales he worked in a factory at the age of 10, in a coal mine at 12, and entered a business house at 13. A local resident for many years he was Labour candidate for the newly-formed Ilford Parliamentary Constituency in the General Election of 1918 (when Sir Peter Griggs was elected). In 1922 he became Member of Parliament for the Consett Division of Durham and from 1929 to 1931 he was Deputy Speaker in the House of Commons. He was a local Councillor and Chairman of Ilford U.D.C., also an Essex County Councillor. Interested in Sport, he was a bowls enthusiast and a great supporter of Ilford Football Club of which he was President. A memorial to him in the form of a handsome pair of Gates stood for many years at Ilford F.C.'s ground in Lynn Road, Newbury Park. They are now at the High Road entrance to the Cricklefield ground. My father knew him well. When in 1924 the Revd. Dunnico wanted to rent a house of which my father had the letting and was asked to provide the customary references he gave the then Prime Minister (Ramsey Macdonald) and the Archbishop of Canterbury. "Would they be satisfactory?" he smilingly enquired. He lived at 74 Wellesley Road and later at 2 Bathurst Road.

Noel EDMONDS Television presenter. Born 22 December 1948 in Ilford he attended the Glade Primary School in Clayhall. As featured in the Recorder 27 April 78, in 1978 he went back to visit the school when he handed over a minibus (which he and the Parents Association had purchased after raising £2,800) to take pupils on school trips.

George J. FAIRHEAD Born in 1881 he learnt the drapery trade in large department Stores including the one-time prestigious firm of Gorringes in Buckingham Palace Road. He opened his own shop at No.33 (now No.64) Cranbrook Road in 1908, and lived at No.6 Granville Road. In 1945 he retired to the South Coast where he died in the 1960's. The business of Fairheads which with Harrison Gibsons and Bodgers is one of the oldest of Ilford's shops still surviving was taken over in 1945 by Mr. Horace Stanley Sweet who was at that time in the drapery business at Maryland Point, Stratford and who lived at 67 Clarendon Gardens. Since the demise of Mr. Sweet Senior the business has been in the hands of his son Mr. Douglas P. Sweet who has recently expanded the business by taking the adjoining premises, No.60 Cranbrook Road – formerly Ashford & Davis the Jewellers.

Harold A. FARAGHER FCIS. Born 20 July 1917 at Reddish near Stockport, Lancs he came to Ilford in December 1928 and has been resident here ever since. A pupil at Ilford County High School (1929-1933) he played football and cricket for the school and ran in the County cross-country championship. In 1935 he played for Lancashire 2nd XI and in 1936 joined Ilford Cricket Club when until 1939 he also played soccer for Ilford F.C.

Harold Faragher – Ilford's "Mr. Cricket".

From 1940 to 1946 he served in the R.A.F. playing cricket for them in England and Germany. Resuming cricket with Ilford in 1947 Mr. Faragher has been active continuously in that sport not only with Ilford C.C. but also with Essex C.C.C., playing for the 1st XI in 1949 and in 1950 when he topped the batting averages, and playing for the 2nd XI over the period 1949-1964 when on occasions he captained the side. A member of the Essex C.C.C. Executive Committee until 1991 he has been a Vice-President since 1978.

In 1957 he founded the Ilford Cricket School and since 1982 he has been President of the Ilford schools cricket association. In addition to his sporting activities Mr. Faragher – affectionately known as "Mr. Cricket" – has been employed in Education in Ilford as a lecturer/teacher in business subjects, as head of Commerce Dept., S.E. County Technical School 1956-62, and Head of Dept. of Business and Management Studies at Barking College of Technology.

Greer GARSON. Born in Northern Ireland 29 September 1908, the daughter of George Garson and Nina Sophia Greer. One of the leading British actresses, playing the lead role in 13 London plays and becoming a famous film star through such films as Mrs. Miniver, Random Harvest and Blossoms in the Dust. She now lives in Texas, U.S.A. For about ten years (1926-1936) Greer Garson's mother Mrs. Nina Garson lived at No.5 Tillotson Road, Ilford where Greer Garson also lived for a time before her first marriage to Edward A. Snelson (later Sir E.A. Snelson). A letter I received from America in October '89 written on her behalf stated that she had recently undergone vascular surgery.

Sir Crisp GASCOYNE JP 1700-1761. Surveyor and Churchwarden for the Parish of Barking (of which Ilford was one of the Wards) which he served for many years. He was Lord Mayor of London 1752-53 and the first occupant of the Mansion House. He gave his name to Gascoyne Road, Barking in which road lived Elizabeth Batts whom Captain Cook, the English navigator, married in 1762 in St. Margaret's Parish Church, Barking.

John Harrison GIBSON was born in the village of Robin Hood's Bay near Whitby, Yorkshire (which town is associated with the famous navigator and explorer Captain Cook). Although John's family were sea-faring folk (Master Mariners) he was apprenticed in the furniture trade to a firm in Whitby and when his indenture was completed he became the youngest ever manager of a ship fitters' department in Newcastle. From there he came to London to become the Manager of a furnishing business in Newington Causeway. When this store was taken over John Harrison Gibson decided that the time had come to set up on his own and in 1902 he opened his store in Ilford when the town's population was just over 42,000 (having increased from just under 11,000 in 1891). (Incidentally it was at this spot that the 7th milestone from London stood).

It was not long before John Harrison Gibson acquired the premises next door and through sheer hard work and by giving good value and excellent service his business expanded until it was one of the largest stores in the town. Not only was it open from 8 am to 8 pm and until 9 pm on Saturdays, he gave free insurance to hire purchase customers, insurance which covered the buyer's indebtedness in the event of death, sickness or other incapacity. Although he had great affection for his horses, all of which he knew by name and which were always handsomely turned out, he was one of the first business men in Britain to foresee the importance of the motor vehicle in commerce acquiring his first runabout in 1910. He died in May 1924 and so was spared the trauma of seeing his store destroyed in the first Harrison Gibson fire which occurred on the morning of Tuesday July 22nd of that year.

Fortunately for the business, his son John E. GIBSON who had served his apprenticeship at Hides of Kingston had inherited not only his father's vision and drive but also his great tenacity. By the following Saturday nearby warehouses were used as temporary showrooms and within a year the store was completely rebuilt. In 1935 he opened his second store at Bromley, Kent and during the War years, 1939-1945, when there was no furniture to be had he scoured the country for second-hand pieces and successfully kept things going.

Meanwhile his son, John (Jack) G. GIBSON, who had trained at the Shoreditch Technical School and at the Ryman School of Display, Westminster was serving in the Army, first with the Essex Regiment and then with the East Yorkshire Regiment during the Allied invasion of France and Holland. After the War he rejoined the firm and in 1947 he took over an existing business in Bedford, in 1953 another in Doncaster, in 1954 a large store in Manchester, and in 1955 one in Halifax. In January 1958 a Harrison Gibson Store was opened in Leeds, and later additional premises in Manchester.

Following the disastrous fire of 16 March 1959 which for the second time destroyed the Ilford store Mr. Jack Gibson was very much involved, as was his father, with the rebuilding, planning and stocking of the large store which stands there today.

The continued success of the business – now part of the Gillow Group – has been in no small measure due to the excellent service given over the years by all members of the staff who have carried on in the tradition of the founder John Harrison Gibson.

One such person is Mr. Leslie Barker who, born in Roman Road, Ilford in 1908 started as a van boy with the firm and rose to become General Manager. In 1968 when the Store was taken over by Waring & Gillow Mr. Barker, then 60, joined Mr. John Bairstow to help set up the Moat House Hotel and Restaurant in Brentwood and later became an Executive Director of Queens Moat Houses plc and as such is still active.

George M. GOTT JP 1850-1913. Born at Mossford Green and educated at the privately-run Ilford House Academy on Ilford Hill he served on the Ilford council for 22 years. A local farmer, occupying Fencepiece Farm, he was elected Chairman of the Works Committee in 1897 and held that position until his retirement in 1913. In 1903 he was also Chairman of Ilford U.D.C. and drove the first tram at the opening of the Tramways system on March 14th of that year. He also opened three parks in one week (South Park, Seven Kings and Barkingside). During his 22 years as a Councillor he travelled from his farm to Ilford in his pony and trap to attend public duties and covered an estimated 16,000 miles on Council Business (no Expenses paid then!). Held in unusually high esteem by his fellow Councillors he died a month after retiring from the Council.

Arthur William GREEN JP Born in March 1872 the son of a Whitechapel grocer he wanted to become a Doctor, an ambition which he was obliged to give up when his father died leaving eight children. Mr. Green came to Ilford in 1896 setting up shop at the corner of High Road and Clements Road (where Dixons now is), the first of a total of his 35 shops in South Essex. He was an Essex County Councillor for 16 years, Ilford Borough Councillor for

23 years and Churchwarden at St. Clements Church for 35 years. Chairman of Ilford Conservative Association for 14 years, a Director of John Bodger Store, and President of Ilford Cricket Club. Mr. Green was also for many years Chairman of the Governors of Ilford Emergency Hospital, and later the King George Hospital (which replaced it). Known as the Admiral of the King George he welcomed King George V and Queen Mary when the newly built extensions were officially opened on July 18, 1931. He was also involved with the Black Notley Sanatorium. Described as the ideal citizen, a great giver, a hard worker and a warm-hearted man he died 27 March 1951 aged 79. For many years he lived at 5 Park Avenue, 24 Coventry Road and latterly at Great Gearies. (Ilford Recorder Obituary/Central Library)

Albert Philip GRIGGS JP Born on 14 November 1879 in Bethnal Green he learnt the trade of a Carpenter and later joined his uncle Mr. W.P. Griggs in the development of the Cranbrook Park Estate and also other Estates in Ilford and Upminster. During the 1914-1918 War he saw active service in France with the Royal Engineers, first in the ranks and later as a commissioned officer. After the War he managed his own business and developed the Highland Estate in the middle and late 1920's and the 1930's. (This Estate is popularly known as the Cathedral estate because the 15 roads on it are named after English cathedral towns and cities.) Mr. Griggs also built St. Andrew's Church with which, including the Church Hall built in 1906, he was closely associated for 46 years. The Church was built "at cost" and the Chapel was a gift by Mr. Griggs to the Church.

An Ilford Councillor from 1925 he was Mayor in 1934/35, was on the Essex County Council for 21 years, Chairman of the Ilford Conservatve Association for 13 years, a Freeman of the Borough of Ilford and of the City of London, a prominent Freemason, a Justice of the Peace on the Stratford Bench and a founder of the local Trustees Savings Bank. He lived at No.5 Cranbrook Rise where he died on 17th February 1953. The site is now occupied by flats (Mistley Court).

W.P. (Sir Peter) GRIGGS MP Born in Hackney November 1st 1853 he had to make his own way in the world his father dying when he was seven years old. He apprenticed himself to the water (Thames river) but left to find a path not quite so rough on firm ground. As W.P. Griggs he was, with A.C. Corbett, one of the principal builders of houses in Ilford in the late 1890's and early 1900's building over 2000 in all. He was an Ilford Councillor from 1899 and an Essex Councillor from 1901. Knighted in 1916 for his services in connection with the First World War he was, in December 1918, elected Member of Parliament for the newly-formed Constituency of Ilford. In addition to being Chairman of various Committees and Associations he was Governing Director of South Essex Recorders. He presented to the people of Ilford the Clock Tower which originally stood in the Broadway and the Clock Tower and Drinking Fountain in Valentines Park. He lived at No.7 The Drive where he died on 11 August 1920. Griggs Approach is named after him.

(*left*) Alderman A.P. Griggs, JP, ECC

(*right*) Councillor W.P. Griggs, ECC, later Sir Peter Griggs MP

Alfred Hugh HARMAN Born in 1841 the son of a bootmaker Mr. Harman first lived at Peckham where he set up in business on his own at a time when photography was very much a do-it-yourself business, making copies and enlargement of photographs and experimenting with different processes. In 1879 he decided to concentrate on the manufacture of photographic dry plates and moved to Ilford as he wanted a site close to London with a clean, dust-free atmosphere. In the basement of a house called "Elmhurst" on the corner of Cranbrook Road and Park Avenue (where The Cranbrook P.H. now is) Mr. Harman with the help of two men and three boys and in busy times, that of his wife and the housekeeper, made photographic dry plates, and drove daily in a horse and trap to London in order to deliver them personally. He then rented a cottage near Roden Street and later purchased houses in Uphall Road from which grew the Britannia Works Company. Following a Court Case the Company's name was changed to Ilford Limited after approval had been sought from the Ilford Council who gave their consent on condition that the word Limited was spelt in full. Mr. Harman subsequently resided in a house called "Langsett" on the corner of Cranbrook Road and Wellesley Road (where McDonald's now is). He died in 1913 and although, sadly Ilford Limited is no longer located in Ilford, or even in Essex (operating now from Mobberley in Cheshire, with a Sales Office in London) they are still an important company in the photographic world with

(*left*) Councillor A.W. Green ECC for many years Chairman of the Board of Management, King George Hospital.

(*right*) Cardinal Heenan: born and lived at No. 33 Ripley Road, Seven Kings, he was a parish priest in Manor Park for many years after being ordained in the church of S.S. Peter and Paul, High Road, Ilford in 1930.

subsidiaries bearing the name ILFORD in twelve overseas countries. (With acknowledgements to Ilford Limited and their book "Silver by the Ton" celebrating their 100 years from 1879-1979)

His Eminence Cardinal John Carmel HEENAN DD, Ph.D 1905-1975 Born in Ilford, he was ordained in 1930 and worked as a parish Priest in Manor Park for many years. Superior of the Catholic Missionary Society 1949-51. Bishop of Leeds 1951-57. Bishop of Liverpool 1957-63. Archbishop of Westminster (Roman Catholic Primate 1963-1975). Author of several publcations and two autobiographies. No native son of Ilford has achieved greater renown. He lived for many years at No.33 Ripley Road.

Watson HORNBY 1863-1942. A painter in water colours and a photographer, he took many photographs of Ilford in the late 1800's and early 1900's. He was in business at No.7 Cranbrook Road (now No.34) selling artists' materials and stationery etc. and living above the shop. He subsequently lived at No.10 Valentines Road.

Some years ago (in the 1960's) the large and probably unique collection of old Ilford photographs taken by Mr. Hornby were given by his daughter-in-law, Mrs. Norman Hornby, to my brother Ben Gunby (Principal of B. Bailey & Co.) who, shortly afterwards, presented them to the Central Reference Library.

Arthur Joseph HUGHES OBE (see also Kelvin Hughes Ltd. of New North Road). Born in 1880 the grandson of the founder of Henry Hughes & Son, navigation instrument makers Arthur Hughes was educated at St. Dunstan's College and Northampton Institute of Science.

Joining the family firm immediately after leaving college he soon began to develop into the scientific research that was to make him famous. From his home at Chigwell he travelled daily to work with a thousand ideas buzzing in his mind – ideas that were later to save many lives.

By the outbreak of the First World War Arthur Hughes had conceived a unique air compass, the aperiodic compass – which saved the lives of countless pioneers in the Royal Flying Corps. It was for this invention that he was made an OBE. His tireless efforts were largely responsible for the discovery of the echo sounder for depth-finding by ultrasonic waves. After the First World War he concentrated even more on research and on the planning of the large factory at Hainault.

By the Second World War he had conceived the air bubble sextant which enabled British fighter pilots to outwit the Luftwaffe by navigating by stars instead of radio. The Americans said it could never be done: Arthur Hughes proved them wrong.

After the War he developed the flow detector which was able to gauge flaws in metal and was used extensively on the axles of London Underground trains.

A regular church-goer at All Saints, Chigwell Row, he was a member of the church council and a Church-warden. Greatly interested in youth and the Air Training Corps. he was also Chairman of the St. Clement Danes sea cadets. He died 4 November 1961 aged 81 at his new home in Hastings.

Baron ILFORD of Bury (life Peer created 1962) was Geoffrey Clegg HUTCHINSON KT, MC, TD Born 1893. Member of Parliament for Ilford 1937-1945 and Ilford North 1951-54. Chairman of the National Assistance Board 1953-64. Hon. Freeman of the Borough of Ilford and of the London Borough of Camden. Died 20 August 1974.

Holcombe INGLEBY JP, MA, MP 1854-1926. Second son of Clement Mansfield Ingleby and Mrs. Sarah Ingleby. Following the death of his mother in 1906 he presented to the people of Ilford 12 acres of the grounds adjoining "Valentines" in her memory. He was the first President of Ilford Golf Club and after taking up residence at Heacham Hall in Norfolk was Mayor of Kings Lynn 1909-10 and 1919-22. Member of Parliament for Kings Lynn 1910-1918, and High Sheriff of Norfolk 1923. Holcombe Road is named after him.

Mrs. Sarah INGLEBY 1823-1906. According to her obituary published in the Ilford Recorder of 5 January 1906 Mrs. Ingleby was resident at "VALENTINES" for over 60 years. Her husband was Mr. Clement Mansfield Ingleby who died at Valentines some 16 years prior to Mrs. Ingleby's demise. Mrs. Ingleby was the Ilford representative at the Romford Board of Guardians where she was a regular attendant and strenuous worker. She was President of the Ilford Philanthropic Society and was involved with the local Primrose League. She paid for the building of the Beehive School (now demolished)

Mrs. Sarah Ingleby, last resident of Valentines Mansion where she died in January 1906. Her husband was Mr. Clement Mansfield Ingleby who died at Valentines some 16 years earlier. (Photo: Local History Room, Central Library, Ilford.)

and largely maintained it. During her occupancy "Valentines" and its grounds were frequently made available for various functions organised by the Ilford Men's Meeting, the local Conservative Association and the Horticultural Society. She was buried alongside her husband at Ovingdean, near Brighton. Ingleby Road is named after her.

Thomas Lascelles IREMONGER MA Educated at Oriel College, Oxford, he served in H.M. Overseas Service (Western Pacific) and in R.N.V.R. (Lieut) 1942-46. Elected Member of Parliament (Conservative) for Ilford North Feb. 1954 to Sept. 1974. PPS to Sir Fitzroy Maclean when Under Secretary for War 1954-57. Served on various Parliamentary Committees. Contested Ilford North as Conservative Independent in March 1978 and again in 1979. Lived at Cheyne Row, Chelsea. Publcations: Disturbers of the Peace 1962, and Money, Politics and You, 1963: an under-writing member of Lloyds, he was married to Lucille Iremonger MA (Oxon) FRSL, author and Broadcaster who died on 7 January 1989. Recreations: Sailing, Riding.

Smart LETHIEULLER 1701-1760 A local Historian, a student of antiquities, and man of literature, examined the Roman coffin found at Valentines in 1729. Explored the site of Barking Abbey employing men to excavate the foundations. In 1754 he purchased the Manor of Barking from the Fanshawes. Lived at Aldersbrook, now the site of the City of London Cemetery. Of Swiss origin, an ancestor of his had been burnt at the stake in Geneva.

Herbert Hope LOCKWOOD BA (Hons) History, associate of King's College, London (born 1917). Formerly lecturer in History and Social Studies at Tottenham College of Technology, is Vice Chairman of Essex Archeological and Historical Congress and President and an active member of the Ilford & District Historical Society and an authority and speaker on the history of Ilford and Barking. His booklets entitled "Where was the first Barking Abbey?" published in 1986 and "Barking – 100 Years Ago" published 1990, are on sale at local libraries. A long-time resident of Ilford he lives at 10 Alloa Road, Goodmayes. Mr. Lockwood's wife, Mrs. Dorothy Lockwood, held until recently for seven years the important honorary post of Secretary to the Essex Archeological & Historical Congress which at one time was held by the late George Caunt OBE.

Admiral Sir Raymond (Derek) LYGO KCB Born in Ilford, 15 March 1925, he lived at No.41 Richmond Road and later at 33 Wycombe Road, Ilford. Attended Valentines School and Ilford County High School. Naval Airman 1942. Commanding Officer HMS Ark Royal 1969-71. Vice Chief of Naval Staff 1986-1989. Freeman of City of London. Chief executive British Aerospace plc. 1986-1989.

Gilbert J. MILES MA. Born in 1904 he came to Ilford in 1925 and taught at Becontree Secondary and Beal Schools, and was later Headmaster of Newbury Park Senior and Becontree Secondary Schools. In 1940 he joined Ilford Borough's Education Department and in 1943 he went to Hornsey to become their Deputy Education Offcer. Returning to Ilford in 1947 as Education Officer he was made Chief Education Officer when Ilford merged with Wanstead and Woodford in 1965. After his retirement in 1969 Mr. Miles took up sailing, taking his boat across the North Sea several times to Holland etc. and into the Baltic. Lives at 38 Water Lane, Seven Kings. Died 24 Feb '92

Revd. Philip MORANT (1700-1770). A learned gentleman (educated at Pembroke College, Oxford) he was a prolific writer of articles and books including his great work "The History and the Antiquities of the County of

Admiral Sir Raymond Lygo.

Essex". Editor of the first records of Parliament covering the period from 1278 to 1413 (requiring a knowledge of Norman French) many of his manuscripts are now in the British Museum. Buried at Aldham (near Colchester) where he was Rector from 1745-1770.

Sir Horatio PALAVICINO. Owner of Cranbrook Manor which he purchased from the Earl of Leicester in 1585 and where he lived until his death in 1600. An Italian, he was naturalised in 1585 and knighted two years later by Queen Elizabeth for his financial services, following the death of Sir Thomas Gresham (English financier and founder of the Royal Exchange). While at Cranbrook Palavicino had custody of four Spanish noblemen survivors from the wreck of one of the Spanish Armada galleons. Three of these noblemen were later ransomed and the other exchanged for a Huguenot prisoner.

The Very Revd. Canon Patrick PALMER. Born in Ireland in 1864 he became the first parish priest of SS Peter and Paul's RC church in Ilford after its completion in 1899. (Previously he had been at Mile End and at a little corrugated-iron church in Bogies Alley at the bottom of Ilford Hill). One of the leading local churchmen of his day he was a man of great ability and acumen. During his 48 years as parish priest in Ilford he was responsible for the acquisition of sites for, and the building of, many Catholic churches and schools in the district. He also organised many fund-raising events and fetes including the several revived Dunmow Flitch "trials" held on the Gordon Road ground in the 1920/30's. Cardinal Heenan in his autobiography "Not the Whole Truth" describes Father Palmer (as he was then) as "the great hero of my youth". The Canon Palmer RC school in Seven Kings is named after him. He died in May 1948.

Joseph PATES 1858-1939. Ilford's Grand Old Man and a great character was, like Mr. Gott, a pupil at Ilford House Academy on Ilford Hill but left school when only 11. After a short period of employment in the City he worked in his father's baker's shop (situated in the High Road opposite Clements Road) getting up at 2 am to help in the bakehouse and delivering bread on his old pennyfarthing. Parish Clerk for 60 years and village postman for 20, sexton, and later Cemetery superintendent, he was a keen cricketer keeping wicket for Ilford Cricket Club. Evacuated to Hampshire at the outbreak of the Second World War – as were many elderly people and school children – he died shortly afterwards on 6 October 1939. He lived at 52 South Park Road.

Frank PEPPER Born in Ilford in 1910 and educated at Ilford County High School, Frank Pepper was the creator of such schoolboy heroes as Rockfist Rogan R.A.F. "the Dare devil Fighter of the Skies and the Boxing Ring" and "Captain Condor, Space pilot of the year 3000". For many years he also wrote the adventures of "Roy of the Rovers" one of Britain's most enduring comic-strip characters. In the course of a long career which began at the Children's Newspaper and Children's Encyclopaedia, Pepper contributed to dozens of magazines and newpapers including Pearsons Weekly, Titbits, John

Bull, Daily Herald, Daily Express, and Daily Telegraph (he employed at least 10 pseudonyms). However, the bulk of his work was done for boys' comic papers including the Champion and when the Eagle was absorbed into the Lion in the 1960's Pepper took on the writing of Dan Dare.

Pepper retired from the comics in 1983 and devoted himself to the compilation of anthologies, publishing 20th Century Quotations, contemporary Biographical Quotations, and a Dictionary of Biographical Quotations. His last book, 20th Century Anecdotes was published as recently as December 1988, shortly after his death. (Details from the Daily Telegraph obituary 13 December 1988: permission to publish received)

Kenneth Bruce PEPPER CB (Companion of the Order of the Bath 1965). Born 11 March 1913 in Hghbury, N. London. From an early age lived at Seven Kings and later at No.9 Fairholm Road, Ilford. Educated at Ilford College and at Ilford County High School, and the London School of Economics. Joined H.M. Customs & Excise 1932 and rose to become Assistant Secretary 1949, and Commissioner from 1957 to 1973. Now living at Anglesey, Gwynedd. (Not related to the foregoing Frank Pepper)

Arthur Alan PRITCHARD CB, JP Born in Ilford 3 March 1922 he lived at No.124 The Drive from 1930 to 1941 and was a pupil at Wanstead County High School. He entered the Board of Trade in 1939, was a RAFVR Pilot during the War years from 1941 until 1952 when he joined the Admiralty of which he was appointed Assistant Secretary in 1964. Assistant under Secretary of State, Naval Personnel and Operational Requirements, M.O.D. 1972-76 and Secretary to the Admiralty Board 1978-81. Deputy Under Secretary of State Ministry of Defence. Now a management consultant and JP for the Ringwood district, he lives at Fordingbridge, Hants.

Eric ROWLAND Was in business as a Butcher with his brother Leslie for many years at No.277 High Road Ilford (opposite the Catholic church) retiring at the age of 70 in 1970. A member of the Ilford Conservative Club, he was active in the local community. Shrewd and careful investments, mainly in Property and Land, resulted in his estate being valued at £3½ million after his death in August 1988 at the age of 88.

Frank SAINSBURY Born in Canning Town June 1915 he has been resident in Ilford since 1946 and is one of the leading local historians giving many talks on the subject including Ilford's Churches. Borough Librarian, West Ham 1956-1965. Deputy Borough Librarian, Newham 1965-1976. Chairman of the County Committee for the Victorian History of the County of Essex. Author of West Ham 800 years, The Church and Parish of St. John the Evangelist, Seven Kings 1904-1929: Six men from Tolpuddle. Editor of "West Ham 1886-1986" Lives at 16 Crownfield Avenue, Newbury Park.

Sir Allen John George SHEPPARD Born in Forest Gate on 25 December 1932 he lived in Ilford (Hainault) from 1937-1963. Educated at Ilford County High School and London School of Economics (B.Sc. Econ). He was with Ford of Britain and Ford of Europe 1958-68, Rootes/Chrysler 1968-71, British

Sir Allen Sheppard

Leyland 1971-75. In October 1975 he joined Grand Metropolitan plc. as a Director and was appointed Chief Executive of Watney Mann Brewers shortly afterwards. In 1982 he became Group Managing Director of Grand Metropolitan and in 1986 Group Chief Executive, and in 1987 Chairman, from which date he has also been Vice President of the Brewers Society. His publications are "Your Business Matters" (written in 1958 when he was only 26) and various articles in professional journals. His involvements include: The C.B.I., London School of Economics (Governor), Royal College of Physicians, Imperial Cancer Research Fund, Royal Society of Arts (Fellow), British Hotels, Restaurant & Caterers Association, and Prince of Wales Youth Business Trust. Recreations: Gardening, reading, and red-setter dogs. (Knighthood announced in the Queen's Birthday honours list 16th June 1990 – Congratulations, Sir Allen!)

Emmanuel SHINWELL Baron (life Peer) created 1970, born London 18 October 1884. Was a resident at No.105 Stevens Road – on the Becontree side of Goodmayes Park – 1924-1927 and in a house (since demolished) in Goodmayes Road. Son of a Polish emigre he was Labour MP for Linlithgow 1922-24 and 1928-31, for the Seaham Division of Durham 1933-50, and Easington 1950-70. He held several important offices in Labour Governments including Minister of Fuel and Power 1945-47. Secretary of State for War 1947--50 and Minister of Defence 1950-521. Was Chairman of the Parliamentary Labour Party 1964-67. Wrote several books (including "Lead with the Left" in 1981). He died in May 1986 when over 101 years of age. I have two letters from him written when he was aged 100.

George Edward TASKER MBE, 27 January 1868-23 September 1925. By occupation a Civil Servant, he was a man of considerable literary attainments.

Author of the very detailed "Ilford Past and Present" which was the first history of events to deal specifically with the town of Ilford up to the time of its publication in 1901. In addition to contributing articles to the local Press he wrote a book on the many walks which could be taken through the countryside around Ilford in the early 1900's. Very much involved with St. Andrew's Church (including the Church Hall built in 1906) he was the first Secretary of the Parochial Church Council, Deputy Editor of the Parochial Magazine and Sidesman. A tablet to his memory is in the church. He lived at 84 Mayfair Avenue.

Miss Eleanor THOMPSON of Clements (a house after which the Clementswood Estate and Clements Road – but not St. Clements Church – were named) was one of the greatest benefactors of old Ilford. Her gifts to Ilford were, mainly, apart from the bells of St. Mary's Church, an Infants School in the High Road which with the Parish Library adjoining was built in 1846 at a cost of £2000, the Reading Room etc. (known as the Thompson Rooms) built in 1858 at a cost of £1000 and used later for general purposes, and the Drill Hall built in 1872 at a cost of £1000 and located at the rear of the Thompson Rooms. Before the Kenneth More Theatre was built in the early 1970's the Drill Hall was in use as the Little Theatre. It stood where Centreway is now. She died in 1878 and the following year the Clements Estate was sold for building purposes. The Head Post Office, Town Hall, Kenneth More Theatre and Central Library all stand on this Estate much of which was the former Clements Farm.

Leonard THOMSON 1914-1986. Was probably the most knowledgeable resident on local public transort. Author of "Ilford's Trams and Trolley Buses". He gave many talks particularly to the patients of Goodmayes Hospital. Was the first Vice-President of the Ilford & District Historical Society.

Neil Gordon THORNE OBE, TD, MP Member of Parliament (Conservative) for Ilford South since 1979 he was born 8 August 1932 and educated at the City of London School and London University, B.Sc., FRICS. Was a member of the Territorial Army from 1952 to 1982, Asst. Adjutant 58 Med. Regt. Royal Artillery B.A.O.R. 1957-59 and C.O. London University O.T.C. 1976-80. Senior Partner Hull & Co. Chartered Surveyors, 1962-76. Councillor London Borough of Redbridge, 1965-68. Alderman 1975-78. Member GLC 1967-73. Chairman of National Council for Civil Defence since 1982, and Ilford Age Concern since 1984. Publications: "Pedestrianised Streets: A Study of Europe and America 1973". NOTE: When I last met Neil Thorne at a funeral some time ago he informed me that he was still living at the same house (60 Gyllingdune Gardens, Seven Kings) in which he was born. 59 years is a long time for anyone to live in the same house and among Members of Parliament today this is probably unique.

Lance (Lancelot O.) TINGAY whose obituary was extensively published in The Daily Telegraph of 12 March 1990 was born on 14th July 1915 and

In the General Election held on April 9th 1992 Neil Thorne lost his seat by 402 vote to Labour's Mike Gapes.

6th June '92. Neil Thorne receives a Knighthood in the Dissolution Honours List published today.

Neil Thorne OBE, TD, MP

educated at Clark's College, Ilford, which was situated in Cranbrook Road near Coventry Road. He was Lawn Tennis Correspondent of The Daily Telegraph for nearly 30 years and was one of the games foremost historians. He was also a considerable authority on Anthony Trollope (1815-82) one of the most prolific of English novelists. Lance Tingay wrote several authoritative books on tennis, including "100 Years of Wimbledon", "The Official History of the Championships", "A History of Lawn Tennis in Pictures", and "The Guiness Book of Lawn Tennis Records". Tingay also published an anthology of his beloved Trollope as well as a limited edition of a short story by the great novelist.

The son of a businessman in the leather trade, he began his journalistic career with Exchange Telegraph the newsagency and served in the Second World War in the R.A.F. Afterwards he wrote on a freelance basis for the Evening Standard and other publications before joining the Telegraph in 1952. He retired in 1981 after never having missed a day of the championships during 43 years of reporting at Wimbledon. Tingay was elected a full member of the All England Lawn Tennis and Croquet Club, of the International Club of France and the International Lawn Club of Great Britain. He also had the signal distinction of being elected to the International Tennis Hall of Fame at Newport Rhodes Island, the highest honour in the American game previously bestowed on only six Britons and never before to a non-player.

Edward TUCK 1819-1907 A teacher in Ilford for 57 years and Headmaster for 48 years of the Boys' National School which stood until 1964 in the High Road near St. Mary's Church. A great humanitarian and benefactor, local historian and geologist he wrote "A Sketch of Ancient Barking, its Abbey and Ilford".

The Revd. Charles H. VINE BA 1865-1930. Minister of the High Road

Congregational Church from 1896 to 1930, he had great influence locally, especially in the early part of the 1900's when the church became one of the strongest in Essex. The Ilford Men's Meetings, with their Orchestra, held at the church, were very popular and there was a membership of 2000 at one time. The organisation undertook a great deal of social work etc. for its members. The church later became known as the Vine Memorial Church. Although this church with its clock tower and steeple which was a prominent feature in the High Road for many years has since been demolished the Revd. Vinc's name has been perpetuated in the new church known as the Vine United Reformed Church in nearby Riches Road.

Mrs. Lucy Bethia WALFORD 1845-1915. Born in Scotland Mrs. Walford was author of over twenty popular novels and numerous short stories which were enjoyed by Queen Victoria, to whom she was presented. Her husband Mr. A.S. Walford (whose grandfather was High Sheriff of Essex in the early 1800's) was a Magistrate at Stratford for ten years. Mr. and Mrs. Walford were the last residents of Cranbrook Hall where Mrs. Walford wrote several of her books and also many articles for magazines, and which they vacated in 1899 when Mr. W.P. Griggs had already commenced the building of houses on the Cranbrook Park Estate.

Sir Frederic WISE DL, JP, MP 1871-1928 Member of Parliament for Ilford from 1920 (following the death of Sir Peter Griggs) until 1928. Created Knight in 1924, he was Charter Mayor when Ilford became a Borough in 1926. See also Ilford in Canada.

Gerald (Gerry) WITHERICK DFM, DFC Born in Ilford in 1915 (he lived at 243 Eastern Avenue) he joined the Royal Air Force in 1936 on a nine-year engagement. A leading aircraftsman with No.47 Squadron in Khartoum when war broke out in 1939 he volunteered as an air-gunner and in 1940 was in operations against the Italians in Eritrea. After taking part in further operations in North Africa he returned to England and took part in numerous attacks on Germany including "Bomber" Harris' celebrated 1000 bomber raids, and in antisubmarine operations with Coastal Command. In addition to his surviving a bailing out, and a runway collision, and a crash landing in Sweden when his plane was shot down during an attack on the German battleship "Tirpitz" he miraculously survived a remarkable 116 sorties (4 operational tours) during the 1939-45 War. After demobilisation he became a publican in Bermondsey, Slough and Burnham, Bucks before retiring to Rustington in Sussex in 1980. He died October 1988, aged 72. (Details from Daily Telegraph Obituary 28 October 88. Permission to publish received)

Peter J. WRIGHT Formerly Secretary and now Chairman of the Ilford & District Historical Society and an active member thereof giving many talks on local history to various Clubs and Organisations. Mr. Wright has recently retired after 40 years in the local public libraries service where he was for many years a most helpful and dedicated Central Reference librarian. Lives at 174 Aldborough Road South, Seven Kings.

(*left*) Sir Frederic Wise, DL, JP, MP Member of Parliament for Ilford 1920–1927. Charter Mayor of the Borough, 1926.
(*right*) Alderman Major A. Young, TD.

This plaque in the Town Hall (which is now registered as a listed building) marks its opening on 5 December 1901.

Major Alexander YOUNG OBE, TD, JP 1879-1960. Elected to Ilford Urban District Council in 1920 he was its last Chairman in 1926. An Ilford Borough Councillor from 1926 to 1930 he was Ilford's sixth Mayor in 1931/32. He lived at No.162 (now No.355) Cranbrook Road.

*　*　*

Well-known sportsmen who have resided in or have been associated with Ilford include (in alphabetical order) in addition to those already mentioned, Nigel Benn, Trevor Brooking, Henry Dodkins, Mark Falco, Graham Gooch, John Lever, John Lyall, Charlie Magri, Bobby Moore OBE and Ian Thompson.

Nigel Benn, who was born in Ilford, was British Middleweight and Commonwealth boxing Champion. On 29th April 1990 he won a world middleweight boxing title at Atlantic City, USA.

Trevor Brooking, ex-West Ham FC and now football commentator was a pupil at Ilford County High School and at one time lived in Marlands Road.

Henry Dodkins was one of the best Amateur footballers in the country for several years and captained not only Ilford FC but England's Amateur XI.

Mark Falco, another Footballer formerly with Tottenham Hotspurs and now with Queens Park Rangers has lived in Clayhall.

Graham Gooch played for Ilford Cricket Club before going on to play for Essex and England as he is still doing – and as captain.

John Lever, another Essex and former England Cricketer also played for Ilford CC. He lives in Ilford and attended Highland and Dane Schools. After 22 years in first-class cricket John Lever – regarded as the model professional – is now coaching at Bancroft's School.

John Lyall, like Trevor Brooking, was a pupil at Ilford County High School and played for West Ham until his playing career was cut short by injury. He was Manager of West Ham United Football Club for over 14 years.

Charlie Magri, former World Flyweight Boxing Champion, lives in Seven Kings. — *Died 24 Feb '93*

Bobby Moore, OBE (ex-West Ham United and Fulham) at one time lived in Glenwood Gardens, Ilford. He played for England 108 times (a record for an England player), 90 as captain. He also captained England Youth at 17 years of age (18 caps), and England U23's (8 caps). Bobby Moore was captain of the England team which won the World Cup in 1966. Two other West Ham players, Geoff Hirst and Martin Peters, were also in the team.

Ian Thompson who played for Ilford Cricket Club from 1946 to 1951 went on to play for Sussex and for the MCC in 1964/65.

Howard Baker, a former well-known band leader also lived in Glenwood Gardens as did Basil Amps.

In addition to the men and women listed it is, of course, appreciated that there are many others who could be included and tribute is paid to them, especially those who through public service, in teaching, in the voluntary services, in the armed or civilian services, or in some other way, have made a valuable contribution to our society.

Members of Parliament representing Ilford during this Century

1900-1906	Mr H Sinclair	Conservative
1906-1918	Mr J H (later Sir John) Bethell	Liberal

During the above years Ilford was part of the Southern Parliamentary Division of the County of Essex

1918-1920	Sir Peter Griggs (died 1920)	Conservative

Shortly before the General Election of December 1918 Ilford was made a separate Parliamentary Constituency. It was in that Election that women (but only those of the age of 30 or over) were eligible to vote for the first time. Just a few years later, however, after the passing of the Equal Franchise Bill on March 29, 1928, all women of the age of 21 or over were given the vote on the same terms as men (and rightly so!). Thus the Suffragettes' campaign finally came to a successful conclusion.

1920-1928	Mr F (later Sir Frederic) Wise (died 1928)	Unionist
1928-1937	Major Sir George Hamilton	Conservative
1937-1945	Mr Geoffrey Hutchinson	Conservative

After the end of the second World War Ilford was divided into two separate Parliamentary Constituencies, Ilford North and Ilford South.

ILFORD NORTH

1945-1950	Mrs Mabel Ridealgh	Labour
1950-1954	Mr Geoffrey Hutchinson	Conservative
1954-1974	Mr T L (Tom) Iremonger	Conservative
1974-1978	Mrs Millie Miller	Labour
1978-	Mr Vivian Bendall	Conservative

In 1974 Ilford North's Clayhall Ward was transferred to the Wanstead &

Woodford Parliamentary constituency (MP Mr Patrick Jenkin until June 1987 since when it has been Mr James Arbuthnot).

ILFORD SOUTH

1945-1950	Mr James Ranger	Labour
1950-1966	Mr A E (Ted) Cooper	Conservative
1966-1970	Mr Arnold J Shaw	Labour
1970-1974	Mr A E (Ted) Cooper	Conservative
1974-1979	Mr Arnold J Shaw	Labour
1979-1992	Mr Neil Thorne	Conservative
1992-	Mr. Mike Gapes	Labour

Chairmen of the Ilford Urban District Council

(from the time Ilford was constituted an Urban District Council pursuant to the provisions of The Local Government Act, 1894)

First meeting 1st January 1895

1895 (Jan to Apr)	Mr Edmund John BEAL
1895-6-7	Mr Edmund John BEAL
1897-8	Mr Edmund John BEAL
1898-9-1900	Mr William Walter GILSON
1900-1	Mr Henry WEEDEN
1901-2	Mr Benjamin BAILEY
1902-3	Mr George William Marshall GOTT
1903-4	Mr John Lawrence BURLEIGH
1904-5	Mr Robert STROUD
1905-6	Mr William Peter GRIGGS
1906-7	Mr John Adams Guy BODGER
1907-8	Mr Thomas PHILPOT
1908-9	Mr James Henry SOUSTER
1909-10	Mr Horace Moore THORNTON
1910-11	Mr George William DAVIS
1911-12	Mr William Joseph HAMMOND
1912-13	Mr Frederick Hopper DANE
1913-14	Mr William James Temple CULLIS
1914-15	Mr William James Oliver SHEAT
1915-16	Mr George GUNARY
1916-17	Mr George CUSHING
1917-18	Mr Frank Douglas SMITH
1918-19	Mr Walter Horace STEVENS
1919-20	Mr George Robert DAVEY
1920-21	Mr Herbert George ODELL
1921-22	Mr Owen WATERS
1922-23	Mr Bertram Sidney John PITT
1923-24	Mr George LEE
1924-25	Mr James William KING
1925-26	Revd. Herbert DUNNICO
1926 (Apr to Oct)	Major Alexander YOUNG

Mayors of the Borough of Ilford

(following the granting of The Royal Charter of Incorporation of the Borough of Ilford under date the 24th August 1926)
Charter Day 21st October 1926. Charter Mayor: Sir Frederic WISE DL, JP, MP

1926-27	Alderman Frederick Hopper DANE MBE, JP, CA (ECC)
1927-28	Alderman William James Oliver SHEAT OBE, JP, CC
1928-29	Alderman George GUNARY JP
1929-30	Alderman Frank Douglas SMITH JP, CA (ECC)
1930-31	Alderman Herbert George ODELL JP
1931-32	Councillor Major Alexander M YOUNG TD, JP
1932-33	Alderman Charles William CLARK JP
1933-34	Alderman Bertram Sidney John PITT JP
1934-35	Alderman Albert Philip GRIGGS JP, (ECC)
1935-36	Alderman James Henry SHIPMAN JP, (ECC)
1936-37	Alderman Henry BILLINGTON JP
1937-38	Councillor John ELBORNE MA, JP
1938-39	Councillor Claude Augustus FARMAN JP
1939-40	Alderman Claude Augustus FARMAN JP
1940-41	Alderman Claude Augustus FARMAN JP
1941-42	Councillor Thomas BRAITHWAITE JP
1942-43	Alderman George John WETTON JP
1943-44	Alderman Russell Stearn DANIELS JP
1944-45	Councillor Mrs B A L A HARDING JP
1945-46	Alderman William Benjamin EKE JP
1946-47	Alderman William Allen Vernon BRYAN JP
1947-49	Alderman Gilbert COLVIN JP, FCIS
1949-50	Alderman Sidney Charles Victor WOODS JP
1950-51	Alderman John BARKER JP
1951-52	Alderman Percy Victor FANING JP, (ECC)
1952-53	Alderman Harold Douglas COWAN JP, FA, CCA, FCCS
1953-54	Alderman Cyril Irving GIBSON JP
1954-55	Alderman Cecil Aubrey HEADLEY JP
1955-56	Alderman Frederick Thomas PEARSON JP
1956-57	Alderman Miss Anne Sylvia TERRY JP
1957-58	Councillor Albert Reginald SHERRELL JP, CA, (ECC)
1958-59	Councillor Frank Robert MASTERS JP
1959-60	Councillor Harold Goldstone ROOT JP

1960-61	Councillor Leslie Victor DREW JP
1961-62	Councillor Owen Francis WATERS JP
1962-63	Councillor Edgar Frank HARRIS JP
1963-64	Councillor Francis Herbert JAMES JP
1964-65	Alderman Mrs Lillian FALLAIZE JP

From 1965 as a result of the re-organisation of London Government in 1964, by which the Borough of Ilford was merged with the adjoining Borough of Wanstead and Woodford, Ilford became part of the newly-named London Borough of Redbridge.

This name was chosen because the original red brick and stone bridge (built in the year 1650) over the River Roding, where Eastern Avenue is now, connected the two districts.

The Coat of Arms of the London Borough of Redbridge dating from 1965 following the merger of the Borough of Ilford and the Borough of Wanstead and Woodford.

Similar to the Coat of Arms of the former Borough of Ilford it incorporates features pertinent to the former Borough of Wanstead and Woodford. These are (1) the cross (supported by the buck) symbolizing the fact that the Manors of Wanstead and Woodford were both originally held by the Abbeys of Westminster and Waltham Holy Cross. (2) In the Shield are three martlets from the Arms of Edward the Confessor and four leopard faces from the Arms ascribed to King Harold. These Sovereigns gave the Manors of Wanstead and Woodford respectively to the Abbeys mentioned. (3) The 12 black symbols – the hurst of trees – represent the oaks of Epping Forest. (4) At the base of the Shield the design now symbolizes both the River Roding and the one-time wells of Woodford.

Mayors of the London Borough of Redbridge

1965-66	Councillor Sydney LOVELESS
1966-67	Councillor H R B ALY
1967-68	Alderman Lionel GOOCH
1968-69	Alderman Sydney G GLEED
1969-70	Councillor I B NATZLER
1970-71	Councillor A J ESCOTT
1971-72	Councillor Charles LOVELESS
1972-73	Councillor Leslie BRIDGEMAN
1973-74	Councillor Mrs Grace M CHAMBERLIN JP
1974-75	Councillor John TELFORD
1975-76	Councillor T Frank COBB
1976-77	Councillor Fred C MOUNTIER
1977-78	Councillor A N BARKER
1978-79	Councillor Bertram HAMILTON
1979-80	Councillor John TELFORD
1980-81	Councillor Miss Joyce M CLARK
1981-82	Councillor Roy C BRIAN
1982-83	Councillor Miss Nancy THURGOOD
1983-84	Councillor Stephen CURTIS
1984-85	Councillor John J M SMITH
1985-86	Councillor Roland E SMITH
1986-87	Councillor Roy W BRUNNEN
1987-88	Councillor Graham F BORRET
1988-89	Councillor Keith AXON
1989-90	Councillor Geoffrey BREWER TD
1990-91	Councillor Mrs Julia ROBERTS
1991-92	Councillor Brian HILL

Councillors representing the Ilford Wards (15 in all)

(following the Elections to Redbridge Borough Council held on 3 May 1990)

WARD	COUNCILLOR	
ALDBOROUGH	Graham Borrot	C
	David Jones	C
	Ernest Watts	C
BARKINGSIDE	Keith Axon	C
	Roy Brunnen	C
	Frank Cobb	C
CHADWELL	Christopher Annal	C
	Robert Cole	C
	Laurence Davis	C
CLAYHALL	Ronald Barden	C
	John Lovell	C
	Alan Weinberg	C
CLEMENTS WOOD	John Hogben	L
	Dr. Faiz Noor	L
	Jackie Woodside	L
CRANBROOK	Charles Elliman	C
	~~Arnold Kinzley~~ *Died 18 March '93*	C
	Asaf Mirza	C
FAIRLOP	Albert Finch	C
	Michael Higgins	C
	Mrs Joyce Ryan	C
FULWELL	Anthony Bramwell	C
	Dennis Candy	C
	Malcolm Stilwell	C
GOODMAYES	John Fairley-Churchill	L
	Mike Fitzmaurice	L
	Paul Jeater	L
HAINAULT	Alan Hughes	L
	Peter McEwan	L
	Miss Linda Perham	L

LOXFORD	Jeffery Edelman	L
	Mohammed Javed	L
	Sid Middleburgh	L
MAYFIELD	Miss Constance Bamford	C
	Trevor Grant	C
	Roland Hill	C
NEWBURY	Harold Moth	C
	Glenn Corfield	C
	John Smith	C
SEVEN KINGS	Provat Das Gupta	L
	Miss Liz Pearce	L
	Resham Mann	L
VALENTINES	Tejinder Ajiz	L
	John Brindley	L
	Andrew Whyte	L

C = Conservative   L = Labour

Total: 45 Councillors (27 Conservatives, 18 Labour). Including the 6 Wards in Wanstead & Woodford represented by 15 Conservative and 3 Liberal Democrat Councillors, the composition of the present Redbridge Council is 42 Conservative, 18 Labour and 3 Liberal Democrat, a total of 63 Councillors.

180

Local Governmental Directorate: Principal Officials

TOWN HALL, ILFORD IG1 1DD

Chief Executive:	G.U. Price
Public Relations Officer:	~~Brian Stone~~ Maxine Norman
Director of Technical Services:	T.K. Jagger, MA
Borough Engineer:	K.W.E. Liddell, C Eng
Borough Recreation Officer:	M.W. Orsbourn, MA
Director of Administration and Legal Services:	G.R. Bassett, LLB (Hons)
Director of Land Management:	W.T. Higham, BA
Borough Planning Officer:	P.W. Clark, MA
Borough Commercial Liaison Officer:	M. Stansbury, MA

17/23 CLEMENTS ROAD, ILFORD IG1 1BL

Director of Personal Services:	J.W. Belcher, BA (Hons)
Environmental Health Serviwes:	J.R. Baxter

22/26 CLEMENTS ROAD, ILFORD IG1 1BD

Director of Finance and Deputy Chief Executive:	M.R. Tilley
Chief Finance Officer:	M. Jennings

LYNTON HOUSE, 255/259 HIGH ROAD, ILFORD IG1 1NN

Borough Personnel Officer:	P.J. Sapwell, BA (Hons)
Director of Educational Services:	K.G.M. Ratcliffe, MA
Chief Inspector of Schools:	J.R. ~~Baxter~~ Gibson, MA
Borough Land Officer:	R.S. Gregory

CENTRAL LIBRARY, CLEMENTS ROAD, ILFORD IG1 1EA

Borough Librarian: N. Maxwell

LEY STREET DEPOT, LEY STREET, ILFORD IG2 7QZ

Borough Works Officer: R.B. Winter

VALENTINES MANSION, EMERSON ROAD, ILFORD IG1 4XD

Housing Services: N. Rudd

QUEEN VICTORIA HOUSE, 794 CRANBROOK ROAD, BARKING-SIDE IG6 1JS

Superintendent Registrar of Births,
Deaths and Marriages: N.D. Stephens
Road Safety Officer: D. Harrington

WOODBINE PLACE, WANSTEAD E11 2RH

Trading Standards Services: J. Frawley

Justices of the Peace in the Ilford area

Mrs V D Bhatia	6 Redcliffe Gardens, Ilford IG1 3HQ
Mr C J Bradley	58 Sunnymede Drive, Barkingside IG6 1LD
Mr L G Bridgeman	7 South Park Road, Ilford IG1 1SZ
Mrs J L Burt	66 Campbell Avenue, Ilford IG6 1EB
Mrs C A Carter	92 Ashburton Avenue, Seven Kings IG3 9EP
Mrs S T Cave	15 Hatley Avenue, Barkingside IG6 1EH
Mr A S J Cross	21 Parkway, Seven Kings IG3 9HS
Mrs P M Dedman	17 Mayfair Avenue, Ilford IG1 3DJ
Mr L Grant	23 Wanstead Lane, Cranbrook, Ilford IG1 3SB
Mr R C Jeffries	37 Spearpoint Gardens, Newbury Park IG2 7SX
Mr D W Leggette	6 Merrivale Avenue, Redbridge, Ilford IG4 5PQ
Mrs J A Maddell	120 Felbrigge Road, Goodmayes IG3 9XJ
Mrs A H Martin	89 Beehive Lane, Gants Hill, Ilford IG1 3RL
Mrs M J Melnick	813 Eastern Avenue, Newbury Park IG2 7RY
Mr J P O'Halloran	599 Green Lane, Goodmayes IG3 9RN
Mr J E Parry	20 Mighell Avenue, Redbridge, Ilford IG4 5JW
Mr R Pizzala	27 Tresco Gardens, Seven Kings IG3 9NH
Mr S C Powell	18 Sussex Close, Redbridge, Ilford IG4 5DP
Dr J J Ridealgh	2 Eastwood Road, Goodmayes IG3 8XB
Mr L E Rogers	113 Balfour Road, Ilford IG1 4HS
Mr J C N Sharma	26 Glebelands Avenue, Newbury Park IG2 7DM
Mr A G Singer	109 Wensleydale Avenue, Clayhall IG5 0ND
Mrs S E Snushall	112 Chester Road, Seven Kings IG3 8PX
Mr M A Stewart	35 Bawdsey Avenue, Newbury Park IG2 7TW
Mrs N E Willis	2 Langham Drive, Chadwell Heath RM6 4TD

Mr C A Wilson	160 Havering Gardens, Chadwell Heath RM6 5AL
Mrs J E Wright	1 Beechwood Gardens, Clayhall IG5 OAE
Mr F R Jones	17 Fowey Avenue, Redbridge IG4 5JT
Mr G W King	85 Christie Gardens, Chadwell Heath RM6 4SD
Mrs J A Liddle	25 Mornington Avenue, Cranbrook IG1 3QT
Capt D E Myers MBE	62 Wanstead Lane, Ilford IG1 3SE
Mrs M Samuels	14 Rochester Gardens, Ilford IG1 3LT
Mrs P White	97 Beehive Lane, Ilford IG1 3RN

Clerk to the Justices Mr M J Faraway	Court House, 850 Cranbrook Road, Barkingside IG6 1HW

An Old Ilfordian's Recollections

I Remember, I Remember, the House where I was Born
the Little Window where the Sun came Peeping in at Dawn
So wrote Thomas Hood, the English Poet, who lived from 1799 to 1845. In the same vein here are some of my early recollections:

I remember, I remember, the house where I was born; it was in Perth Road, Ilford behind which then stood a field of golden corn.

I remember well that house where, in June 1914, I first saw the light of day and the fields nearby in which my sister and brothers and I often used to play.

I remember the soldiers and the large round balloon and the Army tents in the days of the German Zeppelin raids which brought to civilians much fear and suspense.

I remember sitting on the front window sill with a clay pipe and a bowl of soapy water blowing bubbles into the sky – they were critical days for Britain then but I was too young to know the reason why.

I remember the hissing geese at nearby Stringer's Middlefield Farm; being three or four or five years old then I thought they would do me harm.

I remember my father's allotment near where now stands the Cinema at Gants Hill and I remember the large gravel pit where the open-air swimming pool is now – yes, I remember it still.

I remember when milk was brought round on a hand-cart with a large gleaming brass churn and the milkman at the doorstep filling each housewife's jug in turn.

I remember the muffin man with a tray on his head and in his hand a bell, and when winkles were eaten for Sunday tea – yes, I remember it well.

I remember the wooden and iron hoops and the spinning tops we had, and every girl her skipping rope; and marbles, and fivestones, and conkers, and cigarette cards – to amass a large quantity of these was nearly every boy's hope.

I can remember a very early Charabanc outing to Southend with my Mother one sunny day in September – it broke down on the way back leaving us stranded on a lonely road in the dark; how we eventually got home I cannot remember.

I can remember my father playing in Valentines Park with the Ilford Civic Band and the many deck-chairs that were filled on a Bank Holiday around the iron band-stand. I remember how late shops stayed open especially on a Saturday night and I remember the flags we put out on Empire Day: it was a colourful sight. Sadly, I can remember seeing some boys without shoes and stockings on their feet picking up fruit which had fallen off stalls: to them it was no doubt a treat.

I remember, also, the singers begging for money in the street, and some disabled men from the First World War trying, by selling matches, to make ends meet.

I remember, too, when people's general health was not as good as it is today, when ailments, particularly in children, were more prevalent in nearly every way; when defects in eyes, lips, teeth and skin were commonplace and many a child was thin in limb and pale of face.

I remember seeing outside a house the roadway covered with straw; the occupant was ill I was told and it was to reduce the noise of carts passing the door.

I remember when funeral hearses were drawn by teams of magnificent black horses, immaculately groomed, their heads high plumed; the mourners (some veiled but all dressed in deepest black) following in many a horse-drawn black coach; the cortege preceded for the entire journey by the funeral conductor on foot, to warn all ahead of its approach.

I remember the horse and black cab and the driver that regularly stood outside Ilford Railway Station: I remember the Clock Tower in the Broadway, and the Sundays when nearly every Church had a large congregation.

I remember when a friendly bobby on his regular beat was a familiar sight in every street and when postmen were uniformly and smartly dressed and Sunday was basically a day of rest.

I remember the days before Women had the Vote and then only (until 1929) for those aged 30 and over: and I remember the many independent British car manufacturing firms there were, with names such as A.C. Alvis, Armstrong-Siddeley, Bean, B.S.A., Clyno, Crossley, Hillman, Humber, Invicta, Jowett, Lagonda, Lanchester, Lea Francis, Riley, Singer, Standard, Sunbeam, Swift, Talbot, Triumph and Wolseley, as well as Austin, Bentley, Daimler, Jaguar, Morgan, Morris, Rolls Royce, Vauxhall, and Rover.

I remember when British motor-cycles were the best in the world, with names such as A.J.S., B.S.A., Brough, Douglas, Excelsior, Matchless, Norton, Sunbeam, Triumph, Velocette, Vincent and Royal Enfield. Now with the exception of Norton and Triumph their fate has been sealed.

I remember when British-manufactured locomotives were our pride and joy, delighting the eye of many a man and boy: exported all over the world – to Africa, South America, Australia, India – China too, just as our magnificent Ships and our machinery were unsurpassed too.

I remember the first surfacing of Cranbrook Road with hot Tarmacadam – the Italian workmen on their knees, and I remember seeing by the Wash (where the Cran brook once flowed across the road) the felling of some of Ilford's finest trees.

I remember when in 1922 I lived in Belgrave Road where just a few hundred yards away Mr Percy Thompson lost his life, for I remember seeing the detectives lifting the roadside gratings next morning in their search for the murderer's knife. I remember the so-called Cranbrook Castle wherein I played one day before it was demolished in 1923, the ground having been sold to the P.L.A.

I remember also in 1923 – June 12th was the actual date – seeing King George V visiting Ilford on his way to see the new Becontree Housing Estate: with other school-children I stood in the High Road near the junction with Green Lane. I remember, too, the very first Christmas broadcast he made later in his reign.

I remember the building of that fine Cinema known as the Ilford Super – alas, like the Ilford Hippodrome sadly destroyed in the last war – and I remember the thick yellow fogs we had – the notorious "Pea-Souper". Thank Goodness we see them no more.

I remember witnessing the big fire which destroyed Harrison Gibson's first Furniture Store: I stayed away from school that morning – it was July 22nd 1924. (By a coincidence I witnessed also the Harrison Gibson fire in 1959, March 16, after the news had been given out by the BBC on the Television screen).

I remember when school hours were longer and school holidays decidedly fewer and when for indiscipline the cane was considered the cure.

I remember the musical evenings we spent around the Piano with a violinist and other accompanist, and many a vocalist, and I remember the playing by men and women of that then popular card-game, Whist.

I remember the time long before people had Television, and Radio – or Wireless as it was called at first – and when on a hot day plain water was drunk from a public drinking fountain to quench many a child's thirst.

I remember the time long before Penicillin was discovered and when brown, stinging Iodine was used for treating cuts and grazes, and I remember when fields and some lawns were covered with those flowers that are not so common now, namely Buttercups and Daisies.

I remember too the different types of butterflies we saw – unlike today when most are white – and I remember when rabbits and hares and red poll cattle (and not Friesians) in fields and meadows were a common sight.

I remember when food had more taste, and there was less waste, before the days of so many shop-bought ready-made meals, and "away-taking", when there was appetizing home-baking and "in the home making" of meat stews with dumplings, rabbit pie, toast by the fire with dripping (simply ripping!), plum duff, and roly-poly, enjoyed by all whether high or lowly.

I remember when very few people had in their homes a Telephone and when it was quite exceptional for someone to own another then-regarded wonderful invention a Gramophone.

I also remember when nearly every house was plagued by house flies and many that had mice and I remember seeing in some houses other pests too, though to remember them is not very nice.

I remember visiting the British Empire Exhibition at Wembley which opened in 1924 – the vast Stadium there staging the first sporting spectacular the year before. I remember, of course, Ilford's own Trams and Trolley buses about which Len Thomson has written a book, involving Research at which he must have taken an exceedingly close look. Dear old Len and I were classmates at Christchurch Road School around 1925. Now that Len has gone there aren't many of us of that class still alive.

I remember the years I spent as a 4th Ilford cub and scout, for some of the people I knew then were the finest without any doubt. Our meetings at the Wycliffe Church, our Pipe Band, and the hut we used at Clayhall Farm are among the things I most remember, as well as the fires around which we sang at Camps we attended from April through to mid-September.

I remember (whilst at a Scout camp) at Southampton in August 1924 seeing the then 17-years old Cunard liner "Mauretania" which had just crossed the Atlantic in a record time of just over five days: Now the journey by air is accomplished in less than five hours in planes operated by the World airlines such as British Airways.

I remember the General Strike – when few people had cars – in 1926, and those who wanted to get to London to work were in a bit of a fix.

I remember seeing on 21st October 1926, the then Duke and Duchess of York being driven down Cranbrook Road in an open car – I had a very close view: they had brought the new Borough's Charter to Ilford, having just travelled along the first section of the new Eastern Avenue.

I remember when a man earning £6 a week was somebody of importance in the City, and I remember when most homes and street-lamps in Ilford were lit by gas and not by electricity.

I also remember when many homes in rural areas were lit by candles and by oil or acetylene lamps, long before the unit of electrical current – the Ampère – was known by everyone as amps.

I remember when some houses did not even have a bathroom and when outside the house was the usual location of the "smallest room".

I remember when a shower-bath in one's home was almost unknown and when it was to the pawnbroker many people went when in need of a loan.

I remember when it was also almost unknown to have close-fitted (wall to wall) carpeting in one's home: floors then being usually stained bare boards with a rug or two, or perhaps a carpet square, or more often covered with a material seldom seen today called Linoleum.

I remember when a newly-built house could be purchased with a deposit of £25 including road and legal charges, and I remember when the River Roding up to Ilford Bridge was used by small trading ships and numerous large barges.

I remember when decorators made their own paint and walked to their place of work pushing a hand-cart (their equipment their own and not rented); the men must have been strong because their wooden ladders were long – today's lightweight extending ladders and scaffold towers not having then been invented.

I remember the horse-drawn carts which delivered to fishmongers large blocks of ice; and I remember the ice-cream vendors with their tricycles on which were the words "Stop me and buy one". I remember when in the 1920's an old ha'penny would buy a bread-roll or some broken biscuits, or a sticky current bun, which whenever a child was hungry – as children often were – was always welcome and nice.

I remember it was then that a piece of fried fish could be bought for tuppence (2d) and with a penny-worth of chips and a ha'penny roll one had a satisfying meal – more than 60 years on it now seems unreal.

A 2lb loaf of bread then was four pence, and tuppence ha'penny a pint of milk would buy, while freshly grown English fruit and vegetables were plentiful and cheap and the quality high.

A card could be posted for a ha'penny, a letter for a penny (1d), the same amount would buy a daily newspaper of which there were many.

If one had a car or motorbike a gallon of petrol could be bought for just over a shilling, with pumps always attended – no self-service filling!

For sixpence the variety of goods sold in Woolworths was truly extensive and compared with today's prices (which include V.A.T.) were most inexpensive.

In a waitress-service Lyons tea shop tuppence (2d) – which is less than 1p – would buy a cup of tea: now in the local self-service McDonald's a cup of tea I see is 43p.

I remember when ambulances for the general public were very few, and residential homes for the elderly too; and when, as a boy, in exchange for paper, rags, bottles and bones, merchants would give me a welcome penny or two.

I remember when it was unusual to see – apart from in cities – a building more than three or four storeys high and I remember when on a Sunday evening people would stand at certain places just to see the relatively few cars go by.

I remember the old magic lantern shows, the silent films, and later the widely-acclaimed first Talkies.

I remember the strict film censorship then – now that producers have so much license almost anything goes.

I remember when men's clothes were not as casual as they often are today, informal clothes being then restricted to leisure and play; when shoes were polished and trousers pressed (and under the shirt a sensible vest) and a 2-piece or 3-piece suit was universally worn and never soiled trainers and blousons and purposely-faded denim jeans – sometimes deliberately torn!

I remember when some men at weekends wore plus 4's and some with their business and more formal suits wore spats, and I remember the time long before Nylon stockings were invented and when most of our ladies, as did nearly all men, wore hats.

I remember the Terrace by Ilford Station known as Sundown Place where lived workers of the adjoining Paper Mill: its products, like Howards' Chemicals and Ilford Photographics brought to the town some fame. Alas they are all gone now – all that remains is the ILFORD name.

I remember the strong independent nature and self-reliance people had before the days of our present Welfare State and the helpfulness and kindness that existed between neighbours then is something I highly rate.

I remember when the baker's roundsman with fresh, appetising, crusty bread would call on us each day, the bread having been made on the baker's own premises early that morning in the good old-fashioned way.

I remember when I was a boy, singing in Westminster Abbey (being then in the Westminster Abbey Special Choir): our practices held in St. Margarets, facing Parliament Square.

I remember the winter evenings spent at home reading, sitting in a chair by the side of a cheerfully warming, flickering, flaming bright coal or log-burning open fire.

I remember that when I was at school the leaving age was 14 though, of course, even younger than that at one time it had been, and I remember that the opportunity then of a University education was infinitely less than it is today, throughout the nation.

I remember the time before the 5-day working week and when, unlike today there was virtually no assistance when a job one did seek.

I remember when there was not a single Traffic Light, nor a Belisha Beacon or Zebra crossing on any road and the days before Driving and M.O.T. Tests and the introduction of the official Highway Code. I remember how extremely crowded the steam trains were in the morning – no Underground then – going up to work in Town: they were almost as bad coming home in the evenings; it almost got me down.

I remember the many individually-owned ("pirate") motor buses operating before the formation of the London General Omnibus Company which later became the London Passenger Transport Board, and I remember the construction – the piling for which, in a minor way, I was associated – in 1929 to 1931 of the extensive Motor Works at Dagenham (at which over the years many Ilford residents have been employed) a truly remarkable achievement envisaged by the great Henry Ford.

I remember the previous London Bridge across which for several years I walked almost every working day; (opened in 1831 it was demolished around 1971 and is now in Arizona, USA).

I remember the great activity then along the Thames nearby, with ships unloading, and the Billingsgate and Borough Markets with the many porters scurrying, hurrying, and carrying boxes of very wet fish seemingly as heavy as lead, or a stack of round wicker baskets containing fruit or vegetables balanced precariously upon the head. I remember they started work very early in the morning at a time when most people were still in bed.

I remember, in April 1929, going with my father to Highbury and seeing Ilford win the Amateur Cup; it was on his 50th birthday and the win really cheered us both up.

I remember when in 1930 the R101 Airship crashed in flames over France for the newspaper boy coming round that Sunday morning, shouting the news, temporarily stunned us into a trance.

I remember taking part in the "Pageant of Essex" held in Valentines Park in aid of King George Hospital in July 1932: lasting more than a week it was a financial success through and through. In the "Siege of Colchester" episode I was a Royalist soldier and had to feign being killed. I remember I lay for some considerable time on that Melbourne "battle field".

I remember the cycle rides at weekends in the 1930's well into Essex and Hertfordshire and Kent, for I still remember the sweet smell of wood-smoke from country cottages wafting into the air as along I went.

Of course motor vehicles on the roads then were far, far fewer and consequently the country air was so much purer.

I remember when in public places and in the streets there was far less litter – not almost everything, as it is today, being packaged or wrapped – and I remember when nearly all local Authorities' rates or charges were levied within reason, obviating the necessity for any to be "capped".

I remember the many high class shops in Ilford between World War II and World War I; their excellent merchandise and their service to customers being second to none.

I remember not only the larger stores of Harrison Gibson, Moultons, Bodgers, Wests, Fairheads, and C.W. Burnes, but the many shops owned by other local residents such as Mr Green the Grocer, Mr Prentis (Fruiter and Greengrocer), Mr Bott's Ajax Shop, Miss Braund's Le Bon Bon, and Nuttall's, Russell Daniels, and Stearns.

I remember too, Ben Barnes (Ironmongery), Gibson, and Feitelson (Jewellery), Watson Hornby, Adlington the Butcher, and Henderson the Baker, but I cannot recall that in Ilford we ever had that legendary tradesman the Candlestick Maker!

I remember Ashley Russell's (Silks), Jessie Norton (Hats), Owen Clark's, Rugg's Library, Knight Purser, Dunn's, the Fifty Shilling Tailors, Burtons, Woolworth's, Boots, and Photographers Dora Head and Wrights, the Lyons teashops, the A.B.C., Williamson's, Jerrard's, Greenwoods (for leather goods), and for draperies Whites.

There were also Peskett's Dairy, the Maypole, Home & Colonial, Cullen's, U.K. Tea Company, Pearks, Pardey & Johnson, Mac Fisheries, Norman Stanley (radios), Victor Fox (furs), and for cars F.G. Smith, Stewart & Arden and the Ilford Motor Company; while for car hire there were the prestigious firms of Baker's, and Frank Coe. Boyd's and Savilles were the shops for pianos. Lilley & Skinner, Manfield, and Souster for shoes, Edgar C. Porter was the electrician, and Mr King the picture-frame maker, not forgetting of course the man who provides such a useful, though solemn and final service Mr Gilderson the funeral undertaker.

I remember Britain winning the Schneider Trophy three times in succession with speeds never before attained in the air.

I remember Sir Malcolm Campbell breaking both the world's land and water speed records to give Britain possession, and I remember Dorothy Round and Fred Perry winning the Wimbledon singles for Britain. What an exceptional pair!

I remember once visiting that huge and spectacular structure of iron and glass called the Crystal Palace, re-erected on Sydenham Hill there was no building around London that I can recall which was higher: originally housing the Great Exhibition of 1851 located in London's Hyde Park, I remember it meeting its end on the night of December 1st, 1936 in a disastrous consuming fire.

I remember that legendary cricketer Jack Hobbs; born in Cambridgeshire and rejected by Essex he played the game for Surrey: smiling, unruffled, cool, calm, and collected he never seemed to worry. With Sutcliffe the runs scored for England always came in such good measure that the pleasure brought to thousands engendered memories I will always treasure.

I remember the many attempts over the years by the world's athletes to run the elusive 4 minute mile; I remember Sydney Wooderson of Great Britain clocking 4 minutes 6 seconds in 1937 and I remember Roger Bannister in 1954 at Oxford being the first to achieve it with 3.59 in such style.

I remember when Money had real value and most people would respect every penny; when walking was normal and Inflation was Nil and what Public Assistance there was, was small and not for the very many.

I remember the day (in September 1939) when the Second World War broke out and the Air Raid warning that Sunday morning – my Gas Mask I was temporarily without; and, during the War, the many raids by enemy planes, the Flying Bombs (V1's) and V2's, and the death and destruction, the sorrow and grief, the Blackouts, the Rationing, and the censoring of much of the News.

I remember the days before sophisticated dentistry, and when some surgical operations were performed (compared with those of today) somewhat primitively.

I remember the days before domestic Refrigerators, Freezers, Vacuum Cleaners and Washing Machines: when household chores were harder, being performed by manual means: before the many products made of cheerful colourful plastic, and easy-to-clean cooking utensils with their surfaces "non-stick". Before liquid detergents, chromium plating, stainless steel, Gas

Central Heating, and Double or Secondary Glazing. To people then such things would have been undoubtedly simply amazing.

I remember the time long before a passenger travelling daily to town was referred to as a commuter, and when few people had seen a Photocopying machine much less a Fax machine, Video, electronic Calculator, Carphone or Personal computer.

I remember the days long before plastic money in the form of Credit cards – Barclays, Euro, Master or Visa, and before the sponsoring of Football teams, and the leagues with such names as Barclays, Vauxhall, HFS Loans, B & Q and Beazer; when Football was played for the love of the game and players were content to win mere local fame, unlike now when so often Money is the main incentive to play the game.

There are many other events and things I still remember, but they are almost too numerous to mention and it would take far too long and it would indeed be wrong for me to expect your continued full and undivided attention.

LOOKING BACK, it is apparent that it was a different age – a past chapter; the turn of a page of England's Social History which to those who did not live through it may seem very much a mystery. But though some changes have been for the worse there's been many for the Better; a word I would spell with a Capital Letter. Let us hope that the "standard of living improvement" will bring with it increased happiness and greater contentment. What the future holds surely no one can tell but to all of you who will see it I WISH YOU WELL!

Norman Gunby

When you are next in the City look for the blue plaque set in the wall of the Midland Bank in Poultry almost opposite the Mansion House. Here stood the house in which Thomas Hood in 1799 was born.

British Rail's – Anglia Region – Engineering Depot at Ilford

Following the delay brought about by the Second World War this Depot – occupying about half a mile of railway land between Ilford and Seven Kings Station – came into being in May 1949 in preparation for the running of Electric trains on the nationalised and electrified line from Liverpool Street to Shenfield in September of that year.

At that time some 92 units were serviced at Ilford when for the first time BR trains with automatic doors were in use. By 1956 electrification of the line had been extended to Chelmsford and Southend and subsequently to Ipswich, Harwich and Norwich, and to cope with the large increase in rolling stock a third building, the present large inspection shed, was added.

In addition to the servicing of electric trains the Ilford Depot has carried out the modernisation of the fleet of Eastern Region Mark III Trains (with sleeping accommodation) and the training of crews for some of BR's new electric locomotives.

In the early 1960's heavy repairs of units used on the London, Tilbury and Southend line from Fenchurch Street as well as those on the Clacton line began to be undertaken here. The work includes the removal and repairs of the electric motors and bogies. Repairs are also now carried out on units from the Eastern Region at Kings Cross and the London Midland at Euston.

Employing about 600 staff Ilford is a very busy and important Depot within Network South-East and with customer demand on the Great Eastern lines increasing all the time, and with new and more modern units coming into service, the depot has a bright future.

On Saturday 20th May 1989 to mark its 40th anniversary the Ilford Depot for the first time was open to the Public when approx 15,000 people attended to see the rolling stock and locomotives (steam and diesel, as well as electric) on display, and more than £15,000 was raised for various charities.

Based on information contained in the Open Day souvenir booklet. Reproduced by courtesy of Mr E Birchler.

On April 19th, 1991 B.R. chairman Sir Bob Reid visited the Ilford Depot and presented the work-force with a British Standards Certificate 5750 for their overall efficiency.

Ilford Limited

As a result of seeing an advertisement of the ILFORD PHOTO COMPANY of 14-22 Tottenham Street, London, W1 in the Souvenir programme of the Royal Tournament held at Earls Court in July 1989 I wrote to the Company to enquire whether this was now the new name of ILFORD Limited. The reply, dated 2 August 1989, from Mr Philip Wright, Sales Service, stated that ILFORD Limited is still the Company name and that under this banner are sections including ILFORD PHOTO COMPANY which is the selling Company for the UK and which sponsors certain events in the UK.

Mr Wright went on to say that ILFORD Limited is part of the Ilford Group of world-wide Companies which was part of the Swiss pharmaceutical firm of CIBA-CEIGY but which is no longer owned by them, the ILFORD Group having been sold to the International Paper Corporation, the world's largest paper manufacturer, early in 1989.

Ilford Cricket School

Located in Beehive Lane at the rear of the Beehive PH, this indoor cricket school was founded in 1957 by Mr Harold Faragher who is also a Director. The school has produced many players who having come at a young age have progressed through to County and International level. These include Graham Gooch, John Lever, Nasser Hussain, David East, Alan Lilley, Chris Gladwin, and Keith and Ian Pont. For the past 30 years under a scheme arranged with the Redbridge Education Authority local schools have been sending parties of boys and girls to the school each week from September to Easter for practice and coaching. Approximately 500 pupils have attended each week over this period.

Ilford Football Club (1881–1979):
Brief history and some of its achievements

1881 Club founded. Population of Ilford then 7,645. Home matches at first (20 Oct) played on ground now occupied by the Town Hall. Later on other grounds in the High Road – on the corner of Green Lane, and subsequently opposite the "General Havelock".

1885/86 Final of Essex Senior Cup reached at the first attempt. Lose to Old Foresters.

1888 Essex Senior Cup won for the first time beating Upton Excelsior 3-1 in the final at Chelmsford. West Ham Charity Cup also won.

1888/89 Club moves to a pitch in the centre of Ilford Sports Ground situated between Wellesley and Coventry Roads where there are also running and cycle tracks. Essex Senior Cup retained by beating Somerset Light Infantry 2-0 on the Essex CC ground at Leyton.

1889/90 Essex Senior Cup won for the third successive season by beating Romford 2-0.

1890/91 London Senior Cup final reached after beating Millwall (then Amateurs) in semi-final.

1891/92 Essex Senior Cup won again, beating Colchester 3-1. London Senior Cup finalists – lose to Old Westminsters 2-1.

1892 Ilford, with Clapton, take a leading part in discussions which lead to the establishment two years later of the Southern League in which Ilford played for two seasons but then with Clapton had to withdraw because of the burden imposed on the players by the many long journeys.

1895/96 Final of the London Charity Cup reached.

1896/97 Ilford join the London League playing against, among others, Brentford, Queens Park Rangers, and Thames Ironworks.

1897/98 Finalists again in the London Senior Cup – lose to Brentford 5-1.

1898/99 Ilford play in the South Essex League and for the following three seasons.

1901 London Senior Cup won for the first time beating Clapton 2-1.

1901/02 Ilford play friendly matches against such teams as Aston Villa, Nottingham Forest, Brentford and Northampton.

1903/04 Essex Senior Cup won for the fifth time, beating South Weald 7-0. London Senior Cup finalists. Lose to Leyton 1-0.

1904 Ilford Sports Ground sold for the building of houses after the Ilford Club had played there for 15 years.

1904 (1 Sept) Ilford play their first game at Lynn Road, Newbury Park having obtained a 21-year lease on the ground and having to erect fencing, a stand and changing accommodation etc. at a cost of £700. Played in heavy rain the game was watched by 1,000 spectators who saw Ilford win 2-1 against old friends and rivals Clapton. A dinner held afterwards at the White Horse on Ilford Broadway.

1905 Ilford play a conspicuous part in the formation of the Isthmian League in which at first there were only 6 clubs. Win London Senior Cup for second time, beating Ealing 2-0.

1906/07 Ilford head the Isthmian League, winning 8 and drawing 2 of the 10 games played. Ilford Charity Shield won.

1907/08 Essex Senior Cup won for the sixth time beating Walthamstow Grange 3-0.

1910/11 Ilford reach final of the London Senior Cup for the sixth time. They also reach Amateur Cup semi-finals for the third time losing to Bishop Auckland (a strong north of England team). While on tour that season in Belgium Ilford beat Bishop Auckland 1-0 in the final of the Belgian Leopold Cup which Bishop Auckland had won the two previous seasons.

1911/12 Seventh Essex Senior Cup win, beating Romford 3-2. Ilford Hospital Shield also won.

1913/14 Ilford beat Nunhead 2-0 to win London Senior Cup for the third time.

1914-1918 During the First World War 40 Ilford FC players served in HM Forces and J. Dines, W. Deal, H. Fleming, and H. Wright were fatal victims of the carnage. For the duration the Lynn Road ground was used as a drill ground for various volunteer organisations.

1920/21 Ilford are Isthmian League Champions with players such as Baden Herod (later to become a Spurs full-back), Ray Dand (who became a professional with Reading), and W. Gotland an Amateur International.

1921 Ilford FC purchase the leased Lynn Road ground for £3,050 and become one of the first amateur Football Clubs to own their own ground.

1921/22 Ilford are Isthmian League Champions again. London Senior Cup and London Charity Cup also won. Reserves win the London Minor Cup.

1923/24 Essex Senior Cup won again (eighth time), beating Grays Athletic 1-0.

1924/25 In an FA Cup round against Leyton five meetings of the two Clubs were necessary. These lasted 9 hours 43 mins with Leyton eventually winning 2-0.

1925 Ilford beat Ajax FC 3-1 in final of International Tournament in Amsterdam.

1926/27 Essex Senior Cup won again (ninth time in ten finals) beating Barking 2-1.

1927/28 Previous season's Essex Senior Cup win against Barking repeated (2-1).

1928 New Main Stand at Lynn Road opened. Seating 825 spectators it cost £4,250.

1929 (20 Apr) Ilford win the Amateur Cup for the first time beating favourites and holders Leyton 3-1 at Highbury where the 35,034 attendance was a record for an amateur game at the time. Ilford beat Barking 8-1 to win Essex Senior Cup again, and London Caledonians 4-1 to win London Senior Cup for fifth time. Ilford Hospital Shield also won.

1930 Ilford win Amateur Cup for the second successive season, beating Bournemouth Gasworks 5-1 at Upton Park in front of 21,102 spectators.

1931 A motor coach carrying Ilford supporters to Bishop Auckland is involved in a collision near Darlington: many injured. Ilford beat Queens Park Rangers and Fulham to reach London Challenge Cup semi-finals.

1931/32 London Senior Cup and London Charity Cup finalists.

1935/36 Ilford reach final of Amateur Cup losing 2-0 to Casuals at Upton Park after a 1-1 draw at Selhurst Park. Essex Senior Cup finalists:lose to Walthamstow Avenue 3-2.

1936/37 Ilford finalists again in Essex Senior Cup, losing to Harwich & Parkeston 2-1.

1937/38 Ilford win London Charity Cup, beating Dulwich Hamlet 4-2.

1938/39 London Charity Cup finalists again: lose to Waltham Avenue 2-1

1939-1945 Royal Air Force take possession of Lynn Road ground for barrage balloon site. Later taken over by War Department for anti-aircraft guns. Following the cessation of hostilities Ilford Council requisition the Stand to store the furniture of Ilford people whose homes had been wrecked by flying bombs and rockets. One former player E.G. Braund killed while flying with the R.A.F. and Jim Watts seriously injured during an air raid.

1949/50 Ilford win Thameside Trophy beating Romford 3-2.

1952/53 Essex Senior Cup won for the twelfth time, beating Grays Athletic 3-1.

1953/54 Essex Senior Cup win repeated by beating Grays Athletic again (this time 2-0), and London Senior Cup won for the seventh time in 12 finals, beating Hounslow Town 2-0. Victor Linart Challenge Trophy also won, beating Louvain, Belgium 3-1 in France.

1954/55 Ilford beat Hounslow Town 4-1 to win London Charity Cup for the fourth time. Essex Thameside Trophy also won, beating Leytonstone 4-0.

1955 Ilford win Victor Linart Challenge Trophy again in France, beating Maastricht (Holland) 5-4.

1956 75th anniversary of the Club. A Dinner and Dance to celebrate the event was held at London's Coventry Street Corner House and a 32 page Souvenir booklet was compiled for the occasion. The above notes are taken from it.

In more recent times Ilford FC's most notable achievements were in reaching the final of the Amateur Cup on a further two occasions, both matches (which I had the pleasure of watching) being played at Wembley Stadium. In 1958 Ilford played Woking losing 3-0, and in 1974 in the very last Amateur Cup final of all, Ilford played Bishops Stortford who won 4-1.

Considering the many excellent teams throughout the country which have to be overcome in the struggle over several rounds it is no mean achievement for any Club to reach the final of a national tournament such as the FA Amateur Cup and the players of these later years therefore carried on in the tradition of Ilford FC's earlier players by performing so well.

The names of all players, or even the outstanding ones, from 1881 to 1979, as well as the many officials without whom the Club could not have functioned, are too numerous to mention here but tribute is paid to them for the pleasure and pride brought to the citizens of Ilford by their splendid efforts, their dedication and their sportsmanship over the 98 years of the Club's existence. This regrettably ended in 1979 when it ceased to be a separate Club upon merging with Leytonstone FC, and the Lynn Road ground was sold for housing where now only the once well-known name of Dellow has been perpetuated in Dellow Close.

Following the subsequent sale of Leytonstone's ground the Leytonstone Ilford Club merged with Walthamstow Avenue FC which has also since sold its ground. The amalgamated Clubs now play under the name of Redbridge Forest and being groundless are currently playing their home games at Dagenham by arrangement with Dagenham FC whose ground is owned by the London Borough of Barking & Dagenham Council. In December 1990 Redbridge Forest were leaders of the Vauxhall Premier Division and at the end of the Season finished as Champions as they had done the previous season.

Some Ilford players of the past. Back row: Jim Watts, Freddie Drane, Cecil Popplewell, Les Male. Front row: Colin Elsworthy, Ron (Dickie) Winch, Gus Simmons, Henry Dodkins, Roger Meadows.

The Herbert Dunnico Memorial Gates which were unveiled by Sir Stuart Mallinson, President of Essex County Football Association at the entrance to the Ilford Football Club Ground at Lynn Road, Newbury Park, 29 September 1955. The gates are now at the High Road entrance of the council-owned Cricklefield Ground having been retrieved from the yard of a firm of sheet-metal manufacturers at Southend. Unfortunately they are not now hung from a pair of handsome brick pillars and the top part of the backing plate has been lost.

Reverend Sir Herbert Dunnico being received at a dinner by my father and stepmother in 1953, the year Sir Herbert died aged 77. Resident in Ilford for many years he was elected Member of Parliament for Consett in Durham in 1922 and from 1929 to 1931 was Deputy Speaker in the House of Commons.

Kelvin Hughes: Historical Notes

As with the well-known Plessey Company (which has been associated with Ilford since 1923) the smaller but likewise distinguished firm of Kelvin Hughes plays an important role in manufacturing operations in Ilford for its sonar and radar products are used throughout the world on land, on the high seas, and in the air. Additionally it is the world's largest Admiralty Chart agency. For Technological innovation Kelvin Hughes has been honoured by the presentation of two Queen's Awards in 1962 and 1969 – and two for Export Achievement, in 1968 and 1989.

Their association with Ilford, where the firm has its main factory, goes back over seventy-five years to 1915 when during the First World War Hainault Farm was being used by the Royal Flying Corps and by the Admiralty, and Mr Henry Hughes, with Admiralty sponsorship, purchased the present site in New North Road. Development proceeded immediately and his firm, known then as Henry Hughes & Son Ltd., began producing at this factory many thousands of compasses, sextants and semaphores.

But the origin of the firm of Henry Hughes & Son Ltd. goes back over two hundred years to 1780 when it was first registered to manufacture nautical instruments. Records show that in that year Mr Thomas Hughes, a master of the Clockmakers' Company and the originator of the firm of Henry Hughes & Son Ltd., sold a chronometer to Captain Bligh of the Bounty whose voyage in 1789 of over 3,600 miles in an open boat after being set adrift by a mutinous crew is regarded as one of the greatest feats of seamanship and navigation of all time.

In 1835 Mr Henry Hughes, a grandson of Thomas Hughes, started his own business in Commercial Road, moving to No.120 Fenchurch Street in 1837. The shop became something of a Club for the nautical personalities of the day: customers included Sir Henry Stanley the African explorer, Lord Fisher of the Dreadnought, the Antarctic explorers Shackleton and Evans, and Captain Slocum the single-handed sailor.

In 1926 Henry Hughes & Son Ltd. brought out the first Admiralty pattern Echo Sounder which by 1935 had developed to the extent that the wreck of the Lusitania off the southern Coast of Eire was able to be located.

In 1941 the company's London premises were destroyed in an Air Raid. So too, were the premises of a rival firm Kelvin, Bottomley & Baird Ltd. But due to a shortage of accommodation and because friendly relations had existed

Kelvin Hughes, New North Road, Hainault. (Photo: Author.)

between the two Companies for some time both were subsequently re-located in the same building in London. Then followed in 1947 a merger of the two companies which at first was called Kelvin & Hughes Ltd. In 1961 the firm became part of the larger firm of S. Smith & Sons (England) Ltd., which in 1935 had acquired a financial interest in the Company. This in turn, is now part of the multi-national Smith's Industries PLC. Today some 70% of the Division's products are exported, and Agents and Service depots are established in nearly 400 ports in 77 countries throughout the world.

KELVIN HUGHES
Some notable achievements

1936   The introduction and manufacture of Automatic Pilots for use in aircraft.
1938   The first commercial Echo Sounder introduced on the world market.
1948   Marine Radar Type No.1 approved to UK Ministry of Transport Specification. First UK company to achieve this distinction.
1950   "White Line" system introduced on the Humber Fishing system. This patented invention is now used by all other manufacturers.
1955   Production began on the first Slotted Radar Antenna. Now used by all other manufacturers.
1962   Photoplot Radar introduced allowing complete daylight viewing. Awarded The Queen's Award for Technological Innovation.
1966   The 21/16P Radar was the first marine radar to be introduced with integral electronic computer.

1968 The company produced its 10,000th Type 17 Radar. Received the Queen's Award for Export Achievement.

1969 Situation Display Radar, a revolutionary new collision assessment Radar introduced giving full daylight viewing. Received a second Queen's Award for Technological Innovation

1975 The Royal Navy specify Radar Type 1006 and Navigational Echo Sounder Type 780 as standard fit.

1978 The Semi-Automatic Plotting Table system introduced for use in Royal Navy vessels.

1980 Radpak, the first Radar in the Kelvin Hughes' range to utilise fixed coils.

1981 The introduction of Anticol, a total tracking radar plotting aid, primarily designed as a complete package for large ships when used in conjunction with Radpak.

1983 Series 1600, the first marine radar to incorporate electric plotting. This was one of a series of radars introduced to meet governmental legislation for all ships over 500 grt.

1984 Radtrak, a low-cost ARPA (Automatic Radar Plotting Aid) designed for use with Radpak and other radars to provide a complete navigational system.

1985 The first of new navigational radars for the Royal Navy known as Type 1007.
A new raster scan monitor for use in multiple systems with Type 1007.

1987 Concept, a range of raster scan, high definition radars and ARPA displays, plus associated transceiver and antennae.

1989 Received a second Queen's Award for Export Achievement (Navigational Aids).

Based on information kindly supplied by Mr D J Parselle, Director, Product Support, Kelvin Hughes Ltd.

THE PLESSEY COMPANY PLC: See Sir Allen Clark, and John Logie Baird in Notable Residents and Associates Section.
Also Chronicle of Events

Other ILFORDS

There is also an ILFORD in Somerset. It is a hamlet near the River Isle (tributary of the 38½ mile River Passett) and its original name of Ileford, on record in AD 1260, means "ford over the River Isle" (Concise Oxford Dictionary of English Place names). It is not marked on most maps or atlases but I am indebted to Councillor A.L. Goverd of Ilminster Town Council – with whom I have corresponded – for sending me a section of Ordnance Survey Map sheet ST/21/31 which shows that Ilford in Somerset lies between Ilton and Puckington and about two miles north of Ilminster. To the east of the small hamlet of Ilford is the smaller hamlet of Ilford Bridges.

Ilfords Abroad

Ilford in Australia (New South Wales)

It is a small town situated approximately 40 miles north east of Bathurst (Australia's oldest inland city, founded in 1815) and approximately 15 miles from Sofala which is one of Australia's oldest gold towns where gold is still found in the area. Some 35 miles to the north-west of Ilford is the larger town of Mudgee, now noted for its production of Australian wines, and of mead and honey.

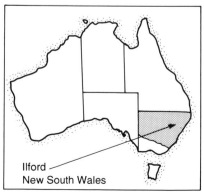

Ilford
New South Wales

(From information and map detail kindly supplied by the New South Wales Government Offices and Australian High Commission, London)

This Ilford in New South Wales was the subject of a letter to the Ilford Recorder of December 5th, 1963 from Mr E.V. Nichols whose address then was 13 Brantwood Gardens, Ilford. In December 1962 Mr Nichols had written to Ilford, New South Wales where lived a Mr Edwin Leader whose grandfather Reuben Leader was married to Martha Robins in St. Margarets Church, Barking in August 1836. In 1849 Reuben Leader with his wife and their five children sailed from London to Sydney. From there they went 139 miles north-west by bullock wagon to a place named Kanes Swamp, now called Ilford. They lived in a shack made of stone and wood. When Mr Nichols wrote to the Recorder in 1963 he stated that there were then in Ilford NSW 3 churches, 2 stores, a school, 2 petrol stations, a community hall and a sports ground and that mixed farming and cattle rearing was carried on. Wool from Ilford, it was stated, tops the wool market in Sydney.

This Ilford in New South Wales was also featured in the Recorder of December 11th, 1986 in a short article by Graham Oates describing a visit there by a Mr Bill Hutchins and Mrs Renee Hutchins of Brentwood who had been on holiday in Australia. They stated that it is in the Blue Mountains and has a population of about 1,000 people with a General Store which serves also as the Post Office. The main road to it is good by outback standards. They described it as a beautiful area where the blue haze over the mountains is caused by the sun on the Eucalyptus trees. In summer the temperature can soar to 100 degrees F or more.

Based on cuttings kindly supplied by Mrs Maureen Bresh, Secretary to the Editor, Ilford Recorder.

Ilford in Canada

There is also an Ilford in Manitoba – one of the ten provinces of Canada. It is a village on the Hudson Bay Rail route which runs from Churchill, on Hudson Bay, down to The Pas – and beyond, through Saskatchewan. It was named after Ilford (Essex) in 1928 at the request of Sir Frederic Wise MP for Ilford at the time, who took a great deal of interest in the building of the railway. Ilford is the railhead for winter freighting operations into the Knee Lake area and the famous God's Lake goldfields.

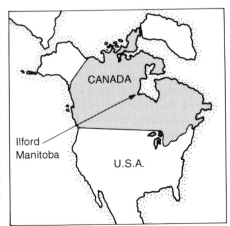

(From the "Place-names of Manitoba" by courtesy of Mrs Anne House, Librarian, Canadian High Commission, London.)

This Ilford in Manitoba was featured in an illustrated article by reporter Steve Holland in the Ilford Recorder of April 7th, 1982 which is basically as follows:

"Deep in the heart of northern Manitoba, Canada lies a small town inhabited by native (Eskimo) Indians. It has a population of 200 who live in timber houses gathered around a lonely railway station – the only link with the outside world as the town has no access by road. A hostile wilderness comprising vast tracts of forest and huge icy lakes surround the township, it is only a tiny spot on the map – an oasis of civilisation in the freezing sub-Arctic circle – 715 miles north-east of Winnipeg.

Described by the Manitoba Tourist Board as a "fairly isolated Indian reservation type of place" it was officially named after our own Ilford at the request of our constituency MP Sir Frederic Wise who in 1903 had founded a stockbroking firm called Wise, Speke & Co. in Newcastle-on-Tyne. His company acted as brokers in the formation of many Canadian firms which have proved to be pioneers. He also helped to raise large sums of money to assist develop Canada Northern and Canada Northern Ontario Railways which have since merged into Canada National Railways. In recognition of his work in opening up this territory the Canadian Government named a town – Wiseton in Saskatchewan – after him.

Ilford began originally as a section house on the railway line where track workmen lived. A gold mine was started at nearby God's Lake and throughout the 1920's and 1930's served as the shipping point for goods, materials, and people to get to the mine. Today there is a great deal of heavy engineering in the area and still some mining. Much of the area is rich in mineral such as nickel, copper and zinc. The local newspaper is the Opasquia Times published 300 miles away by Mr Murray Harvey who was reported as saying that "Ilford is predominately a native settlement with a few white people. The town is snow-free in June, July, August and part of September when the average temperature is 75 to 80 F. The winter average is minus 10 to minus 30 F but on an exceptionally cold day it is around minus 50 F. The area has long daylight hours in summer and in June is light from about 3.30 am to 11.30 pm. But in winter they have only a few hours when they are not in darkness. The locals travel in 'skidoos' – power toboggans – in the winter, and there are also a few cars and trucks for short distance journeys".

Mr Ed Waklenberg who runs the town's only store and his daughter Shelley added that Ilford has a hotel, post office, railway station, a small bar and a pool hall. Most of the native people here fish and trap for a living. "Our trappers go for mink, beaver and wolves and we get moose every year, and there is a lot of fishing done as northern Manitoba is half water and half land", Mr Waklenberg said.

The town has a Mayor and four Councillors and the Gold Trail Hotel which is owned by Mr Kip Thompson who was Mayor for eight years until he resigned in 1977. His wife Mrs Thompson who helps run the hotel and has lived there for 20 years stated that people work in trappping, fishing and construction of the winter roads which are built on top of three feet of ice on the frozen lakes.

Whenever work is available people work but there is a lot of unemployment. Local people make their own entertainment and they have a community hall which shows movies. Bingo and dances are popular. "We have one TV channel and we are happy to have that", said Mrs Thompson. "We have only had television since about 1978 and telephones since about 1976. Despite the sleepy way of life very few young people leave the town. If anyone goes it is usually the older residents who generally move to Thompson which is 100 miles away and has a population of 18,000."

"I don't feel I am missing too much by living here", said Mrs Thompson. "Everyone enjoys the winter and in the summer we can go boating and fishing. The town is remote and peaceful – and that is the way we like it."

Based on feature kindly supplied by Mrs Maureen Bresh, Secretary to the Editor, Ilford Recorder.

* * *

Some Changes in Britain 1938-1991

	1938	*Latest*
POPULATION	47.5 million	57.2 million
WAGE for average male in manufacturing	£3.55p per week	£229.87 per week
CARS	1.9 million	19.2 million
OWNER OCCUPATION	32%	68%
MILK per pint	1.5p.	30p.
EGGS (one dozen)	9p.	£1.20p.
LOAF	1.5p.	65p.
TEA (per 125g)	3p.	53p.
FORD CAR 8hp	£115	£5,199
		(Fiesta Popular)
3-BEDROOMED S/D HOUSE (British average)	£600	£55,000
SEAT AT ROYAL OPERA HOUSE	£1.50	£64
ELECTRICITY GENERATED (Giga watt hours)	24,372	286,275
CRIME PER 100,000 POPULATION	741	7,526

From figures published by Central Statistical Office, London 1991
Note: 1938 prices (then £.s.d.) converted to present Decimal Currency

History Depicted on British Postage Stamps

During the reign of our present Queen Elizabeth II – from 6 February 1952, many of the events or subjects mentioned in this Potted History of Ilford have been commemorated by the Post Office by the issue of special postage stamps. Listed below are those which in some way, directly or indirectly, are associated with or are a part of our history and its people. Illustrations of the stamps can be found in the Colour Checklist published by Stanley Gibbons and entitled "Collect British stamps", a new edition of which appears in the autumn each year.

Event or Subject	*Year of Stamp Issue*
Roman Centurion: 1st Century AD (Romans hereabouts)	1971
Norman Ship and Norman Horseman: 1066 (Normans in the district)	1966
Peasants working in the field (at the time of the Domesday Inventory: 1086)	1986
Freemen working at trades: Domesday 1086	
Queen Elizabeth I (reigned 1558-1603)	1968
Spanish Armada scenes: 1588 (Troop movements in the locality)	1988
Royal Mail (General Letter Post) inception: 1660	1960 (See Footnote)
Oak Tree (many thousands at one time in the Ilford area including the ancient Fairlop Oak: many used for the building of the King's Ships)	1973
Early settlers and Clippers to Australia (from 1788)	1988
Carol Singers: 18th Century	1978
The Norwich Mail Coach (which ran through Ilford on its way to and from London) 1827	1984
Sir Rowland Hill – Postal Reformer: 1795-1879	1979
Social Reformers Robt. Owen, Lord Shaftesbury, Elizabeth Fry (Illustrations of Machinery, Chimney Sweeping and Prison) 1800's	1976

Fishing (Barking, of which Ilford at one time was a part was an important fishing port until the coming of the Railway from London and its extension to Great Yarmouth)	1981
Shire Horses (as used on Ilford's many farms, and in the Ploughing matches held here)	1978
Cornfield, and loaf of bread (wheat, oats, and barley previously grown locally)	1989
Food and Farming (many vegetables grown for the London market on Ilford's farms at one time)	1989
Salvation Army (founded 1865, it has been active in Ilford for well over a century)	1965
Penny Farthing and Safety bicycle: 1884 (cycling was a popular recreation in the late 1800's and early 1900's and there was a cycle track here at one time)	1978
St. John Ambulance Service (commenced 1887): a voluntary service it has been active in Ilford for many years	1987
First motor Fire Engine: 1904 (similar type used at Ley Street Fire Station opened in 1905)	1974
Boy Scout Movement (formed 1908 by Baden Powell following an experimental camp held in 1907)	1982
"Votes for Women" (Suffragettes): early 1900's	1968
British-built Steam Locomotives and Ships (many of which, as well as machinery etc. were exported to all parts of the world) Note: many Ilford residents were associated with the sea or with the London Docks.	1975
Servicemen and Nurse (as in World War I 1914-1918)	1971
Sopwith Camel bi-plane Fighter (as used from Hainault Farm airfield in World War I)	1968
Girl Guide Movement (formed following the Boy Scout Movement. A similar organisation for girls was founded in the USA in 1912)	1982
Horn Loudspeaker 1920's (Wireless coming into people's homes from early 1920's)	1972
Famous British Trains (mainly pre-World War II)	1985
AA (Anti-Aircraft) Artillery (in action in Ilford during World War II also during World War I)	1965
Air battle over London ("Battle of Britain" 1940)	1965
Blitz victim being tended by St. John Ambulance Brigade	1987
Coronation of Queen Elizabeth II: 3 June 1953 A spectacular ceremony televised.	1953
World Cup Football: 1966	1966
England, Cup Winners	1966
Telecommunications (British Post Office technology: 1960's)	1969
British Motor Industry	1966 & 1982

The Anglo-French (BAC/Aerospatiale) Concorde: Maiden flight: April 9th. (Note: on 4 Nov 1970 it exceeded Mach 2 - twice the speed of sound). The Concorde has been seen over Ilford.	1969
80th birthday of the Queen Mother (who has visited Ilford on several occasions during her long lifetime)	1980
Sports centenaries: Running, Rugby, Boxing, Cricket	1980
Wedding of Prince Charles and Lady Diana Spencer: 22nd July (another televised spectacle seen by many Ilford residents)	1981
City of London (in which countless Ilford residents over many years have worked)	1985
Town Letter Delivery	1985
Halley's Comet: 1986	1986
Queen Elizabeth II's 60th birthday: 21 April 1986	1986
Tram as a means of urban transport (Ilford's trams ran from 1903 until 1938)	1988
The Lord Mayor's Show, London 11 Nov 1989 (seen by many Ilford children over the years)	1989
The Queen's Award for Export Achievement, 25th Anniversary (as awarded to Kelvin Hughes and the Plessey Company)	1990
90th birthday of the Queen Mother	1990

Footnote: The Post

Although the third centenary of the establishment of the General Letter Office was commemorated by the issue of two special stamps on 7 July 1960, the history of the post in Britain originates a good deal further back than the year 1660.

It is chronicled that when King Richard III was expecting the landing of Henry of Richmond (later Henry VII) in the year 1484 he followed the practice introduced by Edward IV in 1482 of appointing a single horseman for every 20 miles, along a certain route by means of whom travelling with the utmost speed, and not passing his respective limit, news was always able to be carried by letter from hand to hand 200 miles within two days. These horsemen, at first known as currors or couriers but later as Post boys, who were controlled and paid by an officer of the Royal Household, were the original "Posts". Later (no doubt for security reasons) they were sometimes accompanied by a guide or escort who was referred to as "riding post". The stages at which letters were handed over were houses or inns where a fresh horse was always available for hire. In 1555 on the Dover road, these stages were required to have a hunting horn hanging at their door or a painted sign, to indicate that it was a "Post House".

By the time of Elizabeth I's reign (1558-1603) post roads were established to London from Ireland (via Holyhead) from Falmouth (via Plymouth, Exeter and Salisbury) from Milford, South Wales (via Cardiff and Bristol) and from Carlisle and Berwick (via Newcastle, Doncaster and Stamford) as well as from Dover (via Canterbury and Rochester). The road through Ilford does not appear to have been a post road at that time.

At first only the King's, or Royal packets, were carried but later the letters of other persons were carried also, though at first this was looked upon with disfavour.

Incidentally the old direction on letters was "Haste, Post, Haste" and so the word post-haste (dating from 1545) came to mean "with all possible speed or expedition". The word was used by Shakespeare.

* * *

Local History Quiz

1. From where came some of the earliest settlers to Essex before the Roman occupation?
2. Where in Ilford was the Iron Age Settlement?
3. For approximately how many years did the Romans occupy most of Britain?
4. What were the names of London and Colchester then?
5. When was Essex invaded and settled by the Saxons?
6. Approximately when was the first Abbey at Barking built?
7. When did William the Conqueror pass through Ilford?
8. Where is Ilford's oldest building, the Hospital Chapel?
9. What was the original purpose of the Hospital there?
10. Which King of England spent two days in Ilford in 1321?
11. What was the former name of the River Roding bordering Ilford?
12. Which native bird was abundant here until about 400 years ago?
13. What was the name of the forest hereabouts in the 1600's?
14. Why was Barkingside so named?
15. Which contemporary of William Shakespeare danced through Ilford in 1599?
16. Which famous Diarist recorded dining here?
17. When was Valentines Mansion built and after whom was it named?
18. When was the River Roding made navigable from Barking to Ilford bridge?
19. What, because of its size, would have been a possible entrant in the Guiness Book of Records?
20. What was the origin of the Fairlop Fair?
21. What was the estimated number at the Fair in 1840?
22. When was the so-called Cranbrook Castle (a) built, and (b) demolished?
23. In which year was the cutting taken from the Valentines Vine to become the famous Vine at Hampton Court?
24. In which year were the pre-historic animal remains first discovered in south Ilford?
25. Who, over a period of many years from about 1834 excavated the pre-historic remains in Ilford?
26. How many Stage Coaches ran through Ilford each day to and from London at one time?

27. Whose funeral cortege passed through Ilford in 1821 on is way to Germany via Harwich?
28. Where exactly was Ilford Gaol situated?
29. What was the name of the railway serving Ilford when it was opened in 1839?
30. In which year was an Act of Parliament passed disafforesting much of Hainault Forest?
31. In which year were the remaining 800 acres opened to the public?
32. From where came many of the stones used in the building of St. Peters Church, Aldborough Hatch?
33. When did Doctor Barnardo and Mrs Barnardo start their homes in Barkingside for orphaned and destitute girls?
34. What was the remarkable occurrence when Doctor Barnardo was only two years old?
35. Who came to Ilford in 1879 to manufacture photographic plates and why did he choose Ilford?
36. When did Ilford break away from Barking to become a separate Civil parish?
37. Who opened his first shop in Ilford in 1890 and has an Arcade named after him?
38. Which local resident in 1896 opened the first of his 35 grocery shops and later became known as the "Admiral of the King George"?
39. In which year were Ilford's own newspapers first published?
40. Howards & Sons Ltd. came to Ilford in 1899. For which particular product were they world-famous?
41. When was Ilford's first public park opened and what was its name then?
42. For what purpose was the land where Ilford Golf Club is now previously used?
43. Appproximately how many farms were there in Ilford at the end of the last century?
44. A.C. Corbett built over 3,000 houses here in conjunction with Robert Stroud. What was their price range?
45. Who in 1902 opened a furnishing store in the High Road that was to become widely known?
46. When was Ilford's Town Hall opened and by whom?
47. When did Ilford's tram service (a) begin, and (b) end?
48. Who wrote a book about Ilford's trams and trolleybuses?
49. Which local shopkeeper was an artist in watercolours and took many of the photographs of early Ilford?
50. What is the name of the Roman Catholic Cardinal who was born in Ilford in 1905?
51. Who presented to the people of Ilford 12 acres of grounds in memory of his mother?
52. In which years were the ploughing matches held at Fairlop?

53. Which was the variety Theatre in Ilford where many notable performers appeared?
54. How many Ilford servicemen lost their lives during World War I?
55. For which invention was Arthur Joseph Hughes awarded an OBE?
56. Who was Ilford's first Member of Parliament when it became a separate constituency in 1918?
57. Who was the co-founder of the Plessey Company which set up in Ilford in 1923/24 and where was he born?
58. Which famous television pioneer worked at Plesseys in Vicarage Lane?
59. What was the previous name of Vicarage Lane?
60. Who opened Eastern Avenue in 1925?
61. Which one-time Cabinet Minister lived in the Goodmayes area in the 1920's?
62. Which local resident was Deputy Speaker in the House of Commons from 1929 to 1931?
63. Who in 1926 was (a) Ilford's Charter Mayor, and (b) Ilford's first annual Mayor?
64. In which year did the PDSA acquire St. Swithins Farm in Woodford Bridge Road?
65. Who built the Estate off The Drive with 15 roads named after English Cathedral towns and cities?
66. In which years did Ilford FC first win the Amateur Cup and on whose ground?
67. In which years did Ilford FC play at Wembley Stadium and against whom?
68. At which Church was it at one time necessary to display "Church Full" notices?
69. The collection of books and papers belonging to an outstanding local historian is now the property of the local council. What was his name?
70. How many V1's and V2's fell on Ilford during World War II?
71. For what was part of Fairlop Plain used during World War II?
72. By whom was approx. 5 miles of Underground tunnelling used during World War II?
73. Which Ilford-born television personality flew Spitfires during World War II?
74. How many Ilford civilians were killed by enemy action during World War II?
75. Which Ilford-born airman who died in 1988 survived 116 sorties during World War II?
76. When was the Underground Railway from Leytonstone to Newbury Park first opened for passenger traffic?
77. Who in 1957 founded the Ilford Cricket School?
78. In which year was Harrison Gibsons's second fire?
79. What was the population of Ilford in 1961?

80. What was the Motto of the Borough of Ilford which in 1965 was adopted for Redbridge?
81. Which local resident is a former world-class football referee?
82. What is the name of a top-ranking airman who was born in Khartoum Road?
83. Which famous batsman played for Ilford Cricket Club?
84. Which well-known Ilford and Essex CC bowler lives locally?
85. Which is one of Ilford's finest trees and where is it situated?
86. Where is the animals' cemetery in Ilford?
87. From where does Ilford Limited now operate?
88. Which former Ilfordian commanded the previous Aircraft Carrier HMS "Ark Royal?"
89. When was a section of the High Road closed permanently to through traffic?
90. When was a section of the M11 from Redbridge Roundabout to near Harlow opened?
91. When was the Woodford-Barking relief road opened?
92. When was the new Central Library opened and how much did it cost?
93. Eric Rowland, a local butcher and shrewd investor died in 1988. What was the value of his estate?
94. Which famous steam locomotive was at BR's Ilford depot in 1988?
95. Which former Ilford County High School pupil is now Chief Executive of Grand Metropolitan plc?
96. Which former reporter and local Newspaper Editor died on 10 August 1990?
97. Who are the present Members of Parliament representing Ilford?
98. Who is financing the new £100 million Shopping Complex named "The Exchange" at Ilford?
99. What does the letter "G" in the Ilford post code stand for?
100. From what date did the local telephone numbers change their initial code from 01 to 081?

* * *

Answers to Local History Quiz

1. From the Rhineland and Northern France
2. By the Roding at Uphall
3. Approximately 363 years
4. Londinium and Camulodunon
5. The 5th, 6th and 7th centuries
6. Between 666 and 670 AD
7. In the winter of 1066/1067
8. On Ilford Hill near the Broadway
9. To care for 13 Lepers
10. Edward II
11. The Hyle
12. The Crane
13. Waltham Forest
14. In 1558 some cottages there were marked on a map as being on the Barking side of the Forest
15. Will Kemp
16. Samual Pepys
17. In the 1690's: John Valentine, resident of a previous house there
18. From 1737
19. The Fairlop Oak
20. A private picnic or bean-feast given by Mr Daniel Day of Wapping
21. 200,000 people
22. (a) 1765; (b) 1923
23. 1769
24. 1786
25. Sir Antonio Brady
26. 60
27. Caroline of Brunswick
28. In Romford Road, near the Three Rabbits PH
29. Eastern Counties Railway
30. 1851
31. 1906
32. Old Westminster Bridge
33. 1874

34. He was pronounced dead by two doctors. It was the undertaker who detected a flicker of life.
35. Alfred Hugh Harman. He wanted somewhere close to London with a clean dust-free atmosphere.
36. 1888
37. John Bodger
38. Arthur William Green
39. 1898
40. Aspirin tablets
41. September 16, 1899; Central Park
42. A company-owned Rifle Range
43. 46
44. £217 to £520
45. John Harrison Gibson
46. December 1901; Ben Bailey
47. (a) 1903; (b) 1938
48. Len Thomson
49. Watson Hornby
50. John Carmel Heenan
51. Holcombe Ingleby
52. 1909 and 1911
53. Ilford Hippodrome
54. 1159
55. The aperiodic compass
56. Sir Peter Griggs
57. Allen George Clarke; Massachusetts (USA)
58. John Logie Baird
59. Cauliflower Lane
60. HRH Prince Henry
61. Emmanuel Shinwell
62. Revd. Sir Herbert Dunnico
63. (a) Sir Frederic Wise; (b) Alderman F.H. Dane
64. 1927
65. A.P. Griggs
66. 1929; Arsenal's (Highbury)
67. 1958 (Woking) and 1974 (Bishops Stortford)
68. Gants Hill (Wesleyan) Methodist
69. Frederick Brand
70. 69 (34 & 35)
71. An airfield
72. The Plessey Company
73. Raymond Baxter
74. 552
75. Gerald Witherick

76. 14 December 1947
77. Harold Faragher
78. 1959
79. 178,024
80. In Unity Progress
81. Ken Aston
82. Air Vice-Marshall Sir Bernard Chacksfield
83. Graham Gooch
84. John Lever
85. The Cedar Tree in Valentines Park
86. In Woodford Bridge Road-adjoining the PDSA
87. Mobberley, Cheshire
88. Admiral Sir Raymond Lygo
89. 10 January 1987
90. 14 April 1977
91. 1988
92. 25 February 1986: £4 million
93. £3.5 million
94. The Flying Scotsman
95. Sir Allen Sheppard
96. Basil Amps
97. ~~Neil Thorne~~ Mike Gapes (Ilford South), Vivian Bendall (Ilford North). James Arbuthnot (Clayhall Ward, part of Wanstead & Woodford Constituency)

9/4/92

98. Norwich Union Insurance and the Prudential Assurance Companies
99. The last letter in the name Barking
100. 6th May 1990

A snapshot of a photograph in the Redbridge Central Library (Local History Room) showing the former Fire Station in Ley Street around the year 1920. The Fire Station was opened on 9 November 1905 and demolished in 1990.

The house that was Middlefield Farm House seen from Valentines Park. (Photo: Author.)

The Great Vine at Hampton Court Palace. Grown from a cutting taken from the black Hamburgh Vine at Valentines in the year 1769 and planted at Hampton Court it is said by the famous landscape gardener "Capability Brown" (1716–1783), this vine now 222 years old is still producing grapes in abundance to this day – as many as 600 bunches in a good year. (Photo: Crown Copyright. Courtesy of Mr. Glyn George). Note: a plaque commemorating the Valentines Vine (which was in a hot house and was also a prolific producer of grapes but has long since gone) can be seen in the wall of the gardens adjoining Valentines Mansion – north side. It was placed there by the Council on behalf of the citizens of Ilford in 1951, the year of the Festival of Britain.

(see colour photographs in centre pages)

Timber from our neighbouring forest was used not only for the building of ships – as recorded by Samuel Pepys – (and many trees would need to be felled for just one ship) but also in the construction of houses. One such house in which timber from the forest was used is the Queen's House at Greenwich, the first wholly classical building in England. Designed by Inigo Jones in 1616 for the extravagant and pleasure-loving Queen Anne of Denmark, wife of James I, it was completed in 1635 for Queen Henrietta Maria, wife of Charles I. The National Maritime Museum photograph shows the gallery of the Hall supported on oak cantilevered brackets, as well as the frieze, cornice and enriched ceiling beams.

A Potted History of Ilford

The recently cleaned Town Hall – now nearly 90 years old – showing the new front steps and ramp, the brick-paved area and the new revolving clock. (Photo: Author.)

The pedestrianised section of Ilford High Road with the Harrison Gibson building and Lynton House in the distance. (Photo: Author.)

The Central Library (opened 1986) in the extended Clements Road. (Photo: Author.)

The Kenneth More Theatre in Oakfield Road. (Photo: Author.)

The pedestrianised precinct looking towards Ilford Broadway. (Photo: Author.)

Ilford Hill from the Broadway. (Photo: Author.)

The new Ilford Railway Station entrance and booking hall. (Photo: Author.)

Cranbrook Road from the Station. (Photo: Author.)

Looking across the Broadway towards Ilford Lane. (Photo: Author.)

Installing one of the fibreglass columns to the High Road entrance to "The Exchange" shopping complex. (Photo: Author.)

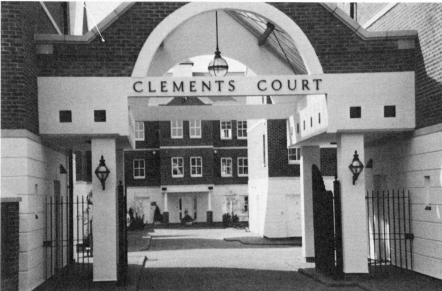

(*Above*) Looking across Ilford Broadway towards Cranbrook Road. The Ilford Hippodrome occupied the site to the right. Built in 1909, it was severely damaged when a rocket projectile fell on cottages at the rear on 12 January 1945. (*Below*) The entrance to a new office complex off Clements Road. Built by Countryside Properties, it was opened in May 1990 by the Mayor of Redbridge, Councillor Geoffery Brewer. It stands on the site of Clements Farm which following the death of Miss Eleanor Thompson in 1878 was the first of many farms in Ilford to be sold for house-building. (Photos: Author.)

The former Wycliffe Congregational Church now Wycliffe House, an office complex. (Photo: Author.)

The V.I.P. plot, Buckingham Road Cemetery. Grave of Sir Peter Griggs in centre. (Photo: Author.)

The paved courtyard to the Hospital Chapel. (Photo: Author.)

Memorial at the Hospital Chapel, Ilford Hill (founded circa AD 1145. Reconstructed AD 1927).
Photo: Author

The Baths, Ilford High Road. (Photo: Author.)

Ilford Fire Station (opened 21 January 1987). (Photo: Author.)

Bus standing in the Bus Terminus on the site of Tyne Hall (on the corner of Ley Street and Hainault Street), the Harrison Gibson building in the background. (Photo: Author.)

The Boating Lake in Valentines Park. This lake, having an area of over 7 acres was within the grounds of "Valentines" of which 47½ acres were purchased from Mrs. Ingleby by the Ilford Urban District Council to become the first part of our present Valentines Park opened 16 September 1899 and originally called Central Park. (Photo: Author.)

Ilford CC's ground in Valentines Park where in 1978 former Ilford cricketer Graham Alan Gooch (born 23 July 1953, Leytonstone) shared with K.S. McEwan a second wicket partnership of 321 for Essex against Northants. (Photo: Author.)

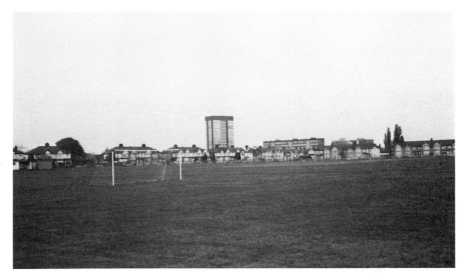

P.L.A. Ground looking towards Beehive Lane/Eastern Avenue. (Photo: Author.)

The P.L.A. Ground. This land was part of Highlands Farm and was the site of Cranbrook Castle built in 1765 and demolished in 1923 following the purchase of the land by the Port of London Authority in 1923. (Photo: Author.)

Swimming and Recreation Centre, High Street, Barkingside. (Photo: Author.)

Public Library, Barkingside. (Photo: Author.)

Animals' Cemetery adjoining P.D.S.A., Woodford Bridge Road, Ilford. (Photo: Author.)

Grave of "Simon" the HMS *Amethyst* cat adjoining P.D.S.A., Woodford Bridge Road, Ilford. (Photo: Author.)

Times past – but not forgotten

Extract from Ilford Recorder dated 9 November 1961:

An 85-year-old woman who was born in a little wooden house in what is now the site of The Olde Red Cow in Ley Street, died in Southwick, Sussex on Monday while visiting a sister. She was Mrs. Caroline Stursberg who lived in Airthrie Road, Goodmayes.

Mrs. Stursberg was born in 1876 when water was brought to the house from a pump in Ilford Broadway and sold at the door for a farthing a bucket and when there were water-cress beds in Ilford Lane.

*   *   *

A letter I received in February 1982 from Miss Ivy Assiter-Field of 143 Thorold Road, after I had written to the Ilford Recorder regarding some early local event, stated that she was born in the same house in which she had lived all her life and which her father had bought new in 1898. She said that nearly everybody then in Thorold Road kept a uniformed maid and that all the rooms in the house had bells which were used to ring for the maid. In those days businessmen used to go to their offices in top hats and morning coats. Cleaning women would scrub the tiled paths leading from the front door to the gate, charging 6d for a long one and 3d for a short one (2½p and just over 1p in today's money).

Miss Assiter-Field added that very few people had a telephone and Mr. Keeble who kept the Basford Arms and who had a telephone used to take and deliver messages for many of the nearby residents. The annual Hospital Carnival procession was led by a man on a white horse and went along most of the roads in the neighbourhood. In those days Vicarage Lane (where Plessey's is now) was a country lane where Mr. Prentis, the local greengrocer grew his own vegetables.

*   *   *

Extract from Leonard Thomson's Introduction to his "Trams and Trolley-buses in Ilford" published 1979:

My acquaintance with the Ilford trams came late in the 1914/18 war when I was but a child. My family lived in Ley Street and trams passed by every few minutes, a few hundred yards away from Ilford Broadway where cars belonging to East Ham and West Ham Corporations, as well as those of the L.C.C. could be seen.

In those far-off days working hours were longer and the week-end relaxation seemed very attractive. The crowd movement on a Saturday afternoon to the local football ground was fascinating to observe, and many people would take a tram on a Sunday to journey to Barkingside as a starting point for rambles to Hainault Forest and beyond.

The tramways did not have a long span of life but played a large part in the development of the district and in the day-to-day needs of the people. On a summer's day to alight at "The Horns" and walk across the fields to Victoria Road, accompanied by the song of the skylark, was a stroll of sheer delight. Today the fields have gone, the trams have gone and the lark is seldom heard in these parts.

*   *   *

Food for thought

Following the Great Fire of London when St. Paul's Cathedral was being built in the late 1660s – approximately 300 years ago when most of Ilford was forest-land – Sir Christopher Wren, while surveying from the south side of the River Thames the building and the spread of London beyond the old city boundaries, is reputed to have said to his companion "Where will it all end!". Most of the present-day Ilford has been built within the last 100 years. What will it be like in another 300 or even 100 years' time I wonder?

Aerial photograph taken in 1989 showing re-developed Ilford Town Centre with Winston Way, Chapel Road and the Woodford-Barking relief road. (Photo: Aerofilms Ltd.)

Aerial photograph taken in 1987 showing centre of Ilford. (Photo: Aerofilms Ltd.)

Notes

Coat of Arms of the former Borough of Ilford
(1926–1965)